The 1980s was a decade of upheaval unprecedented since the conclusion of World War Two. In 1980, superpower detente had been abandoned and there was no sign of an end to the competition and conflict between the United States and Soviet Union. Yet by the end of the decade the Cold War was officially declared to have ended. Communist elites had been overthrown in Eastern Europe, the Soviet Union was in a state of disintegration, and the two superpowers had embarked on a process of unparalleled international cooperation. The suddenness and rapidity of change took most observers by surprise, and led many to reassess their assumptions about global politics.

This volume brings together a number of scholars who review their own ideas alongside the writing of others (such as Kenneth Waltz, John Lewis Gaddis and Stanley Hoffmann) to discuss how well their international relations theories have survived the collapse of the Cold War. It asks a number of relevant questions about how the Cold War should be conceptualized; why theorists overlooked the potential for change in Eastern Europe; why the Soviet Union shifted its foreign policy; the contribution of radical and feminist theory; and the future of international relations theory itself.

CONTRIBUTORS: Robin Brown, Fred Halliday, Michael Cox, Richard Crockatt, Mike Bowker, Marysia Zalewski, N. J. Rengger.

FROM COLD WAR TO COLLAPSE: THEORY AND WORLD POLITICS IN THE 1980S

Cambridge Studies in International Relations is a joint initiative of Cambridge University Press and the British International Studies Association (BISA). The series will include a wide range of material, from undergraduate textbooks and surveys to research-based monographs and collaborative volumes. The aim of the series is to publish the best new scholarship in International Studies from Europe, North America and the rest of the world.

Cambridge Studies in International Relations

FROM COLD WAR TO COLLAPSE: THEORY AND WORLD POLITICS IN THE 1980s

Edited by
MIKE BOWKER and ROBIN BROWN

CAMBRIDGE
UNIVERSITY PRESS

Published by the Press Syndicate of the University of Cambridge
The Pitt Building, Trumpington Street, Cambridge CB2 1RP
40 West 20th Street, New York, NY 10011–4211, USA
10 Stamford Road, Oakleigh, Victoria 3166, Australia

First published 1993

Printed in Great Britain by Redwood Press Limited, Melksham, Wiltshire

A catalogue record for this book is available from the British Library

Library of Congress cataloguing in publication data

From Cold War to collapse: theory and world politics in the 1980s / edited by
Mike Bowker and Robin Brown.
    p. cm. – (Cambridge studies in international relations: 25)
    Includes bibliographical references and index.
    ISBN 0 521 41596 9 hbk 42512 x pbk
    1. World   politics   –   1945- 2. International   relations.   3. Cold
War. I. Bowker, Mike. II. Brown, Robin. III. Series.
D843.F757   1992
327'.09'04 – dc20   92–2717 CIP

ISBN 0 521 41596 9 hardback
ISBN 0 521 42612 x paperback

CE

CONTENTS

CONTRIBUTORS

MIKE BOWKER Lecturer in Politics at the University of East Anglia

ROBIN BROWN Lecturer in International Studies at the Institute for International Studies, the University of Leeds

MICHAEL COX Senior Lecturer in Politics at Queen's University, Belfast

RICHARD CROCKATT Lecturer in American Studies in the School of English and American Studies, University of East Anglia

FRED HALLIDAY Professor of International Relations at the London School of Economics

N. J. RENGGER Lecturer in International Relations in the Department of Politics, University of Bristol

MARYSIA ZALEWSKI Lecturer in Sociology at the University of East Anglia

ACKNOWLEDGEMENTS

This volume was conceived whilst the two editors were temporarily employed in the now sadly defunct International Relations Section of the Department of Linguistics and International Studies at the University of Surrey. The two major concerns of this book, the Cold War and International Relations theory, roughly reflect the division of our teaching duties at Surrey. It seemed a good idea to bring the two topics together in one volume in the light of the extraordinary events in international politics which were occurring during our stay in Guildford.

Five of the seven chapters collected here were first presented as papers to the British International Studies Conference at Newcastle University, 17–19 December 1990. The editors would like to thank all the contributors for their diligence and hard work. Particular thanks are also due to Professor Steve Smith of the University of East Anglia for his unstinting help and encouragement throughout the project.

MIKE BOWKER and ROBIN BROWN
November 1991

1 INTRODUCTION: TOWARDS A NEW SYNTHESIS OF INTERNATIONAL RELATIONS

ROBIN BROWN

The 1980s was a decade of upheaval unknown since the end of World War Two. The decade began with the onset of the Second Cold War and ended with unparalleled cooperation between the superpowers. In 1980, the Soviet Union had just invaded Afghanistan, and many in the West feared this action reflected Moscow's heightened global ambitions. Meanwhile, the American military establishment had become gravely concerned over the USSR's first strike nuclear capability, and urged the American president to take urgent countermeasures. The Soviet Union, for its part, believed the West was embarking on a renewed arms race in a desperate bid to attain strategic superiority. Moreover, the Kremlin feared a newly emerging encirclement, at Western instigation, among neighbouring states hostile to Moscow.

The two superpowers appeared to be locked in a relationship of tension and danger from which there seemed no escape. Yet, by the end of the decade, the Cold War was officially declared to be over. Moscow had pulled its troops out of Afghanistan, the old communist elites in Eastern Europe had been toppled by popular revolution, and even the USSR itself had begun the process of disintegration. Both superpowers were cutting their nuclear arsenals, while all the time calling for bigger reductions and new initiatives. The United States and the Soviet Union no longer saw each other as enemies. Instead, the mood was in favour of cooperation and mutual aid. The Cold War system, with which the world had grown so familiar since its formation in the late 1940s, had suddenly collapsed. The future, in the post-bipolar world, looked very uncertain.

The rapidity of the change took participants and observers alike by surprise. Although many doubts had been expressed about the stability of the Soviet position in Eastern Europe, few imagined that the leaders of the USSR would permit such rapid dismantling of the 'gains of socialism'. This surprise, even among the experts in the field, led many to challenge academic understanding of global politics and the

1

utility of International Relations Theory. Many questions were raised. How do the ideas of the main IR theorists stand up to the test against the realities of global politics? Can they account for the radical changes in the 1980s? What limitations have been revealed? And in what directions should the discipline move to remedy any perceived weaknesses? These questions form the central focus of this volume. The papers collected here represent a first attempt to answer them.

Despite the variety of answers to the questions, these papers share several assumptions and can be seen as part of an emerging synthesis of some of the apparently contradictory approaches to the subject. Approaches to world politics are increasingly seeking to link the international and the domestic, the societal and the transnational in a way that incorporates some of the elements of traditional Realism. The remainder of this chapter outlines the background to this synthesis and some of the other issues which need consideration.

The emergence of Neo-Realism

The story of the emergence of International Relations as an academic discipline is a familiar one and there is no need to repeat it here. It need only be noted that during the 1980s, it became conventional to divide theoretical approaches to the subject into three categories: the Realist, Pluralist/Liberal, and Marxist/Structuralist 'paradigms'. But what concerns us most in this chapter is the shifting interaction between these approaches in the last ten years, and the state of the dialogue between them.[1]

Realism, which had emerged back in the 1940s, remains to this day the dominant paradigm in International Relations. However, Realism has changed its form constantly over time. There is a world of difference, for example, between a behaviouralist treatment of the balance of power and Morgenthau's *Scientific Man Versus Power Politics* in their assumptions about the nature of international politics and the best approach to its study. This capacity for transformation is one of the reasons for the continuing hegemony of Realism within anglophone International Relations. Nevertheless, it is still possible to define a core of common interests in Realism. These are: the state, anarchy of the international system, power and security.[2]

During the 1960s and 1970s, Realism came under attack from two directions. Firstly from the behaviouralists, who regarded the founding texts of Realism as impressionistic and unscientific. This, in part, stimulated the so-called 'Great Debate' in the discipline between 'scientific' and 'classical' approaches. Looking back, twenty-five years later, it is clear that the debate has resolved nothing.[3]

The second assault from the 'transnationalists' was more substantive. They attacked the Realist model on two fronts. The first attack referred to an alleged change in the basic nature of world politics. While the Realists may have been correct in their emphasis on power and security back in the 1940s, the world of the 1970s had changed to such an extent that Realism no longer provided a 'usable map of the world'. It had been overtaken by new actors and new issues. The new international actors included terrorists, multinational corporations, intelligence agencies and drug dealers, and they were operating, without heed to borders, on a global scale. It was further argued that these new actors had a significant impact on world politics. Partly as a result of the emergence of these new actors, a new set of issues arose which could be bracketed under the heading of 'interdependence'. Issues like pollution, overpopulation, nuclear proliferation, resource depletion and poverty, it was said, could no longer be resolved satisfactorily within the confines of the state unit. Thus, transnationalist writers either predicted and/or advocated the demise of the nation-state as the dominant form of political organisation.[4]

The second thrust of attack was one based on method. This was part of a more general movement in political science towards the disaggregation of the state and analysis in terms of political systems and interest groups. In International Relations, this movement was reflected, not only in the writing on transnational relations, but also in Foreign Policy Analysis which utilised bureaucratic politics models and decision-making analysis.[5]

The most carefully considered response to the critics of Realism came from Kenneth Waltz. In his book, *Theory of International Politics*, published in 1979, Waltz effectively set the agenda for mainstream International Relations in the 1980s. Waltz's responses can be considered on three levels: his method; his substantive response to the Realist critics; and his conclusions.[6]

The methodological style of Waltz's work derives from his concept of theory. The quality of a theory, in his view, is a function of its breadth of applicability. The wider the range of cases that it can explain, the better the theory. The starting point for a theory of International Relations is the recurrence of patterns of behaviour over time. For Waltz, the dominant pattern in international relations is the balance of power. Therefore, a good theory of international relations is one which will explain balancing in the whole range of cases in which it occurs, not just some of them.[7] Consequently, he rejects

'reductionist' theories which explain events in terms of the characteristics of the members belonging to the international system. If balance
or power politics operated in the Ancient Greek states-system, then
attempts to explain them by reference to the characteristics of modern
states, for instance by explaining imperialism by reference to capitalism, become unnecessary. For this reason, he argues that the importance lies, not in the characteristics of the units of the system, but in the
structures of the system itself. In other words, there is something about
the structures of international relations that cause states to act in the
way that they do.[8]

Waltz takes micro-economics as his model. Micro-economics, he
claims, is able to explain outcomes on the basis of the structure of the
market, be it monopolistic, duopolistic, oligopolistic, or one of perfect
competition. This can be done without reference to the characteristics
of the firms, beyond the limited assumption that they will act in a
rational profit-maximizing way.[9] In the case of International Relations,
political structure is defined in terms of three criteria. Firstly, is the
organising principle one of hierarchy or anarchy? Secondly, what is
the differentiation among the units? (Or, in other words, what is the
division of labour?) Finally, what is the distribution of capability or
power? Waltz answers that the organising principle is one of anarchy,
and there is no division of labour, since states are essentially the same
kind of entity. As a result, the crucial factor in the international system
is the distribution of power which is determined by the number of
poles or great power states existing at any one time. Given this spartan
definition of structure, Waltz could point to only one major change in
the international system since 1648 – the transition from a multipolar
system to a bipolar one at the end of the Second World War.[10]

Two things were of particular importance about Waltz's work.
Firstly, from a very simple basis, he was able to generate considerable
explanatory power. Secondly, he made an explicit attachment to the
methodology of economics with its assumptions of rational choice and
its employment of model-building. This enabled him to abandon the
more questionable assertions on human nature which traditional Realists, such as Morgenthau, had used as a basis for their theoretical
model.

The substantive content in the book was rigorous, albeit perhaps
rather artificial. It stated that the rise of transnational activity had not
changed the ordering principle – the division of labour or distribution
of power in the international system – and was consequently unimportant. Waltz demonstrated that the degree of economic interdependence between the Great Powers was lower in the late 1970s

than it had been before 1914. As the distribution of capabilities in the system narrowed, the importance of the Great Powers inevitably increased. As a result, low interdependence was only to be expected. Therefore, the substance of Waltz's analysis was an attack on the theories of transnationalism and interdependence.[11] In his conclusion, Waltz stated that bipolarity was extremely stable; therefore, it was likely to endure. Bipolarity provided the best framework for dealing with the problems of interdependence because cooperation, which was deemed necessary to cope with the new international issues, was easiest with a small number of actors. Hence, two Great Powers were better than three or five.[12] In sum, Waltz suggested that the Cold War system had its merits. In the nuclear age it was perhaps the best option available.

There were many critics of Waltz. One critique, however, deserves special attention here. This concerned his reification of the postwar bipolar system. Waltz, these critics maintained, omitted any discussion in his work on the dynamic of systemic change. How could the system have been transformed in the past? How could it be transformed in the future? Moreover, the abstraction of his theory meant that it had nothing to say about the everyday interactions of international relations.[13]

The Rise of International Political Economy (IPE)

To some extent these shortcomings were compensated by the other key strand of Neo-Realism, the attempt to develop a better understanding of the interaction of the state and the economy in world politics. One of the main criticisms of Realism was its lack of attention to economic issues, which the interdependent theorists argued were becoming vastly more important in the international system of the 1970s. The critics often quoted Henry Kissinger as an example of an American foreign policy-maker who showed a lack of interest in economic issues while in government.

Like all the main schools of thought in International Relations, the rise of interdependency theory had deep intellectual roots. Theorists of interdependence drew on the liberal distinction between state and society. They assumed that the development of a modern economy would produce a more pacific world order since the state's freedom of action would be constrained by transnational activities and the resultant interdependence.[14] In some versions of the argument, the end result would be either the replacement of the state by large-scale international integration or the rise of the multinational corporation.

5

Realist IPE rejected the assumption that there was any fundamental tension between economic activity and state power. Indeed, they went further and argued that the two belonged together. States used their power to secure favourable economic conditions. The growth of transnational activities was a function of the kind of policies preferred by states. The modern state had been forced to take responsibility for the economic well-being of its citizens. Therefore, it sought to create the conditions for economic success. Despite this common interest, states have different types of economy, different resources and different levels of development. As a result, different states favoured different types of economic activity, using political means to promote their economic goals. The obvious example of this was the nineteenth-century German analysis of Britain's commitment to free trade. According to this view, free trade was promoted for purely national reasons since it worked to the advantage of the British as the world's strongest industrial power. These kinds of arguments began to surface again with new formulations in the mid to late 1970s. They appeared in the work of Robert Gilpin and Stephen Krasner in the International Relations literature, whilst Charles Kindelberger was prominent in the field of economics.[15]

The centrepiece of the Realist reinterpretation of the global political economy was the 'hegemonic stability thesis'. Drawing on rational choice theory, the central argument stated that in a world of egoists, cooperation will always be difficult. No member of a group can be sure that cooperative projects will not be sabotaged by the defection of one of the other members of the group. Consequently, each will be prepared to defect given the chance. This, it was argued, described the economic behaviour of the Great Powers during the 1930s. While free trade benefits all, it does so unequally. Each state may be better off if it can pursue protectionist policies, provided the others play by the rules of free trade. Attempting to do this produces a situation where everybody defects and everybody is worse off. In the 1930s, global depression had been encouraged by the widespread adoption of 'beggar-my-neighbour' policies. Kindelberger argued that in the post-Second World War period the United States had acted as 'hegemon' in the system. The other Western states had accepted US leadership because they concluded that it was in their interest to do so. It was true that Washington had provided both negative and positive incentives for cooperation, but Kindelberger wondered if these cooperative arrangements could survive if the relative power of the United States declined. Would the loss of hegemony allow the basic difficulties facing cooperation to re-emerge? This argument led to the development of two sets of literature – one exploring the problems of cooperation with and without a hegemon; the other, the decline of American power.[16]

Robert Gilpin, in his book, *War and Change in World Politics*, pointed to the danger that the cost of defending America's dominance in world politics could in itself lead to it losing that very position. In many respects pre-empting Paul Kennedy's *The Rise and Fall of Great Powers*, he argued that economies and states have a life-cycle.[17] The history of international relations can be seen as a series of hegemonies. A state's political influence expands as a result of its domestic strength. However, the process of expansion unleashes countervailing forces both at home and abroad.[18] Abroad, the state acquires a broader range of commitments that have to be defended, but at the same time it comes up against the other members of the system who are in a position to copy the economic, administrative and military innovations of the dominant power. At home, rising political and military commitments damage economic strength. Thus, the cost of defending the positions acquired during the period of expansion becomes increasingly debilitating. The great power, therefore, begins to lose its dominant position. Furthermore, Gilpin notes that the major wars that have occurred are those that took place when a declining hegemon was challenged. Gilpin relates this to the current position in the international system of the United States, and before that to the United Kingdom.[19] Gilpin saw world politics as an arena where Waltz's balance of power was only one aspect of an international system where competition was taking place on economic terms, not simply in the pursuit of wealth, but as a means to political power. Whereas Waltz abolished history, Gilpin returned to Machiavelli's cycles of growth and decay. In so doing, he provided a motor for change in the Neo-Realist perspective.

The debate over hegemony had several sides to it. Although some advocates of the stability thesis could point to a variety of indicators that suggested the decline of American power, others called into question the pessimists' notion of power. For despite America's decline in relative terms, the United States still retained disproportionate means for influencing the world political economy, and its hegemony was never seriously under threat.[20] A second optimistic response to the doom-laden pronouncements of Kindelberger and Gilpin came from those Robert Keohane liked to call, the 'neoliberal institutionalists'. While in terms of the inter-paradigm debate, neoliberal institutionalists can be located in the Realist camp, Keohane distinguished them from the Neo-Realists. For him, Neo-Realism posited an international system with a single variable – the distribution of power.

Institutional arrangements in any issue area would reflect that distribution, and as it changed, so would those arrangements. In Keohane's view, however, those institutional arrangements were important in themselves. Over time, a set of rules, practices and understandings (or regimes) evolved which regulated behaviour. As a result, changes in the distribution of power were mediated by the pre-existing regimes, so that the relationship between power and outcomes is less direct than Realists suggest.[21] The institutionalist perspective on the American decline argues that during the period of US hegemony, institutions were created which may have simplified the problems of cooperation to such an extent that a hegemon is no longer required.[22] Whatever the labels, however, the institutionalist analysis, like the Neo-Realist, is based on rational choice theory, and in particular on Robert Axelrod's work on the evolution of cooperation.[23]

The key development in mainstream (American) International Relations during the 1980s has been the development of Neo-Realist IPE. The scope of Realist analysis has been extended into areas where it was thought to lack purchase. Even the cooperative aspects of world politics can be treated within the framework of anarchy, power and security. For cooperation is a direct result of state power. Three aspects of IPE deserve special mention. Firstly, the recognition that the state is as much an economic actor as a military one means that it will act to preserve national interests in a number of ways. Secondly, the above suggests that insecurity can be used to explain international outcomes that go beyond military threats.[24] Thirdly, this change of perspective has important consequences for the concept of 'power'. In this view, power is seen as essentially variable and dependent on specific issues. As a result, power is as much a matter of societal structures and procedures as military force. Thus, the traditional view of Realism can be extended to one that acknowledges, in principle at least, the relevance of the internal workings of states and their interaction with societies.

Although Gilpin identifies three paradigms in IPE: the Realist (otherwise known as the Nationalist or Mercantilist), the Liberal and the Marxist, the relationship between the first two is hardly exclusive.[25] Gilipin is not an advocate of Mercantilism, which is the subordination of economic well-being to the needs of national power. His work is more about the interaction between a set of economic actors – individuals and firms, and self-interested political actors – states, which attempt to manipulate the world economy to their own interests. The self-interest of the economic actors might give rise to a liberal global economy, but the states have national interests which they seek

8

to advance often at the expense of the wider international perspective. The basic propositions of Realist IPE emerge from the interaction between these two sets of actors, and the processes they initiate.

Marxism and the rise of the state

A second strand of the new synthesis can be found in Marxism and more generally in historical sociology. There is a cliché that Marxism has nothing to contribute to International Relations because of its focus on class and economics. This can be supported by the fact that the most prominent school of Marxist writing on world politics – dependency theory – is only tangentially concerned with relations between states.[26] It can be argued that relations between states are determined by class interests, hence there is no need for a theory of relations between states, and indeed the attempt to formulate one simply serves to disguise the true nature of the capitalist global social system. In other words, relations between states is simply another aspect of capitalism. However, it can be demonstrated that implicitly, at least, Marx and Engels separated the question of inter-state conflict from that of capitalism. For in their writings, it is implicit that the existence of independent communities is in itself sufficient for conflict to occur.[27]

Despite this, most Marxist writings have tended to follow Lenin in reducing international relations to class interests. They have, to coin Christopher Chase-Dunn's useful expression, come to treat the inter-state system and the global economy as possessing one logic rather than two. Put more plainly, in the traditional Marxist view, class conflict takes primacy over inter-state conflict.[28] Wallerstein's Modern World System accepts the one logic concept. It claims that the states-system is purely parasitic on capitalism, and as such, could be incorporated into the wider framework. However, the past decade has seen the emergence of a body of writing, within the Marxist school, which challenges the single logic model. Such writers have come to acknowledge the importance of inter-state relations, but they have attempted to formulate the interaction within historical materialist categories. This group has joined the growing number of Marxists who accept the concept of 'the relative autonomy of the state'. Therefore, they are able to concede that inter-state relations represent an important dynamic in understanding change within societies.[29] This critical view was a response to the renewed East–West conflict in the early 1980s. The oppressive and militaristic nature of the Soviet regime made many theorists unwilling to seek explanations simply in terms of capitalism.

9

Instead, explanations were sought in the nature of the states-system which promoted militarism.[30]

This view grew out of, and in turn stimulated, a wider move in the social sciences to 'bring the state back in'.[31] The habit of ignoring the state in favour of other concepts, such as class, was perceived to have been premature. The 'state' remained a distinctive entity. Within sociology it had become commonplace to discuss 'society' as something contained within national boundaries. This ignored the fact that society was defined by boundaries which had been determined by the power of the state, and its interaction with others. It also downplayed interaction between the societies themselves. Thus, capitalism remained an important, but not sufficient, explanation of state structures.

In the case of Europe, states developed through competition with each other. This competition could take several forms, from war and the preparation of war, at one end of the spectrum, to trade at the other. In order to compete more effectively, states had to change or improve the internal functioning of the state. This could involve administrative techniques, labour discipline or scientific research and development. Therefore, it became illusory to study either the European state or the European states-system separately. They existed in an essentially symbiotic relationship.[32] Consequently, historical sociology took a renewed interest in the area conventionally covered by International Relations – the analysis of the modern state, not only as a function of capitalist modernity, but also as a function of the states-system. Such writing has brought many insights into the subject, but it should be noted that the school owed as much to Weber as to Marx.

The Gramscian school represented a second type of Neo-Marxism. The main figure in this school is Robert Cox, whose work, like Robert Gilpin's, was concerned with the rise and fall of hegemony.[33] Hegemony is a term used in Gramsci's writing which indicates a domination maintained through ideologically based consent, rather than force or repression.[34] Cox's work attempted to outline the development of the global political economy in terms of three levels of analysis: the organisation of production, the form of the state, and the form of the world order. Interestingly, in the end, Cox concluded that the single most important factor in the overall pattern of global politics was the form of the state.[35]

Critical International Relations Theory (CIRT)

There was a striking congruence between the concerns of Realism and historical materialist writings on world politics during the 1980s, in that both emphasised the inter-action of the states-system within a wider social and economic context. However, despite the overlap in approach, a set of issues remain unresolved. The main one concerns the fundamental question of method. What can a theory do? What is it unable to do? How should it be constructed? Essentially, Critical International Relations Theory was raising again many of the questions of the earlier 'Great Debate'.

Critical International Relations Theory draws on a variety of sources from philosophy and sociology. What these approaches have in common is a high degree of scepticism concerning the objectivity and detachment of theory. Theory is not, as Gadamer puts it, 'rendered anonymous'.[36] In other words, theory is not constructed in a vacuum. On the contrary, it is always constructed by an individual with definite views, from a particular background, and at a certain time in history. Therefore, theory cannot be objective and detached. Instead, it is there to serve a particular purpose. Thus, Morgenthau's Realism justified America's role in the Cold War, while Gilpin's theory on hegemony legitimised the United States continued dominance of the international system.

Consequently, CIRT strongly suspects that conventional International Relations theory is part of the problem rather than part of the solution. Waltz is the subject of particular criticism. CIRT draws its inspiration from two sources, the loosely Marxist-derived work of Habermas and Gramsci, and post-structuralist scholarship. The underlying assumptions of these two approaches differ, but both provide a powerful critique of orthodox International Relations theory.[37]

The crucial difference between the 'Marxist' critical theorists and their more conventional counterparts lies in their differing assumptions about the nature of the social world. For the latter, the world exists independently of the individual. It is possible, therefore, to accumulate and analyse objective data on the workings of the international system. For the critical theorist, this commits a basic error by treating institutions, which are the product of human activity, as if they are normal or natural entities. These institutions, which include states and the states-system, exist solely as a result of the beliefs and actions of individuals and communities. For critical theorists, it is always important to consider both the factors that sustain these institutions as well as the potential for change. Thus, CIRT has two main criticisms of the Realist view of international relations. Firstly, Realism assumes that politics is, and will always remain, a struggle for power. Secondly, Realists are prone to declare the existence of immutable truths, such as that above. Critical theorists, on the other hand, perceive change as a central element in social existence. Therefore, an

11

analysis of dynamic forces, such as capitalism, is essential to a full understanding of social existence and the modern world.[38]

The second strand of CIRT belongs to post-structuralism or post-modernism. This represents a more radical break with conventional conceptions of theory. According to this view, in International Relations, as in other fields of knowledge, what is being purveyed is not knowledge of the world, but representations of the world. Thus, in a book like Morgenthau's *Politics Among Nations*, a post-structuralist is not interested in the substance of the work, but in the claims that it makes, the simplifications that it imposes, and the rhetorical strategies that it employs. Hidden within the text are a whole set of assumptions about the world which are taken for granted. Post-structuralism attempts to make these clear and to locate them within a wider context of power and knowledge.[39] For as Foucault claimed, power and knowledge are inextricably linked. To claim knowledge is to claim power.[40] For the post-structuralist, the social world is a collection of textual practices. A statement about the nature of political relationships is significant, not because it tells us how things are, but because of what it tells us about itself. What is interesting, for example, is not whether Realism is an accurate description of the world, but the way in which it seeks to represent the world. Such representations interact with others in society and affect thought and action. As a result, language is very important. Furthermore, changes in language have an importance far beyond the academic discipline of linguistics. They can reflect basic changes in our view of society and state. Thus, the post-structuralist considers the study of language as central to an understanding of social life.

Due to these radical assumptions, post-structuralism can produce apparently random reflections on themes such as the relationship between sport and international relations. For, the world is simply a collection of interpretations.[41] To an even greater extent than the Neo-Marxist variant of critical theory, post-structuralism represents a radical break with the positivist pursuit of reliable, cumulative knowledge of the dynamics of international relations. The rigid categorisation of much IR study is seen as an obstacle rather than an aid to research. At best, it simplifies and obscures the complexities, particularities and ambiguities of real life.[42]

This criticism is the most valuable contribution of post-structuralism to IR theory. It alerts us to the nature of the language that we use, the assumptions built into it and the importance of 'silences', i.e. what the theory leaves out or takes for granted. The work of Richard Ashley and others simply point out that the literature of International Relations is

12

littered with frequently repeated clichés which are taken as true. For example, Ashley questions the claim that the international system is an arena of anarchy which, as such, contrasts sharply with the stable and ordered existence in domestic politics. This, he says, is a fiction which serves to legitimise the state.[43] On the other hand, the charge that post-structuralism is nihilistic has a certain degree of force. While it is capable of detecting the limits of any particular 'text' by identifying origins, assumptions and silences, what it cannot do is deal with the political problem of International Relations. That is, it has little practical to say on the division of the world into a variety of groups with differing perspectives and cultures. Post-structuralism is of value in attacking the preconceptions of particular cultures, it is of little use in the political sense of coping with a divided world. Nevertheless, Critical International Relations Theory has the potential to revive the 'Great Debate' of the 1960s, for it raises the same issue about the status of IR theory. Can there be a science of international relations? And should IR aim at explanation or interpretation? The critical theory debate goes further, however, since it points to the differing conceptions of the social world which underlay the differences between the classical and scientific schools.[44]

The new interdependence

While Realism was resurgent during the 1980s, eclipsing the transnationalist approaches, in the latter part of the decade it became possible to see evidence of the re-emergence of writing which emphasised interdependence. This was hardly surprising, given the expansion of international communications. However, the new writing moved away from the simple equation made by the earlier transnationalists which stated that the rise of interdependence meant the decline of the state and its eventual replacement by other actors. The new interdependent theorist directs attention to what might be called the world politics of everyday life. The main aim of this school is to explore how the apparently mundane elements of life all around the world reflect the influence of international and transnational processes. Key examples of this type of thinking are found in the work of Cynthia Enloe and R. B. J. Walker, although they both might reject such classification.[45] Enloe's exploration of the impact of international processes on women shows how the living conditions of women on one side of the globe, for instance in garment manufacturing, are crucially shaped by the demands of women in the developed countries.[46] This exploration is a radical break with the traditional agenda of world politics which focused on war and conflict. However, it remains part of the new debate which perceives a dialectical relationship between the processes of social and economic change and the states-system.

From the above it is clear that the 1980s was a decade of upheaval just as much in the academic discipline of International Relations as in the so-called real world of global politics. The chapters collected here aim to reflect that fact. The four chapters that follow consider the Cold War system quite explicitly, and looking back, examine the failures and weaknesses of political analysis and International Relations theory. The final two chapters by Marysia Zalewski and N. J. Rengger look forward and attempt to suggest possible future directions for the discipline.

Fred Halliday's chapter provides a general treatment of the nature of 'cold war'. In his recent work, Halliday has led the call for a treatment of world politics that integrates the state and the social level, arguing that the treatment of the 'state' in International Relations writing is inadequate.[47] Here, he calls for an analysis of the Cold War that recognises it as an 'inter-systemic' conflict which involved, and was driven by, the competitive interaction between two different forms of social system. Foreign policy behaviour was seen as a product of the nature of distinct social systems, not of the international system as such. Relations between social systems were a product of their internal formations, so 'foreign policy' between states was not seen to be an adequate conceptualisation of the US–Soviet relationship. In the Cold War, Western wealth and consumption were weapons as much as military equipment. Halliday emphasises the importance of asymmetries in the Cold War, and points to the need for an analysis that can draw on a wider historical framework than Realism. He suggests one derived from historical materialism or Weberian historical sociology, and one which can operate on three levels of interaction between systems: inter-state, inter-socio-economic and inter-ideological. While the Cold War had its own specific features, a concept of inter-systemic interaction has wider applicability. For example, it could help in the analysis of relations between European states, as well as formations such as the Chinese and Ottoman empires. In Halliday's perspective, the Cold War was fought between two incompatible social systems. The capitalist West was the winner, but more because of its tee-shirts than its military might.

Halliday's earlier work looms large in Michael Cox's analysis of the attempts by radicals to explain the international events of the 1980s, and in particular the nature of the 'Second Cold War'. This essay provides a considered view of the attempt by one set of theorists to make sense of a particular period of international relations. Cox points out differences among these writers regarding the substance of the Second Cold War, but all were agreed that the collapse of detente was a consequence of American actions. US claims about Soviet provocation were deemed groundless, and so, from the radical viewpoint, America remained the main threat to peace. Cox's main criticism, however, is that the expectation of the radicals that the Second Cold War would become a permanent feature of the international system was false. Moreover, it was false for identifiable reasons, namely the radicals' inadequate understanding of three things, the Soviet Union, Ronald Reagan and nuclear weapons. Cox, therefore, performs an exercise which happens all too rarely in the social sciences – a post-mortem on performance in the field. International Relations will always make mistakes in predicting the future, but a systematic review of how those predictions turn out can only be of benefit in alerting us to the limits of current analytical frameworks. As Wittgenstein observed:

> When we think about the future of the world, we always have in mind its being at the place where it would be if it continued to move as we see it moving now. We do not realize that it moves not in a straight line, but in a curve and its direction constantly changes.[48]

Cox himself, along with Waltz and Gaddis, are the subjects of Richard Crockatt's chapter, in which he examines how these three writers explain the stability of the Cold War system. Crockatt argues that the work of Waltz and Gaddis failed to provide any purchase on the sources of change in the Cold War system. Like the subjects of Cox's critique, they failed to understand the forces of change inherent in international relations. To correct this imbalance, Crockatt concludes that there is a need for analysis in terms of processes as well as structures, and that the evolution of the Cold War system must be understood, not only in terms of inter-state interactions, but also in terms of the tangentially related development of capitalism.

The emphasis of Halliday, Cox and Crockatt on the dynamism of the Western system and the inability of the Soviet Union to compete effectively is partially rejected by Mike Bowker's consideration of the forces for change in Soviet foreign policy during the 1980s. Many of the pressures for change had a longer history than the Reagan era, and elements of Gorbachev's 'new thinking' in many cases reached back into the 'period of stagnation'. What is clear, however, is the dependence of change at the inter-state level on socio-economic problems in the USSR. The choices made by the Soviet leadership were influenced, rather than determined, by external events.

Marysia Zalewski's chapter shifts the focus from the Cold War to gender issues in International Relations. Her chapter is important as it represents a part of what has since become known as the post-positivist debate. As such it poses a challenge, not only to the assumptions and mode of theorising in mainstream IR, but also to the agenda of International Relations itself. From its original concern with war and diplomacy, it has taken a considerable period of time for questions of political economy to find a place on the IR agenda, despite a certain congruence between the theories of mercantilist political economy and Realism. It has proved long and difficult to develop ideas on the impact of global processes on everyday life too. To develop a treatment of gender promises to be even more of a challenge, albeit one potentially full of insights. Zalewski notes that its greatest impact is likely to be as a contribution to the post-positivist debate.

The volume ends with N. J. Rengger's study of the problem of order in the 1990s. While Rengger's concern is with the future and with the normative aspect of international order, a common thread that connects his work to the earlier chapters is the recognition of the linkage between domestic and international order. He stresses, for example, the tension between the upholding of human rights and the maintenance of stability in the international system. While the states-system does much to manage conflict between independent communities, it is limited in its response to the frequent cases where problems arise within boundaries. This is a problem which is likely to dog the practice and the theoretical treatment of world politics for some time to come.

Conclusions

The essays collected here provide a critical interpretation of the ways in which scholars have sought to comprehend the events of the last decade. Despite certain differences, the chapters have a common core. They claim, firstly, that an analysis limited to the state system is of limited value during a revolutionary upheaval; secondly, that socio-economic factors are of vital importance; and, thirdly, that the interdependence of states has grown and become more significant. Finally, this chapter has shown that the conventional tripartite division of the discipline into Realist, Pluralist and Structuralist paradigms needs rethinking. This is because there is an emerging overlap between Realist attempts to come to terms with socio-economic factors and the efforts of historical sociology to integrate ideas on the states-system. The major difference today lies between the positivist and the post-positivist approaches to International Relations theory.

It is also the view of the authors that the actual practice of international politics has often been neglected by the theorists. This volume represents a first attempt to remedy this. The ideas outlined here would suggest that this needs to be developed beyond the traditional conception of Foreign Policy Analysis or Strategic Studies. New times require new thinking. The questions remain: what practical lessons can we learn from the events of the 1980s? and what are the limitations of the theoretical frameworks that they have revealed? This is the task that needs carrying out. The lessons identified in this volume can only be a starting point.

Notes

I would like to thank Mike Bowker for his useful comments on a draft of this chapter.

1 On the emergence of International Relations, see William C. Olson and A. J. R. Groom, *International Relations Then and Now: Origins and Trends in Interpretation* (London: Harper Collins, 1991); K. J. Holsti, *The Divided Discipline: Hegemony and Diversity in International Relations* (Boston, MA: Allen and Unwin, 1985); Michael Banks, 'The evolution of International Relations Theory', in Banks (ed.), *Conflict in World Society: New Perspectives on International Relations* (Brighton: Wheatsheaf, 1984). On the three paradigms see Michael Smith et al. (eds.), *Perspectives on World Politics* (London: Croom Helm, 1981); Michael Banks, 'The inter-paradigm debate', in Margot Light and A. J. R. Groom (eds.), *International Relations: A Handbook of Current Theory* (London: Pinter, 1985); R. D. McKinlay and R. Little, *Global Problems and World Order* (London: Pinter, 1986).

2 Holsti, *Divided Discipline*, see also Michael Doyle, 'Thucydidean Realism', *Review of International Studies*, vol. 16, no. 3, July 1990; Justin Rosenberg. 'What's the matter with Realism?', *Review of International Studies*, vol. 16, no. 4, October 1990; Hans J. Morgenthau, *Scientific Man versus Power Politics* (Chicago: University of Chicago Press, 1946).

3 The papers that made up the debate are collected in Klaus Knorr and James N. Rosenau (eds.), *Contending Approaches to International Politics* (Princeton, NJ: Princeton University Press, 1969). Some recent comments on the aftermath of the debate can be found in Fred Halliday, 'The pertinence of International Relations', *Political Studies*, vol. 38, no. 3, September 1990, p. 507; Richard Little, 'International Relations and the methodological turn', *Political Studies*, vol. 39, no. 3, September 1991.

4 A useful compilation of this literature can be found in Smith et al., *Perspectives*, pt. 2.

5 On Foreign Policy Analysis, see Christopher Hill and Margot Light,

'Foreign Policy Analysis', in Light and Groom, *International Relations*; and Halliday, 'Pertinence', pp. 507–8.

6 Kenneth N. Waltz, *Theory of International Politics* (Reading, MA: Addison-Wesley, 1979).

7 *Ibid.*, pp. 65–7.

8 *Ibid.*, pp. 67–73.

9 *Ibid.*, pp. 89–91, 93–4.

10 *Ibid.*, pp. 88–99, 162–3.

11 *Ibid.*, ch. 7.

12 *Ibid.*, pp. 204–5.

13 See Robert O. Keohane (ed.), *Neorealism and its Critics* (New York: Columbia University Press, 1986), especially the contributions by Ruggie and Ashley.

14 On the roots of transnationalism, see F. Parkinson, *The Philosophy of International Relations: A Study in the History of Thought* (Beverly Hills, CA: Sage, 1977), ch. 6.

15 See for instance Stephen Krasner, 'State power and the structure of international trade', *World Politics*, vol. 28, no. 3 (1976), and *Defending the National Interest: Raw Materials Investment and US Foreign Policy* (Princeton, NJ: Princeton University Press, 1978); Robert Gilpin, *US Power and the Multinational Corporation: The Political Economy of Direct Investment* (New York: Basic, 1976); Charles P. Kindelberger, *Power and Money* (London: Macmillan, 1970).

16 Statements of this thesis include, Charles P. Kindelberger, 'Dominance and leadership in the international economy', *International Studies Quarterly*, vol. 25, no. 2, 1981; Robert Gilpin, *US Power*, and *The Political Economy of International Relations* (Princeton, NJ: Princeton University Press, 1987).

17 Robert Gilpin, *War and Change in World Politics* (Cambridge: Cambridge University Press, 1981), pp. 10–11; Paul Kennedy, *The Rise and Fall of Great Powers: Economic Change and Military Conflict from 1500 to 2000* (London: Unwin Hyman, 1988).

18 Kennedy, *Rise and Fall of Great Powers*.

19 *Ibid.*, chs. 4–5.

20 Susan Strange, 'The persistent myth of lost hegemony', *International Organization*, vol. 41, no. 4, 1987, and *States and Markets* (London: Pinter, 1988), pp. 235–40. Also see the discussion in Michael C. Webb and Stephen D. Krasner, 'Hegemonic Stability Theory: an empirical assessment', *Review of International Studies*, vol. 15, no. 2, 1989.

21 Robert O. Keohane, 'Neoliberal institutionalism: a perspective on world politics', in Keohane, *International Institutions and State Power* (Boulder, CO: Westview, 1989), and *After Hegemony: Cooperation and Discord in the World Political Economy* (Princeton, NJ: Princeton University Press, 1984). On regimes, Stephen D. Krasner (ed.), *International Regimes* (Ithaca, NY: Cornell University Press, 1983).

22 Keohane, *Hegemony*, pp. 244–5.

23 Robert Axelrod, *The Evolution of Cooperation* (New York: Basic, 1984).

24 Barry Buzan, *People, States and Fear: An Agenda for International Security Studies in the Post-Cold War Era* (Hemel Hempstead: Harvester Wheatsheaf, 1991).

25 Gilpin, *Political Economy*, pp. 25–41, also *US Power*, pp. 26–32.

26 A restatement of this view is Holsti, *Divided Discipline*, p. 80.

27 W. B. Gallie, *Philosophers of Peace and War* (Cambridge: Cambridge University Press, 1978), pp. 74–9.

28 Martin Shaw, 'War imperialism and the state system: a critique of orthodox Marxism for the 1980s', in Shaw (ed.), *War, State and Society* (London: Macmillan, 1984); Christopher Chase-Dunn, 'Interstate system and capitalist world economy: one logic or two', *International Studies Quarterly*, vol. 25., no. 1, 1981.

29 A useful short introduction to the 'Modern world-system' is Immanuel Wallerstein, *Historical Capitalism* (London: Verso, 1983). Among the critics are: Aristide Zolberg, 'Origins of the modern world system: a missing link', *World Politics*, vol. 33, no. 2, 1981, Theda Skocpol, 'Wallerstein's world capitalist system', *American Journal of Sociology*, vol. 82, no. 5, 1977; D. P. Rapkin, 'The inadequacy of a single logic', in W. R. Thompson (ed.), *Contending Approaches to World System Analysis* (Beverly Hill: Sage, 1983), Giddens, *Nation-State*, pp. 167–8.

30 Michael Mann, 'Capitalism and militarism', in Shaw, *War, State and Society*, p. 44.

31 P. B. Evans et al. (eds.), *Bringing the State Back In* (Cambridge: Cambridge University Press, 1985); John A. Hall (ed.), *States in History* (Oxford: Blackwell, 1986).

32 Giddens, *Nation-State*, pp. 22, 30–1.

33 Robert Cox, *Production, Power and World Order* (New York: Columbia, 1987). Other key writings by Cox are 'Social forces, states and world orders: beyond International Relations Theory', *Millennium*, vol. 10, no. 2, 1981, and 'Gramsci, hegemony and International Relations: an essay in method', *Millennium*, vol. 12, no. 2, 1983. Other Gramscian works are E. Augelli and C. Murphy, *America's Quest for Supremacy and the Third World: A. Gramscian Analysis* (London: Pinter, 1988); Stephen Gill and David Law, *The Global Political Economy: Perspectives, Problems and Policies* (Hemel Hempstead: Harvester Wheatsheaf, 1988).

34 Cox, 'Gramsci', pp. 163–4, 169–72.

35 Cox, *Production*, p. 399.

36 Cox, 'Social forces', p. 128: Hans-Georg Gadamer, 'Philosophy or theory of science', in Gadamer, *Reason in the Age of Science*, trans. Frederick G. Lawrence (Cambridge, MA: MIT, 1983), p. 166.

37 On the quasi-Marxist approaches, see Mark Hoffman, 'Critical Theory and the inter-paradigm debate', in Hugh C. Dyer and Leon Mangasarian (eds.), *The Study of International Relations: The State of the Art* (Basingstoke: Macmillan, 1989); on post-structuralist approaches, Pauline Rosenau, 'Once again into the fray: International Relations confronts the humanities', *Millenium*, vol. 19, no. 1, 1990.

38 These considerations became clear in the treatment of Waltz's *Theory of International Politics*, see Cox, 'Social forces', and his 1985 postscript in Keohane, *Neorealism*, pp. 239–49; Richard K. Ashley, 'The poverty of Neorealism', *International Organization*, vol. 38, no. 2, 1984, and Ashley, 'Political Realism and human interests', *International Studies Quarterly*, vol. 25, no. 2,

1981. A useful perspective is provided by R. B. J. Walker, 'History and structure in the Theory of International Relations', *Millennium*, vol. 18, no. 2, 1989.

39 The most extensive attempt to apply poststructuralist ideas to international relations is James Der Derian and Michael Shapiro (eds.), *International/Intertextual Relations: Postmodern Readings of World Politics* (Lexington, MA: Lexington, 1989), see also the special issue of *International Studies Quarterly*, 'Speaking the Language of Exile: Dissidence in International Studies', vol. 34, no. 3, 1990.

40 Michel Foucault, *Power/Knowledge: Selected Interviews and Other Writings, 1972–1977* (New York: Pantheon, 1980).

41 Michael J. Shapiro, 'Representing World Politics: The Sport/War Intertext', in Der Derian and Shapiro, *International/Intertextual*.

42 See Richard K. Ashley, 'Untying the Sovereign State: A Double Reading of the Anarchy *Problematique*', *Millennium*, vol. 17, no. 2, 1988.

43 Ashley, 'Untying', pp. 255–9.

44 See Walker, 'History and Structure'; and Martin Hollis and Steve Smith, *Explaining and Understanding International Relations* (Oxford: Clarendon, 1990).

45 Cynthia Enloe, *Bananas, Beaches and Bases: Makaing Feminist Sense of International Politics* (London: Pandora, 1989); R. B. J. Walker, *One World, Many Worlds: Struggles for a Just World Peace* (London: Zed, 1988).

46 Enloe, *Bananas*, ch. 7.

47 Fred Halliday, 'State and Society in International Relations: A Second Agenda', in Dyer and Mangasarian, *The Study of International Relations*; '"The Sixth Great Power": On the Study of Revolution and International Relations', *Review of International Studies*, vol. 16, no. 3, 1990.

48 Quoted in Richard Rorty, *Philosophy and the Mirror of Nature* (Oxford: Blackwell, 1980), p. vii.

2 COLD WAR AS INTER-SYSTEMIC CONFLICT: INITIAL THESES

FRED HALLIDAY

The Cold War: two debates

In the academic and policy related literature on Cold War and East–West rivalry since 1945 there have been two main debates: one, a historical argument, concerning the causes and 'responsibility' for cold war, the other, framed partly in the language of the peace movement and partly within International Relations (IR) itself, on the underlying dynamic of the conflict. The former debate fell into three main phases – the initial anti-communist consensus, the 'revisionist' challenge, and a new 'post-revisionist' consensus.[1] Although developed around the First Cold War of 1947–53, the same debate, about causes and responsibility, elaborated simultaneously rather than sequentially, can be identified with regard to the Second Cold War, of 1979–85.

Rich as it was in historical detail, this debate on cold war suffered from two obvious limitations: on the one hand, it arose out of a specific political conjuncture and was dominated by the concerns of that situation – as much for the 'revisionists' as for the anti-communists; secondly, it was conducted in almost complete innocence of theoretical issues as such, reflecting the empiricism both of Anglo-Saxon historiography and of the, off-stage, political debate itself.

The second debate, on the dynamic of East–West conflict, contains some greater awareness of theoretical issues but in neither of its two contexts, the peace movement or the IR literature, was the theoretical underpinning substantially developed: some specific aspects of the conflict – the role of ideology, the arms race, crisis management – did receive theoretical treatment within IR, but not the Cold War as a whole. The analysis of what cold war was remains very much at the pre-theoretical level, in the sense of having implicit rather than explicit theoretical positions and of failing to ask what the implications of the Cold War for IR theory as such might be. Abstracting from this literature, however, this second debate can be said to encompass four main approaches. For the sake of convenience, and at the risk of some foreshortening, these can be categorised as: realist, subjectivist, internalist, inter-systemic.[2]

For Realism, and those such as the historical sociologists who have recently adopted it, the Cold War was a continuation of great power politics, albeit with certain additions such as nuclear weapons, arms racing and capitalist–communist ideological rivalry. The assertion of this continuity within international conflict was facilitated by focusing on the foreign policy of the USSR itself, which was seen as continuing the foreign goals of the pre-1917 regime, and/or of the USA, which was seen as just another imperial power, not only *vis-à-vis* the third world or the Europeans and Japanese, but also *vis-à-vis* the USSR.[3]

By 'subjectivist' is meant those theories that analysed the Cold War in terms of perception and misperception. The IR literature on perception developed in the 1960s and 1970s in the writings of such people as Janis and Jervis.[4] It suggested that foreign policy in general, and foreign policy mistakes in particular, could to a considerable extent be attributed to the perceptions held, individually and collectively, by those making foreign policy and by the populations that influenced or constrained them. This argument was not specifically directed to discussion of cold war, but had implications for it. Whether the argument was explicitly extended in this way or not, it paralleled and reinforced an argument common amongst liberal writers on the Cold War, and on revolutions generally, to the effect that the conflict could be avoided if only each side had been better informed about the other (a 'different' policy towards Russia after 1917, China after 1949, Cuba after 1959, or, for that matter, France after 1789).[5] Such arguments tended to downplay the necessity of ideological commitments on either side (to world revolution, solidarity/rollback, intervention and so forth) and to stress the need for better information and contact between states supposedly, but not really, committed to each other's transformation.

The term 'internalist' denotes those approaches that locate the dynamic of Cold War within rather than between the contending blocs. This approach has several variants: it can locate the source of conflict either within the domestic politics and socio-economic structure of the two major states themselves, and, by extension, within the other constituent states; or it can do so within the internationally constituted bloc itself, seen as an ensemble where cold war is functional to the maintenance of bloc cohesion and the hegemony of the dominant states within it. The most straightforward version of this is Chomsky's 'two dungeons' thesis, according to which the USA and the USSR pursued the Cold War in order to discipline their own societies and their respective junior partners.[6] Mary Kaldor's work has a similar thrust to it.[7] Arguments such as those of Alan Wolfe, which attribute Cold War to the workings of US domestic politics, are an alternative version.[8] Many expositions of the 'internalist' thesis focus on the pressure for confrontation from economic sectors, characteristically the 'military-industrial' complex. Thompson's theory of 'exterminism' is one of the more elaborate variants of this thesis, since it sees the arms race not just as the product of what arms manufacturers themselves want, but of a dynamic that has come to characterise the societies in question as a whole.[9] 'Internalist' arguments tend to deny the efficacy of East–West conflict as such and to imply a degree of homology between the foreign policies and internal structures of the two blocs.[10]

The 'inter-systemic' argument can be quickly distinguished from all three of the other approaches: in contradistinction to realism it denies that East–West rivalry is merely a continuation of traditional great power politics, not only by questioning the validity of this supposedly universal and classical model, but by allotting a central place in the conflict to the diverse, heterogeneous, character of the competing states, at both internal and international levels; in opposition to theories of misperception, it asserts that the competing political programmes and ideological perspectives of the two blocs are to be taken seriously, while not at face value, and that the states comprising the blocs were, in broad terms, committed to their realisation; as against the internalists, the 'inter-systemic' approach asserts that international conflict does have a reality, in other words that the two blocs are concerned not just with internal issues, profits, hierarchy or 'order', but also with improving their relative positions *vis-à-vis* each other and with prevailing over the other.

Inter-systemic theory can be summarised in terms of three core propositions: (a) East–West rivalry is a product of conflict between two distinct social systems; (b) this competition involved a competitive and universalising dynamic; and (c) it can only be concluded with the prevailing of one bloc over the other. The term 'system' is not used here to denote the 'international system' in general, as designated in conventional IR theory, nor 'the Cold War as system', in the sense of mutual reinforcement characteristic of the internalists, but to denote the internal organisation of the societies and polities of each bloc.

There was, consequently, something specific and necessary, an underlying contradictory and universalising dynamic in East–West relations. Cold War was, above all, a product of heterogeneity in the international system – to repeat, in both internal organisation and international practice – and could only be ended by the attainment of a

23

new homogeneity. The implication of this was that, *as long as two distinct systems existed*, cold war conflict was bound to continue: cold war could not end with compromise, or convergence, but only with the prevailing of one of these systems over the other. Only when either capitalism had prevailed over communism, or the other way around, would inter-systemic conflict cease.

Issues in inter-systemic theory

While present in an implicit way in some discussion of the Cold War, inter-systemic conflict theory was little represented in either IR literature or peace movement writing. If it draws its most obvious inspiration from Marxism, it can also be seen as a continuation of a strain of argument within IR that has little or nothing to do with Marxism and which stresses the importance of ideological difference in international conflict.[11] The reasons operating against its acceptance were several. Itemising them may help not only to clarify the claims of the 'inter-systemic' approach, but also to identify what some of the underlying issues within IR theory raised by this issue may be.

For conventional Realist theory, as in Bull and Waltz, the issue of internal systemic determination of foreign policy is irrelevant, indeed technically inconceivable: since all that matters are relations between states no such admission of the relevance of internal processes, causes or consequences, is allowed within such theory. Relations between 'states' can be analysed irrespective of internal correlates. Moreover, by positing an abstracted 'international system', which determines the behaviour of states and imposes certain rules on component members, Realism denies the possibility of fundamentally variant forms of international conflict.

To argue for inter-systemic theory in its fullest form, requires having an adequate concept of the difference between the systems, not just in terms of some international slogans and goals, but in terms of the constitution of the societies themselves and the basis of their disagreement. Here the very strong resistance of IR theory to the concept of 'capitalism' becomes relevant: a naive visitor to the field of international relations might think that if anything characterised the development of the international system over the past 500 years it would be this phenomenon. It is at least as important as war, nationalism, statehood and the other familiar terms: yet it is almost never mentioned, except in muffled formulations about the 'development of the international economy' and, latterly, 'interdependence'. To develop a concept of inter-systemic theory involves, however, having some

24

concept of what constitutes the West at both the internal and international levels, namely 'capitalism', and of its comparatively short-lived twentieth-century challenger, whatever the latter may be called. This is something which can be provided either within Weberian sociological or Marxist theory, yet, precisely because of IR's silence, it is almost impossible to do within mainstream international theory.

Even where the internal is considered relevant, as in foreign policy analysis, there is little support for the inter-systemic approach: on the one hand, what are seen as transnational 'linkages' are limited, specific, forms of interaction quite different from the comprehensive view of inter-systemic interaction envisaged here, and based on an often flimsy, behavioural, concept of society; on the other hand, empirical correlations carried out within foreign policy analysis do not confirm any distinct correlations between type of political system (e.g. monarchical/republic, totalitarian/democratic) and foreign policy output. Since totalitarian societies can be aggressive or defensive the issue of systemic determination does not arise.

A theory based on inter-systemic conflict is all the more unattractive because of what it appears to resemble: it can easily be assimilated to either, or both, of the paradigms of old Cold War thinking itself, i.e. dogmatic Soviet conceptions of the 'two camps' and of a capitalism–socialism conflict, or Western presentations of the Cold War as a conflict between two rival political and economic systems, a 'free' world versus one of a communist dictatorship. The compulsion to distance themselves from both of these stereotypes does much to explain the espousal by liberal and peace movement writers of approaches involving a degree of causal, and ethical, symmetry, i.e. the subjectivist and internalist. A similar concern can be seen in the liberal writings that accompanied the end of the Cold War in the late 1980s when it was suggested, in the face of all evidence, that somehow *both* sides had been exhausted by the Cold War and were therefore the losers: of course the USA had paid the cost, but it was not Soviet bankers who were coming in to supervise the US transition to socialism. Those using Marxist categories to explain the Cold War were almost inevitably assimilated to orthodox Soviet pre-1985 analyses: this was not only because of bias in those making this assimilation but also because the theoretical underpinnings of their analysis were not made sufficiently clear.[12]

One of the central themes of inter-systemic theory, that cold war is a product of heterogeneity, does not necessarily command assent. As against the supposedly intuitive view that heterogeneity makes for instability and homogeneity for stability, there is the counter-view,

25

equally intuitive, that it is heterogeneity that makes for stability. In Realist theory this informs the view, espoused by Waltz and others, of the stability of bipolarity. In regard to systemic heterogeneity it is the assumption implicit in the 'two dungeons' theory: it is not explicit in most IR theory, since this is only concerned with relations between states, but in the now fashionably resurrected German theorist Carl Schmitt, who argued the need for an 'adversary' in political life, domestic and by extension international, and earlier, in the general thesis popularised by Arnold Toynbee of 'challenge and response'.[13] Schmitt, like the inter-systemic theory, has suffered by association, in this case with Nazism: but, as the presence of this thesis within the benign liberal and peace movement writing indicates, his argument has broader relevance or at least unacknowledged following. It reinforces the view, initiated by denying that capitalism or communism have any serious universalising dynamic, that East–West conflict was a mirage, and was really functional for ruling groups on both sides.

Differing theoretical approaches aside, there are obvious historical, indeed common sense, reasons for denying the validity of the inter-systemic approach. On the one hand, there appears to be little reason to attribute conflict to the inter-systemic when modern history is so full of conflicts between homogeneous states: from the inter-capitalist explosions of 1914 and 1939 to the disputes and wars of the socialist bloc. On the other hand, the pattern of postwar alliances, and informal strategic alignments, suggests that heterogeneity is no obstacle to such collaboration: thus a capitalist India collaborated with a socialist USSR, while a socialist China aligned with the USA.

Core propositions

The difficulties with the inter-systemic approach are, therefore, considerable: there are at least three major alternative approaches to analysing cold war; there are strong reasons, theoretical and empirical, for rejecting it; it has unsavoury political associations. Above all, however, it is underdeveloped in its own terms: those who have espoused it have thrown out occasional arguments as to its validity and components, or have implied that there is a read 'off the shelf' theory within Marxism for explaining such a phenomenon. Once an attempt is made to lay out what the claims of the inter-systemic theory are then it becomes evident that even greater theoretical complexities underlie it and inhibit its adoption. It is, however, only through such a construction and identification of the broader theoretical implications that the argument can be taken further. In the light of this discussion, the inter-systemic argument would seem to rest on five core propositions.

(i) *The socio-economic heterogeneity of 'East' and 'West', i.e. of communist and capitalist societies:* This pertains, at least, to the economic and political levels within each state and bloc. The starting point for the inter-systemic argument is this difference, in fundamental, constitutive, terms, between the two kinds of society and polity. This 'difference' may be formulated in Weberian or Marxist terms, but does involve some conception of the political and social system as a whole. Constitutional or behavioural political science approaches, theories based on convergence, or those which saw the USSR as just another form of 'capitalist' society, deny this heterogeneity and will necessarily preclude analysis on inter-systemic lines, as will those that, for tactical or 'fairness' reasons, treat the two symmetrically. If it is not admitted that the Soviet and US blocs were fundamentally different in international constitution then the argument cannot proceed.

(ii) *This socio-economic and political composition must be shown to be determinant, in a broad sense, of foreign policy and international relations more generally.* There is no 'foreign policy' as such, but only the foreign policy of specific kinds of state and society. This thesis of determination in some ways overlaps with, but is theoretically quite distinct from, that found in foreign policy analysis with its examination of the domestic determinants of foreign policy output. The difference lies in the conception of what constitutes relevant domestic determinants, and in the (unstated) differences in what constitutes the state-society relationship: as in the discussion of heterogeneity, the discussion inevitably leads back to the general conception of society and polity.

(iii) *The thesis of inter-systemic conflict implies an internationalising and indeed universalising dynamic within each bloc and system:* in other words, it implies that each bloc is impelled to seek not only to protect its own state and economy, to maximise its advantage within the constraints of a 'balance of power', and to appear to challenge the other for reasons of ideological credibility within, but to dominate as much of the world as possible, and to undermine and hopefully abolish the alternative system. Such an argument goes against the orthodox IR conception of international relations tending to preserve whether by design or of necessity, a 'balance of power', and also against the liberal assertion that neither side had any compelling ideological aspirations and that the conflict was all about power maximisation. Yet, apart from a rather large amount of historical evidence with regard to the drives of capitalism, elements of this universal dynamic are recognised in existing theories: the drive of capitalism to maximise markets and access to raw materials, the commitments of the USSR to world revolution, the competition of each for allies in the Third World to enhance their military and political security and strength. But these are at best fragments of a broader theory of universalisation, which is as yet obscure.[14] For example, the drive of capitalism is not merely economic: otherwise it would have been quite content to leave the communist states with their political systems intact provided trade was conducted between them. This drive to universalisation is the issue that lies at the core of the heterogeneity issue, since it is claimed that each system, beyond any immediate compromises or obstacles, was committed to the transformation of the other. The least that can be said about the outcome of the late 1980s is that, at first sight and more, it lends credence to this.

(iv) *Inter-systemic conflict operates on multiple dimensions not just that of inter-state relations as conventionally conceived: the issue of what 'foreign policy' states pursue compromises only a part of how each of the two socio-economic systems operated internationally.* Inter-systemic competition took place at three main levels: that of inter-state relations as such, i.e. 'foreign policy' conventionally conceived; that of socio-economic interaction more broadly interpreted, to include the actions of entities other than states/governments, most notably financial and industrial enterprises; that of ideological interaction, and in particular the impact on one society of the example, the demonstration effect, of others. A clear example of this triple interaction, with the mutual reinforcement of each level, was that of FRG–GDR (West German–East German) relations in the late 1980s, up to and through the collapse of the East German regime in 1989–90: the project of the FRG as a whole was, in the classic Clausewitzian wrestling sense, to defeat, not annihilate, i.e. to 'throw down' (*niederwerfen*) the GDR. This was inter-systemic conflict in its rawest form and operated at all three levels: the undermining of the GDR, the mobilisation of a pro-unification majority within it, the discrediting of any socialist or neutral option, were accomplished by the pressure on the GDR on the three levels. In contrast to what conventional realist theory, with its stress on inter-state conflict, might suggest, the role of the Bonn government was perhaps the least important and that of West German business secondary: the most influential level was the impact on millions of East Germans of the image they had of the West and then, once the frontier was opened, of visiting the West. This demonstration effect was certainly compounded by the pressures of West German banks and businesses on the GDR economy, whether or not this pressure was formally coordinated with Bonn, and the specific actions taken by Bonn itself: conditionality for economic aid, encouragement through automatic citizenship and welfare benefits to the GDR population to leave, fostering of rumours about imminent collapse of the GDR economy and so on. It would have been rather difficult to interpret this instance of inter-systemic conflict without some reference to the tendency of capitalism to expand, a tendency realised not just through the actions of states as such but also through the broader social and ideological interactions.

(v) *Heterogeneity of internal socio-economic systems implies heterogeneity of international relations, conceived in terms of broad goals and mechanisms of internationalisation.* The interests of the two blocs were fundamentally opposed, and the kinds of world they aimed to create diverged as indicated. From this it followed that there would be other differences in the foreign policy and international extension of these systems. This did not necessarily entail, in the narrow sense in which this is conventionally phrased within IR, that they pursued different kinds or styles of foreign policy, i.e. that the instruments, conventions and operating procedures of foreign policy themselves were heterogeneous. This is left open: the states involved in the conflict may, or may not, have been socialised in the Realist sense of the term. The argument cannot be settled by looking at 'socialisation' in the formal sense, of whether they had the same kinds of diplomatic conventions or respected sovereignty. The Realist argument about 'international society' and the socialising effects of the system is relevant in limited terms, but does not answer this broader question. On the other hand, the heterogeneity of goals in general, since it arises from a heterogeneity of system, is accompanied by a heterogeneity at at least three other levels: first, heterogeneity of cause – the underlying reasons for the universalising dynamic may well be different in different socio-economic systems, being more or less economic in one, more or less military or political in the other; secondly, the mechanisms for, and commitment to, creating an international homogeneous bloc around a core, hegemonic, state may well differ, as is at least evident from the very different political and economic policies of the USA and USSR within their respective blocs – the forms of integration and mechanisms of hierarchy were not identical; thirdly, the mechanisms for competition with the other bloc may also be asymmetrical – this asymmetry reflecting not just differences in 'power' generally conceived, but the varying salience of different components of a system's *modus operandi*, e.g. economic, ideological, military, as reflected at the international level. The relative balance of economic and military power in the influence of the Soviet Union and USA was very different, just as was the degree of direct political control exercised by each over their respective bloc clients. The competition of blocs may, therefore, involve not just a conflict of goals, but a conflict of the reasons for which, and the mechanisms by which, international relations were conducted.

Future directions

This outline disinterment of the components of the inter-systemic theory inevitably raises more questions than it answers. Two points are immediately evident: first, that whatever its analytic and theoretical strengths, inter-systemic theory is a far from adequate development. The appearance of such a development in earlier Soviet dogma concealed more than it revealed – not least because of the immanent teleology within its concept of 'correlation of forces', which implied that history was moving inexorably towards the triumph of the Soviet over the Western blocs; secondly, any elaboration of a theory of inter-systemic conflict entails a broader theoretical framework, loosely derivative of either Weberian sociology or historical materialism. Concepts such as 'state, system', the 'international' while apparently common currency between mainstream IR and sociology/historical materialism are on closer examination not.[15] More important still, as the above outline makes clear, and not for reasons of canonical deference, the starting point for any theory of inter-systemic conflict is not a vague difference in foreign policy goals or styles, or a divergence derived from geo-strategic asymmetry, but the difference in the constitution of society itself, in both domestic and international variants. The starting point for any related theory of IR is, therefore, the concept of what in Marxist theory is 'the mode of production' and of the relations between this and 'the state': without these the theory of inter-systemic conflict is unthinkable. No ecumenical defusing of differences between an IR mainstream which precludes such concepts and these other theories is possible. There can be no analysis of inter-systemic conflict that cannot admit the category 'capitalism' and its, variously named, contrary.

If this argument is valid, then in addition to the development of a theory of international conflict and international relations generally based on social systems, there are at least three other areas of theoretical development suggested by inter-systemic conflict theory.

Dimensions and mechanisms of international interaction

If, as already indicated, inter-systemic conflict can be seen as operating on three levels – inter-state, inter-socio-economic, inter-

30

ideological – then it becomes necessary to analyse how these interact and how the relative balance shifts from period to period, for any specific state, and as between different kinds of state. What is entailed here is nothing less than a proper sociology of international relations: not in the sense of tacking on some off-the-shelf IR theory to existing sociology, or of making some broad and possibly inapposite generalisations about how international relations have social aspects (law, ideology, convention etc.), but in the sense of how within an international system, constituted by different states, the socio-economic determines both the individual states themselves and, transcending the states, the system as a whole. In the light of the history of the last 500 years, and of the outcome of the Cold War itself, there is a special need to re-examine and elucidate the universalising drive of capitalism itself, both in terms of why it seeks to mould the world in its image, and the variant mechanisms of so doing: if pop music and tee-shirts are the gunboats of the late twentieth century, there is an underlying continuity in the multi-layered and aggressive drive of capitalism to destroy all rival socio-economic systems.

Inter-systemic conflict and anti-systemic movements

The conflict of social systems, embodied in and mediated through states (the USA, USSR etc.) in Cold War has been accompanied by broader movements within and between states directed against these states and the international orders they embody. In the course of this century, these have taken a variety of forms (revolutions, strikes, guerilla wars, ideological challenges etc.) and have been directed against the hegemonic orders in both blocs. Three standard analyses of these anti-systemic movements are available: the conventional IR approach, which subordinates them to states, and denies their relevance to international relations except where they receive the backing of states – viz. the almost complete silence of IR literature on revolutions, and trades unions;[16] the orthodox Soviet approach which assimilated non-state anti-systemic movements to the state interests of the USSR itself, thus dissolving the issues of autonomy and contradiction involved in the relationship; and the conventional 'alternative' approach (e.g. that of Arrighi, Wallerstein and Hopkins), which sees anti-systemic movements as the motor of international history and as capable of overriding the powers and fragmentations of states.[17] In the case of the latter, and analogous writings from the peace movement, these anti-systemic movements are seen as directed against what is still one, homogeneous, system, the divergence of capitalism and communism being denied. Thus the workers' movements in Poland and South Africa are part of one 'anti-systemic' dynamic.

The comparative study of inter-systemic conflict

The focus of this analysis has been on inter-systemic conflict of the postwar period, that between the communist and capitalist blocs. This has certain specific features not found in earlier epochs: the technological and economic dimensions of its military competition, the specific ideological forms of hegemony claimed by both sides, the mobilisation of large masses of population into systemic and anti-systemic activity. This particular inter-systemic conflict would appear to be yielding one other unique feature, namely the historically contra-cyclical outcome whereby an already established system, capitalism, generated and then suffocated its newer-emerged rival. Yet in other respects inter-systemic conflict is by no means specific to the Cold War epoch: the conflicts of societies based on feudalism and capitalism from the fourteenth century in Europe to the last redoubts of pre-capitalism in the Third World in the late twentieth century would bear comparative analysis, as would more specific localised conflicts between slave-owning and free labour exploiting societies. The means by which capitalism has encircled, undermined and then crushed the Soviet bloc have something in common with the earlier capitalist assaults on the Chinese and Ottoman empires, not least in the way alarmed reformers within the besieged bloc, in trying to alter their own system in order the better to compete, have accelerated the decomposition of their social and political systems.

Only spasmodic mention has been made of the outcome of the Cold War, with the rapid demise of Soviet power in the late 1980s. It would, however, appear plausible to argue that in certain important respects this bore out the suggestions of inter-systemic conflict theory: first, in that the collapse of communism came not through the conventional mechanism of inter-state conflict, namely war, nor through the erosion of the Soviet bloc's territory by Western military or commercial pressure, but rather through the undermining of the system through the demonstration effect of Western success in the social, economic and political fields;[18] secondly, that the form in which the Cold War ended was not that of a balance of power, or of a mutual exhaustion, but of the prevailing of one bloc over the other, in other words a systemic victory. Other interpretations of this outcome, and indeed of the underlying character of the Cold War, are certainly possible: the hope must, however, be that at least, even if rather late in the day, the underlying theoretical assumptions and implications of this, the overriding dimension of international conflict in the post-1945 era, are examined.

Notes

This summary argument is an attempt to make explicit the assumptions underlying a number of my earlier writings on cold war, notably *The Making of the Second Cold War* (London: Verso, 1983), and 'The Ends of Cold War', *New Left Review*, no. 180, March–April 1990. I would like to thank in particular Simon Bromley, Margot Light, Justin Rosenberg, Mike Rustin, Gautam Sen for comments on an earlier draft as well as Paul Lewis for his careful assessment and critique of my *Second Cold War* in his Open University reader *Global Politics, Block II: Superpower Rivalry and Global Political Competition*, Paper 2, Open University, 1988, and Mick Cox for many stimulating exchanges on these issues.

1 J. L. Gaddis, 'The Emerging Post-Revisionist Synthesis on the Origins of the Cold War', *Diplomatic History*, vol. 7, Summer 1983.
2 For earlier discussion of this literature, see Halliday, *The Making of the Second Cold War*, ch. 2, and 'Vigilantism in International Relations: Kubalkova, Cruickshank and Marxist Theory', *Review of International Studies*, vol. 13, no. 3, 1987.
3 Thus in his textbook of realist theory, *The Anarchical Society: A Study of Order in World Politics* (London: Macmillan, 1977), Hedley Bull treats East–West conflict in the postwar period as illustration and confirmation of this broader argument. Many others, for example, Morgenthau and Waltz, did likewise. There was no problem.
4 Irving L. Janis, *Victims of Groupthink: A Psychological Study of Foreign Policy Decisions and Fiascoes* (Boston: Houghton Mifflin, 1972); and Robert Jervis, *Perception and Misperception in International Policies* (New Jersey: Princeton University Press, 1976).
5 The argument that the conflict between revolutionary and status quo powers was in some sense avoidable is found, *inter alia*, with regard to the French revolution in Kim Kyong-won, *Revolution and International System* (New York: New York University Press, 1970), and with regard to Iran in James Bill, *The Eagle and the Lion* (New Haven: Yale University Press, 1988).
6 Noam Chomsky, *Towards a New Cold War* (New York: Pantheon Books, 1982).
7 Mary Kaldor, *The Disintegrating West* (London: Penguin, 1979); and *The Imaginary War: Was There an East–West Conflict?* (Oxford: Blackwell, 1990).
8 Alan Wolfe, *The Rise and Fall of the 'Soviet Threat'* (Washington, 1990).
9 E. P. Thompson et al., *Exterminism and Cold War* (London: Verso, 1982).
10 For an attempt to engage with Chomsky on these issues, see my discussion with him in Bill Bourne, Udi Eichler and David Herman (eds.), *Writers and Politics* (Nottingham: Spokesman Books, 1987).
11 Two classic discussions of heterogeneity within mainstream IR literature are Richard Rosecrance, *Action and Reaction in International Politics* (Boston:

Little Brown, 1963); and Raymond Aron, *Peace and War* (London: Weidenfeld and Nicholson, 1966), pp. 373–81.

12 Vendulka Kubalkova and Albert A. Cruickshank, 'The "New Cold War" in "Critical International Relations Studies"', *Review of International Studies*, vol. 12, no. 3, July 1986.

13 Carl Schmitt, *Concept of the Political* (New Brunswick, NJ: Rutgers University Press, 1976); and Arnold J. Toynbee, *Study of History* (12 vol., London: Oxford University Press, 1934–61).

14 A powerful historical account of the universalising drive of capitalism can be found in Eric Hobsbawm, *The Age of Empire, 1875–1914* (London: Weidenfeld and Nicolson, 1987). What is striking is that this generally accepted historical thesis, and one eloquently stated in *The Communist Manifesto* should have so little impact on left-wing writing on cold war in the 1980s: asserting that capitalism did have a tendency to prevail over alternatives to it, and for global hegemony, seemed to play into the hands of Soviet policy; instead we had the debatable symmetry of the internalists.

15 The Soviet term, 'correlation of forces', a supposedly more dynamic and materialist alternative to the 'balance of power' was never taken seriously in the West and was abandoned in the 1980s in the USSR: in fact, it has proved its validity, precisely because it did take socio-economic and ideological factors in international competition into account and did see the possibility of a decisive shift in favour of one bloc. That it mistook which bloc would benefit from a shift in the correlation was perhaps a secondary oversight. For a lucid analysis of the concept, see Margot Light, *The Soviet Theory of International Relations* (Brighton: Wheatsheaf, 1988).

16 Fred Halliday, '"The Sixth Great Power": On the Study of Revolution and International Relations', *Review of International Studies*, vol. 16, no 3, July 1990.

17 Giovanni Arrighi, Terence Hopkins and Immanuel Wallerstein, *Anti-Systemic Movements* (London, Verso, 1989).

18 For applications of these ideas to the collapse of the Soviet bloc, see Halliday, 'The Ends of Cold War', *New Left Review*, no. 180, March–April 1990, pp. 35–50; and 'A Singular Collapse: the Soviet Union, Market Pressure and Inter-state Competition', *Contention* (Los Angeles), vol. 1, no 2, Fall 1991.

3 RADICAL THEORY AND THE NEW COLD WAR
MICHAEL COX

Introduction

During the 1980s there were, in effect, two quite distinct phases in the relationship between the United States and the Soviet Union. The first – corresponding more or less to President Reagan's tenure of office between 1980 and 1985, saw the return to Cold War policies and rhetoric that many assumed (or at least hoped) had died a death after the Vietnam disaster. The second, stretching from Gorbachev's rise to power in the middle of the decade to the Bush presidency, not only witnessed the speedy and unexpected termination of this 'New' Cold War, but following the collapse of Soviet power in Eastern Europe in 1989, the disintegration of the Cold War as a system. By any stretch of the imagination the eighties were an extraordinary decade, undoubtedly the most turbulent and revolutionary of any since the end of the war.

Making sense of the eighties is thus absolutely crucial and in this chapter I want to examine how one particular group of writers – loosely described here as radicals – sought to comprehend this transitional period. As I shall try to show, radicals presented a picture of US–Soviet relations during this period that was both internally coherent and intellectually distinct – at times suggestive and original as well. However, as I shall also demonstrate, their reading of these years was flawed in a number of important ways and left them open to serious attack from their academic adversaries. Here, however, intellectual history was only repeating itself, for an earlier generation of radicals had also attempted (and failed) to demonstrate that they had a better appreciation of the Cold War than their less critical peers. Let us therefore briefly examine the original surge of radical writing on the 'First' Cold War, before going on to examine the new wave that later attempted to understand the 'Second'.

The rise and fall of radical revisionism

In the period between the US decision to escalate the war in Vietnam in 1965 and the final collapse of American power in South-East Asia, radicals effectively dominated the debate about the origins of the Cold War, much to the chagrin of conservative scholars. Building upon the earlier work of the grand old man of revisionism, William Appleman Williams, writers such as Horowitz, Kolko, LaFeber, Gardner and Chomsky set the intellectual pace during these years by challenging established truths and asking awkward questions about the dynamics of American rather than Soviet imperial expansion in the postwar period, and the degree to which the US rather than the USSR bore the major responsibility for postwar tensions. To those reared on established truths about the origins of the Cold War the revisionists seemed naive at best, mere apologists for the USSR at worst. However, for a critical generation grown tired of the Cold War, radicals appeared to have the most persuasive intellectual answers to the big problems of the day.[1]

There were a number of reasons for the remarkable success of radical discourse during those years, particularly in the United States. First, and perhaps most importantly, critical scholarship on all aspects of United States foreign relations (and not just the Cold War) was stimulated and broadened by the controversy over Vietnam: in part because the war in South-East Asia radicalised a large section of the American intelligentsia, but also because it brought into question the original doctrine of containment which many assumed was the ultimate cause of the débâcle in Vietnam.[2]

However, to conclude that in the absence of Vietnam radical revisionism would not have arisen would be misleading. Other factors also helped weaken the hold of orthodoxy upon American academia. One, undoubtedly, was the intellectually one-sided character of the traditional interpretation of the Cold War which dealt almost exclusively with Soviet actions after 1947 while ignoring the mainsprings of American policies. Another was the longer-term erosion of the Cold War consensus within America itself, the result firstly of major changes in the communist world since the late fifties, and secondly of an increasing discomfort in the United States with some of the consequences of the Cold War, notably high military spending.[3] Finally, revisionism was but the more radical expression of an ongoing debate already taking place within the foreign policy and academic community in the sixties about the future relationship between the USA and its main communist rivals. Long before Vietnam, in fact, sections of the liberal establishment were already beginning to challenge and question traditional Cold War shibboleths. As they did so, this fed into the broader academic discussion about the causes and consequences of a conflict that many now saw as irrelevant.[4]

In the latter half of the seventies radical analysis of the Cold War was not so much defeated, but castrated and incorporated by an emerging generation of liberal scholars led by John Gaddis. They had two distinct advantages over the new left: one, a stronger attachment to the norms of academic scholarship, and secondly, a greater sensitivity to the complexity of the postwar period. In comparison to the one-sided picture provided by the revisionists, the post-revisionist's account of the origins of the Cold War certainly seemed more balanced. Moreover, the fact that the revisionists had said little that was seriously critical of Soviet policies after the war left them open to the damaging charge they had previously levelled against their orthodox enemies: that they were apologists for one of the two sides in the Cold War.

Revisionism thus lost its star-billing (although revisionist accounts of the Cold War still continued to appear) and post-revisionist analysis – which emphasised the political rather than the economic taproots of US foreign policy, and maintained that both powers shared responsibility for the Cold War – became dominant in the academic community. Whether the new school represented a modified form of revisionism or a recycling of the old orthodox tale with footnotes remained an open question however.[5]

Changes in the international political scene probably did as much to undermine the radical's control of the intellectual agenda as did the obvious academic strengths of post-revisionism.[6] First, by 1975 not only was Vietnam a dead political issue in the United States, but the new left was beginning to lose its influence on American campuses. Moreover, by proclaiming the virtues of detente with both Russia and China in the seventies, the foreign policy elite temporarily, but successfully, undercut the radical claim that the US was addicted to Cold War policies. In addition, by emphasising the importance of human rights around the world, the Carter administration not only forced the Soviet regime onto the defensive, but many on the left as well, particularly those who earlier had defended the very regimes (like Vietnam and Cambodia) that now turned out to be so inhuman in the treatment of their own citizens.[7] Finally, in the later seventies, the intellectual shift to the right in the West – particularly in the United States and France – proved too much for many on what was fast becoming the 'old' new left, and some of the most influential (notably

Ronald Radosh and David Horowitz) simply shifted sides and joined the camp of the neo-conservatists. A few even made it into the outer fringes of the Reagan administration.[8]

Reaganism and the radical revival

Ironically, the election in 1980 of an American president determined to rebuild US power in the world gave a major boost to the radical cause. In many ways Reagan was a gift to the left. Patriotic, prone to the wildest Cold War rhetoric, apparently indifferent to the plight of the Third World, and to all intents and purposes ignorant of Europe, he was almost the identikit ugly American – easily caricatured by his enemies as 'that cowboy' in the White House with a flair for articulating all that was least attractive about America. According to his critics (many of whom were not radicals, of course) Reagan had too many simple answers to too many complex problems. Thus, instead of addressing the social and political causes of instability in the Third World, he blamed it all on the Cubans or the Soviets. Moreover, from his rhetoric it was difficult not to conclude that he had complete faith in the virtues of military power to resolve most, if not all, international problems. Most worryingly of all perhaps, Reagan seemed to think that the Cold War itself had been a golden age in American history when the country had been united and US power had been respected around the world.

What caused most concern, however, was not Reagan's understanding of the past, but his administration's contemporary pursuit of what many saw as destabilising nuclear policies. The new team's apparent endorsement of game plans designed to fight and prevail in a nuclear encounter, the political influence of the Dr Strangeloves who staffed right-wing think tanks close to the White House, and the development of a new generation of first strike weapons created concern at home and sent a political shiver across the Atlantic. This found its expression in the exponential growth of a mass West European peace movement. It was in Europe, in fact, rather than in the United States that Reagan's nuclear policies probably had their most radicalising impact – partly one suspects because Reagan tapped a deep well of anti-Americanism on the continent, but also because many Europeans believed that the deployment of new nuclear weapons on their soil (notably cruise and Pershing II) was simply an artful American dodge that would enable it to fight a 'limited' nuclear war in Europe without it spreading to the US mainland. Indeed, it was somewhat ironic that the least important component of the Reagan nuclear programme should have become the *raison d'être* for the anti-nuclear campaign across Western Europe after 1979.[9]

While radicals on both sides of the Atlantic were agreed that the New Cold War constituted a new and potentially very dangerous stage in superpower relations, they were by no means united in their analysis of events.

Some like Edward Thompson, assumed that Europe was the main battlefield in the Cold War and that it was here that the real struggle would have to be fought. Thompson even took the opportunity presented by the collapse of superpower detente to launch a strong critique of the new left for having abandoned Europe in the seventies for more exciting terrain on the periphery of the international system.[10] Others however insisted that it was on this so-called periphery – the Third World – that the New Cold War would be at its most intense. It was in the Third World, after all, that American imperialism had suffered its most important reversals in the seventies. It was thus likely to be there that the New Cold War would be fought most bitterly.[11]

Nor was there complete agreement either about the underlying meaning of the New Cold War. According to Mary Kaldor and Noam Chomsky for instance, the Reagan foreign policy had very little to do with containing the Russians. Rather it was a conscious attempt by Washington to reassert American power after a period of decline.[12] Fred Halliday, on the other hand, took an altogether different approach. The Second Cold War, he maintained, had little if anything to do with US decline. On the contrary, it was exactly what it appeared to be: a US attempt to contest the Soviet Union more forcefully after a period in which there had been important military and political gains for the USSR. Of course Halliday agreed that the 'threat' was not as great as neo-conservatives claimed. Nor did he deny the fact that conjunctural factors (such as the shift to the right in the United States in the late seventies) contributed to the New Cold War. Yet Reagan's rhetoric reflected a genuine US concern, the expression ultimately of an American antagonism to the Soviet Union – a new form of society opposed to and by Western imperialism.[13]

Radical analysis and the New Cold War

While the left may have disagreed about the underlying meaning of the New Cold War, and were divided as to where the main geographical site of the conflict should be located, nevertheless it is still possible to identify a relatively coherent radical analysis of superpower relations in the late seventies and eighties. This consisted of a number of important propositions, the first being that America bore the ultimate responsibility for the collapse of superpower detente. Soviet actions before 1980 may have contributed to this, but the main cause (or causes) of the demise of the Kissinger–Nixon 'grand design' had to be sought in the United States rather than the USSR. Radicals identified a number of factors that had undermined attempts to normalise US–Soviet relations in the seventies, including internal opposition in the US to detente by Cold Warriors who believed that the USSR remained and would always be a serious threat to the West; antagonism by the US military to a policy that might weaken their position; the 'aggressive' human rights drive pursued by Carter under the urging of his NSC adviser Brzezinski after 1978; the central role played by the Committee On The Present Danger in the whipping up of anti-Soviet hysteria in the latter half of the seventies; and finally the deliberate manipulation of the Soviet threat by the intellectual advocates of 'revitalised containment' – the same people of course who advised Reagan on foreign policy before 1980 and who, after he came to power, filled key positions within his administration.[14]

For radicals the collapse of superpower detente was thus the result of American pressure rather than Soviet actions. This in turn related to a second crucial point emphasised by radicals: that the driving force behind the 'Second' Cold War (as it had been behind the 'First' in 1947) was the more powerful, rightward moving United States.[15] America indeed had a vested interest in a New Cold War. It would legitimise its more assertive stance in the broader world system. It would also reinforce the unity of the West after a period of drift. And it would strengthen the forces of conservatism globally. The USSR by contrast had no interest in a breakdown of relations; quite the opposite, in fact. Moreover, whereas the US seemed to have a dynamic strategy in 1980, the USSR had no strategy at all – other than to limit the potential damage that might be inflicted upon its international position by the new American offensive. Soviet policy in short was essentially reactive and defensive; America's on the other hand was active and aggressive.[16] Even Thompson, who was critical of both superpowers, agreed that US intentions were 'more provocative and dangerous' than those of the USSR.[17]

The radical view that the primary responsibility for the New Cold War lay with the United States was not only based upon a particular reading of US intentions however: it was also premised upon an empirical, comparative assessment of American and Soviet capabilities. According to the left, the USSR was simply too weak to be a threat to the more powerful United States.[18] Indeed, not only was the US much more of a 'superpower' than the Soviet Union, the latter faced so many problems that it could not even claim superpower status. Its economy was inefficient and burdened down by excessive military spending. Its new friends in the Third World were poor. Its traditional allies in Eastern Europe remained hostile. China was an enemy. And as a model of society the USSR inspired and attracted nobody. Furthermore, even though Soviet military power may have grown since the sixties, the USSR remained militarily inferior in several important ways. Soviet military supremacy in other words was a myth.[19]

The emphasis placed by radicals on Soviet weakness was by no means an innocent academic ploy. Its 'function' was to undermine the most central of all right-wing claims: that there was an extremely serious Soviet threat to the West to which the US was legitimately responding under Reagan's leadership. This, it was argued, was either a gross exaggeration, or, in fact, a carefully constructed device whose purpose was to justify American imperial strategy. Indeed, according to some on the left, the superpowers – far from being enemies – were actually informal partners in the joint management of a bipolar international system from which they both benefited. Thus how could the USSR be a threat to the United States when both worked in tandem to preserve the status quo?[20]

Radical scepticism about the Soviet threat was central to its understanding of the Second Cold War, for having proved that the Reagan administration's foreign policy was based upon a myth (or even a fabrication), it could then set about attacking it more effectively. It also lent credibility to the radical claim that the principle threat to world peace was the United States rather than the USSR. It was American policy, they argued, that was leading to renewed tensions in the Third World. It was also the US that was challenging the legitimacy of the USSR – and not the other way round. And of course it was the United States that was seriously intervening into the internal affairs of other people's countries and once again escalating the arms race.[21]

Radicals and the arms race

Nowhere was American responsibility for increased tensions so evident – according to the left – than in the field of nuclear weapons and arms control. Here there was no doubt as to who was the more aggressive of the two powers. The main driving force behind the arms race had always been, and still remained, the United States. The US had led in the development of military technology and weapons production throughout the Cold War – and still did. And through the

41

promotion of successive myths such as the bomber and missile gaps in the fifties, and the 'window of vulnerability' in the seventies, it had been responsible for every major escalation of the arms race.[22]

It was true of course that the US had promoted some form of limited arms control in the seventies. However, it had not been really serious about regulating the arms race according to radical commentators. Indeed, in the so-called era of detente, the US had seen arms control not as a way of promoting disarmament, but as a means of managing Soviet foreign policy through the dubious strategy of linkage. Reagan had now even abandoned that charade and was proceeding with an unprecedented military build-up. Believing that the US could either outspend the USSR and impose enormous strains on the Soviet economy, or that it might achieve nuclear superiority over the Soviets, the White House was pursuing a policy of military coercion whose ultimate goal was the recreation of a position of strength which the US had once held in the halcyon years of the Cold War.[23]

What, however, set the radical critique of American nuclear policy apart was not just its analysis of US goals, but the political conclusions it derived from that analysis. Many 'moderate' opponents of the Reagan administration were against its nuclear programme; however, they still believed in deterrence and the doctrine of mutually assured destruction. Radicals on the other hand questioned both. Thus deterrence, according to the peace movement's most influential spokesperson, Edward Thompson, was one of the biggest and most expensive lies in history – less a theory, more a rationalisation that could neither be proved nor disproved.[24] Moreover, it only had to fail once. It was also irrelevant in the modern era when weapons were being developed not to deter the Russians, but to prevail over them in a nuclear exchange.

Herein perhaps was the most important point of all. According to more mainstream analysts, nuclear war remained unthinkable. Radicals however insisted that new weapons and doctrines being developed on the American side made it increasingly likely. The struggle against the Cold War therefore was not just a struggle against one (or both) of the superpowers, but a desperate battle for survival against the threat of the nuclear holocaust. Indeed, according to Thompson, World War Three was nigh imminent. As he argued in 1980: 'The present nuclear status quo is inexpressibly dangerous and increasingly unstable. It is exceedingly probable that it will at some time detonate in global nuclear war, whether through accident, miscalculation or hysteria.'[25] The logic of the arms race could in fact only lead to one conclusion according to Thompson: the extermination of humanity.

Simply by preparing for war – even though they assumed they would never have to fight it – the US (and the USSR) were making it virtually inevitable. Thus there was only one solution: the elimination of all nuclear weapons.

The Cold War – and beyond

The collapse of superpower detente and the subsequent pursuit by the United States of an uncompromising anti-Soviet strategy, convinced radicals that the New Cold War would remain in being for a very long time. Indeed, there was an implicit assumption in most radical commentary that while there was something distinctly artificial about detente, an ongoing Cold War conflict between the two sides was almost normal.[26]

There were several reasons why the left assumed the Cold War would persist. Firstly, according to radical analysts, there had been a decisive shift to the right in the West in the period between the Vietnam war and the Soviet invasion of Afghanistan. This had brought new political forces to the fore, sympathetic on the one hand to the economic doctrines of Hayek, and opposed on the other to all forms of socialism. This would feed the Cold War it was felt because the politicians who championed the new right doctrines – notably Thatcher and Reagan – linked their own fate with the cause of anti-communism. Once elected therefore there was little chance (or so it was assumed) of the anti-Soviet policies they supported being abandoned.[27]

Secondly, what convinced the left that the New Cold War would endure was its view that there were powerful forces at work within America opposed to any form of coexistence with the USSR. The American system, it was pointed out, had been shaped by and defined in terms of its postwar conflict with Soviet Russia. Moreover, by the end of the seventies, the US was a wounded nation desperately seeking to find new certainties in an increasingly uncertain world. The 'new right' effectively provided these, and as a result built up a powerful coalition of Americans supportive of both a conservative domestic programme and a hawkish foreign policy. This trend was in turn reinforced by a move rightwards within the American elite itself. By the beginning of the eighties power had shifted (or so it was argued) from a liberal eastern establishment which favoured good relations with the USSR, to a more conservative bloc based in the Sunbelt states who were hostile to any compromise with America's traditional communist foe abroad.[28]

43

But this was not all. According to the left there were even deeper sources of the Cold War that made 'a rapid end' to the conflict 'almost impossible to imagine'.[29] Halliday assumed that the chasm-like differences between the US and Soviet systems would keep the Cold War going almost indefinitely. Others, however, believed it would continue not because it was the reflection of differences between the two powers, but because both superpowers actually 'needed' it: either to maintain discipline at home or to control unruly allies. As Chomsky argued in 1982: 'The cold war is a highly functional system by which the superpowers control their own domains. That is why it continues and will continue.'[30]

Not surprisingly, because radicals saw the Cold War as having very deep roots, they believed it could only be overcome as a result of a profound restructuring of the international system as a whole. Inevitably, because many regarded NATO and the American presence in Western Europe as the principle problems, they argued for the disbandment of the former and the withdrawal of the latter from the continent.[31] Others took the view that this one-sided approach simply would not work: nor would it be acceptable to most West Europeans. The only solution was for both superpowers (and not just one) to disengage, leaving Europe whole and free from all outside influence.[32]

In the last analysis, however, most radicals held that the only real long-term solution to the problem was socialist renewal on both sides of the iron curtain. Only with the elimination of capitalism in the West and Stalinism in the East could the logic of the Cold War be undermined.[33] Then, and only then, would the way be open for the establishment of a more secure, rational and less dangerous world. In fact, all radicals agreed that the end of the Cold War promised great things. It would inevitably release resources for use in more productive or ethical ways. It would also make life better for the people of the Third World. It would in turn lead to the creation of less distorted societies – on both sides of the divide. Above all it would mean a more peaceful international environment.[34]

Radicalism and the Cold War – a critique

The revisionist account of the 'First' Cold War – we should recall – temporarily gained the intellectual and moral high ground primarily, if not only, because of a crisis in the Cold War system occasioned by the Vietnam war. Similarly, radical analysis of the 'Second' Cold War exercised its greatest influence in the early eighties when there was yet another international crisis, caused this time by the election of an American president determined to rebuild US power globally. Radical theory, it seemed, was most popular when times were turbulent. However, radicals were not just successful because they expressed the critical spirit of their age, but because they challenged the orthodox at the level of ideas (some would say overwhelmed them completely), and advanced what many regarded as an alternative, intellectually superior analysis of world politics. This had been true of an earlier generation who had sought to reinterpret the First Cold War. It was equally true of those who now sought to understand the turn in superpower relations in the early eighties. Nor was this so surprising. Chomsky's morally charged attacks on US interventions in the Third World, Thompson's poetic critique of the arms race, and Halliday's tightly organised discussion of the origins of the Second Cold War (to take but three examples) were by any measure powerful and well-written accounts. The fact that they each became best-sellers for a period also appeared to demonstrate that they supplied what many demanded: accessible and critical assessments of international politics in a period of rapid transition. Even more mainstream commentators who did not agree with either their method or conclusions, were forced to take radicals seriously.[35]

However, temporary popularity is no guarantee of wisdom, and the question arises firstly of how adequate or complete the radical account of the New Cold War actually was – or is. Here, I want to suggest that the strengths of radical analysis should not blind us to some of its self-evident weaknesses. Three deserve mention: its failure to provide a proper critical discussion of Soviet behaviour in the seventies; its refusal to take Reagan's Russian policy seriously enough; and a very incomplete (often misleading) analysis of nuclear weapons in general and the reasons for the deployment of cruise and Pershing II in particular. Let us deal with each in turn.

Soviet behaviour in the 1970s

At the heart of the radical account of the superpower relationship in the early eighties was a simple but important message: the New Cold War was primarily the fault of the United States. This of course did not make radicals apologists for the USSR. Nor did it mean the Soviet contribution was ignored entirely. However, even amongst those who saw the USSR as a problem – and here one is thinking particularly of Halliday's analysis – there was still an assumption that America bore the major responsibility for the collapse of superpower detente and the subsequent breakdown in

US–Soviet relations. There are, I would suggest, some real difficulties with this account of things.

Firstly, in their attempt to designate 'blame' many radicals more often than not ended up substituting moral judgement for proper analysis. In this respect they made exactly the same mistake as their intellectual enemies on the right. Moreover, even though they were not actively or subjectively pro-Soviet, the fact that their critical comments were directed more against the US than the USSR, tended to make it appear as if they were. Radicals may not have cheered the Soviet Union; yet because they booed every move made by the United States, it looked very much as if they were supporting one side rather than the other. This then left them open to one of two damaging charges: that they were openly hostile to Western democracy, or 'objectively' on the side of the USSR.

Secondly, while we do not have to accept the alarmists' overdrawn picture of Soviet intentions and capabilities in the seventies, the fact remains that Soviet actions during the decade actually did a great deal to undercut support for superpower detente in the United States. The American perception of a Soviet Third World offensive may have been overdrawn. However, there is little doubt that Soviet military involvement in Third World conflicts did come to assume an 'increasingly prominent place in the US foreign policy agenda'. By means of diplomacy, military advisers, arms shipments and support for proxies, the USSR, in fact, attempted to influence the course of at least eight localised conflicts in the seventies – and all this before Afghanistan.[36] Whether these actions seriously undermined the balance of power is questionable. This was not the point however. The fact was that the USSR was clearly acting against Western interests, and the United States appeared unable to do anything about it. Thus, it was reasoned, some policy – other than a failed detente – would have to be found to contain Soviet ambitions.[37]

The radical failure to understand the sources of US concern was in the last analysis, a function of one particular problem: a desire on their part to deny that there was any Soviet threat. Indeed, as we have seen, most radicals either assumed there was no such threat, or minimised its importance. At one level, of course, this was quite reasonable given exaggerated conservative claims about the Soviet Union. On another, it was absurd to argue that these had no substance at all. After all, here was an antagonistic, if not necessarily revolutionary Soviet system, with a sizeable (and growing) military capability, giving support in the seventies to forces and regimes hostile to the United States. Moreover, it was doing so when traditional means of dealing with the USSR had all but collapsed as a result of Vietnam and America's loss of military superiority.[38] Hence, the question was bound to arise: how should the US respond to what many genuinely did see as a new Soviet challenge? This brings us, logically, to Reagan's much maligned Russian policy.

Reagan's Russian policy

The left had a somewhat contradictory attitude towards Reagan. On the one hand, they seemed to treat his administration's statements about revitalising containment very seriously. On the other they viewed his policies towards Russia as being either irrational or unintelligent: irrational in that they were premised upon dealing with a threat that did not really exist, and unintelligent because Reagan was literally stupid – certainly the least intellectual president to have occupied the White House in the twentieth century. The contemptuous attitude which many radicals seemed to have towards Reagan undoubtedly led them to underestimate the coherence of his administration's approach to the USSR. Reagan, it is true, may have spoken in rather simplistic terms about the USSR. His advisers, however, understood the difference between rhetoric and reality – and a careful reading of the situation led them to the inescapable conclusion that because of its many problems the USSR was now peculiarly vulnerable.[39] Even Reagan grasped the point. Indeed, in his speech to the British parliament in 1982, he employed the language of Marxism to explain the underlying cause of the crisis of totalitarianism. The 'decay of the Soviet experiment', he argued, was more or less irreversible. Why? Because there was a fundamental contradiction in the Soviet system between the 'political structure' and the 'economic base'. As a result 'the productive forces' of the USSR could no longer develop or be developed.[40]

On the basis of what turned out to be an extraordinarily prescient analysis of the Soviet crisis, the Reagan administration then attempted to develop a viable strategy. This again was far more rational than its critics were prepared to concede at the time. Believing (correctly as it turned out) that the USSR was in economic decline, the US set out to accelerate the process through a policy of economic denial and military squeeze. Of course this approach had its limits. Nor was Reagan's tough line the only factor that later forced the USSR to moderate its foreign policy and contemplate far-reaching economic reform. However, it would be naive to think that there was no connection between American policy in the eighties and the Soviet response after

47

1985. Reagan may not have been the architect of perestroika. Yet, by narrowing down Soviet options and increasing the costs of the Cold War, his administration undoubtedly kept the USSR in the corner into which its own problems had already forced it – and over time impelled it to seek a new deal with the West.[41]

The left's analysis of nuclear weapons

This brings us to the problem of nuclear weapons. The radical case against nuclear weapons was both morally powerful, and when it dealt with some aspects of the Reagan nuclear programme, intellectually persuasive as well. Politically, moreover, there is little doubt that the radical left did a great deal to undermine the legitimacy of nuclear weapons in the early eighties. The fact that their opponents were often forced to resort to smear tactics (even using the old chestnut that they were in the pay of the Russians), only seemed to prove that the anti-nuclear forces had pushed the establishment into a corner. Yet, in the end, the left was routed on this issue, not because of political attacks launched by simple-minded enemies, but because of basic flaws in the original radical argument.[42]

Firstly, while many may have shared the radical concern about nuclear weapons, few were convinced that there was a serious alternative. Nuclear weapons after all could not be disinvented. Moreover, if they were abandoned this would have undoubtedly led to an increase in military spending for the simple reason that 'nukes' were relatively cheap, while conventional weapons were hideously expensive. Furthermore, the Soviets showed no sign of getting rid of their strategic arsenal – thus why should the West dispense with its forces?

Secondly, in spite of radical arguments to the contrary, most people remained convinced that there really was a Soviet threat to the integrity of Western Europe – and even if there wasn't, the USSR still possessed massive conventional capabilities. The problem then arose: how could Soviet power be effectively neutralised? Most radicals of course had no answer, for they doubted that there really was a Soviet challenge. Others, who were prepared to address the issue, unfortunately put forward 'alternative' defence strategies that were simply not credible: partly because they were premised upon a reading of the Soviet Union that always assumed the best about its intentions, and partly because they presupposed defence without nuclear weapons against an enemy that still possessed them. To the average voter (let alone a hostile defence establishment) this was not only woolly-minded but dangerous as well. If the 'Russians' had nukes then 'we' needed them too, went the simple, but popular refrain of the time. More mainstream strategists, on the other hand, proposed what looked like a crude but credible answer to the defence conundrum: that is, maintain a serious nuclear deterrent and threaten to use it (first if need be) if the USSR stepped over the line – the assumption being that the Russians would not step over the line precisely because of the threat of nuclear retaliation. Such a threat, it was pointed out, had kept the peace for forty years; and there was no reason to suppose it would not continue to do so.

This in turn led to a much bigger question about the conditions for peace in the modern world. On this subject critics of the radical school made a simple, but important historic point: before the development of nuclear weapons there had been two world wars; however, in the postwar nuclear age there had been none. Thus conventional weapons, it was evident, had not been able to prevent global conflict between 1914 and 1945, whereas nuclear weapons after 1945 had. Hence, why get rid of something that had contributed (possibly been the main reason for) international order in the second half of the twentieth century?

Moreover, try as they may, it was difficult for the left (as indeed it was for Ronald Reagan and the 'star warriors'), to seriously challenge the related doctrines of deterrence and mutually assured destruction. While the nuclear hostage relationship may not have been a very comfortable one, it nevertheless impelled both sides to act with extraordinary caution towards each other. Thus, far from being a source or cause of conflict, nuclear weapons made the two powers exceedingly careful – even when relations were tense, as they undoubtedly were in the years of the New Cold War.[43]

This brings us, finally, to the vexed question of Euromissiles. Here, radical analysis was probably at its most bizarre. Thus it was simply not true (as many on the left seemed to think) that the original pressure to deploy cruise and Pershing came from an arrogant and assertive America determined to show the West Europeans who was boss. In fact, as Garthoff has demonstrated, the United States was by no means convinced at first (if ever) that new long-range theatre nuclear forces were needed at all.[44] Furthermore, the idea that such weapons were then deployed so that at some future date the US could fight a limited nuclear war in Europe was to stand 'reason, logic and history on its head'. Indeed, as one of Edward Thompson's more formidable opponents argued at the time, the object of these weapons was not to make a limited nuclear war feasible, but impossible.[45] Intermediate-range weapons stationed in Western Europe, but under American control and capable of reaching targets in the Soviet Union, would in fact guarantee that a nuclear confrontation could not be limited to Europe. The reason was obvious. Confronted with an attack by US systems under US command the Soviets would respond not just by launching a nuclear attack on Western Europe, but against the US as well.[46]

From New Cold War to superpower *rapprochement*

As we have seen, the majority of radicals assumed the New Cold War would continue for a very long time indeed. This prognosis however turned out to be quite wrong, for by the summer of 1984 a trend in Soviet policy towards some form of accommodation with the United States was clearly detectable. Then in September, Foreign Minister Gromyko conferred with both Reagan and Schultz, and it was agreed that both sides would resume arms control negotiations – something that began, to the surprise of most observers, six months later in March 1985. On 12 March, at Chernenko's funeral in Moscow, Bush also delivered an invitation from Reagan to Gorbachev for a summit meeting which the Soviet leader promptly accepted. On 3 July, a Reagan–Gorbachev summit was finally agreed to in Geneva on 19–20 November 1985.[47]

These early signs of superpower *rapprochement* were not taken too seriously by those grown used to the New Cold War. Yet they soon led to bigger things, and in the two-year period following the first summit, relations between the United States and the Soviet Union improved dramatically. Indeed, by the time Reagan left office in January 1989 they had been radically transformed – so much so that when Bush entered the White House, Moscow and Washington were probably closer than at any time since the Yalta conference in early 1945. The New Cold War had simply withered away.[48]

The reasons for this metamorphosis in the superpower relationship have been the subject of a good deal of investigation and speculation – not least by the same radicals who had previously denied that such a change was possible. To be fair, most radicals had been sensitive to the fact that the outcome of the New Cold War might be very different to that planned by the Reagan administration in 1980. For example, in his provocative study on the politics of containment, Jerry Sanders predicted that American policy in the New Cold War might easily founder on what he termed the 'shoals of reality', a view also supported by both Chomsky and Halliday.[49] However, these were qualifications to the main radical thesis that the roots of the Cold War went deep and thus its speedy termination was most unlikely.

Radicals responded to the new situation hesitantly. The first instinct was to ascribe the new international environment to political and economic problems on the US side. Others (grasping at straws, one suspects) insisted that the new superpower amity was in part the result of earlier work done by the peace movement.[50] Halliday took a rather different approach, denying in fact, that anything of real import had actually taken place during Reagan's second term. Thus in summer 1988, he still maintained that 'image and mood [had] changed' in the superpower relationship 'more than substance'.[51] A year later, in his new study on the Third World, he implied that the conflict between the US and the USSR in the underdeveloped countries was still very much alive – a somewhat bizarre view given the degree of superpower collaboration over regional issues in the latter half of the decade.[52]

The key question, obviously, is why did radicals seem to get it so wrong? Part of the answer, surely, is that their underlying theory (or theories) of the Cold War all seemed to lead them to predict continued conflict rather than *rapprochement*? After all, if as they suggested, one or both of the superpowers required the Cold War for either domestic or international reasons, or the antagonism itself was the expression of some deep unbridgeable economic gulf, then it was hardly surprising they were unable to predict the thaw in US–Soviet relations.

Radicals, I would suggest, also failed to draw the correct lessons from the first superpower detente. According to their reading, there was something almost deviant about the Kissinger–Nixon 'grand design'. But this was a serious misjudgement, for detente was not some odd detour in the superpower relationship, but reflected, rather, fundamental and irreversible changes in the postwar international system that forced both states to redefine their position towards each other. The fact that detente imploded (Gaddis wonders whether it was ever seriously tried), did not mean that the underlying pressures impelling the US and the USSR towards a new relationship had gone away; only that it could not be constructed in the seventies.[53]

Firstly, there was the simple but inescapable fact of nuclear parity. In 1969 Kissinger had accepted that superiority was impossible: after four years in office Reagan was forced to the same conclusion as well. Kissinger moreover understood that without arms control Western public opinion would turn against nuclear weapons: Reagan was soon impelled to the same conclusion after having attempted to escape from the logic of arms control during his first term.[54] More generally, the Nixon administration realised that the costs of being both world

51

policeman and international fireman were rapidly outstripping America's ability to play (or pay for) such a role. By the middle of the eighties the Reagan administration confronted the same inescapable reality, and was impelled to recognise that there was a clear 'gap' between what America ought to be doing and what it could afford to do. Indeed, by his second term, it had become clear that the Reagan effort to 'revitalise containment' was beginning to impose a burden on the US economy that demanded two things: a reduction in military spending and some form of 'new deal' with the USSR to ensure continued international stability – not surprisingly the same policies outlined by Nixon and Kissinger in the early seventies before their strategy disintegrated.[55]

Thirdly, most radicals probably took Reaganism as an American phenomenon far too seriously. What they saw and heard in the early eighties was the flag-waving and the patriotic, anti-communist rhetoric and concluded that this was the 'true' expression of 'real' America. However, as a number of studies showed at the time and have demonstrated since, electoral support for Reagan was by no means overwhelming. Certainly the 1980 and 1984 elections did not reveal a fundamental realignment in US politics.[56] Moreover, like any American president, Reagan was as prone to political disasters as any of his predecessors. Nixon we know was destroyed by Watergate. Reagan was then seriously undermined by Iran–Contra. Neither event could have been forecast, but both undercut support for the two men and their associated policies.

Finally, radicals clearly failed to discern the depth of the Soviet crisis and the impact this was to have upon Soviet policies in the latter half of the decade. In this of course they were not alone. Indeed, just before Gorbachev came to power, the CIA released a study of the Soviet economy which concluded that the USSR could easily 'muddle through'.[57] Yet the question still remains as to why the left in particular failed to understand the sheer scale of Soviet problems. There were three reasons, I think. Firstly, they actually knew very little about the USSR, and in a sense didn't need to know because they assumed that the US was the main mover in international affairs. Secondly, some at least still believed that the Soviet system – in spite of its deformations – was either superior to, or at least as viable as Western capitalism. And finally, for political reasons the left simply could not concede that the neo-conservatives in the Reagan administration (notably Richard Pipes) actually had a better appreciation of the USSR than they. Moreover, if the right's arguments about the irreversible crisis of communism were correct, then the administration's tough policies towards the USSR were less irrational and more coherent than the left had ever been prepared to admit.

After the Cold War

This leads, finally, to the question concerning the end of the Cold War. The left always assumed that the termination of the US–Soviet conflict – if and when it ever came – would by definition involve profound international change. In this respect they were proved correct. Yet the end of the great contest did not result from a radical restructuring of the continent as radicals had hoped, or socialist advance in the world, but 'bourgeois' triumph in Eastern Europe and an American victory over the Soviet Union globally. Thus, far from marking a radical breakthrough, the end of the Cold War coincided with and was caused by an apparent collapse of the whole radical project. Indeed, if anybody 'got it right', it was not those in the early eighties who looked forward to radical renewal in the world, but George Kennan the conservative who in his original article on the 'sources of Soviet conduct' predicted that a successful containment of the USSR would lead to both a 'mellowing' of the communist system and a Soviet withdrawal from its overextended positions abroad.[58]

But shouldn't radicals be able to share in the spoils of peace? After all, the end of the Cold War could, and in time probably will lead to less military spending not to mention greater democracy on a global scale. It should also mean of course better, more stable relations between the US and the USSR – something which all self-respecting radicals have been clamouring for since 1947. Perhaps so, but many have their doubts as to whether the termination of the 'Great Contest' will not also release contradictions hitherto contained within the stable framework of Cold War bipolarity. As Mearsheimer has observed, we might all soon be missing the Cold War.[59] Even those – like the Germans and the East Europeans – who are the most obvious beneficiaries of the new era, face an extremely uncertain future. In addition, the possible fragmentation of the Soviet Union could conclude in civil war or even new inter-state conflicts. But if radicals (amongst others) had examined the structure of the Cold War a little more carefully, they may have been able to predict all this.[60] However, this would have then posed a real dilemma, for they might have been forced to the uncomfortable conclusion that the system to which they were so opposed (and had done their best to destroy politically), had probably done more to contain conflict than unleash it, and that its passing therefore would almost inevitably lead to a world less peaceful than the one that finally disintegrated in the latter half of a most turbulent decade: a decade that began with Reagan in the White House, and ended with his successor and Mikhail Gorbachev working together to oppose Iraqi expansion in the Middle East.[61]

Notes

1 The best guide to revisionist writing on the Cold War is almost certainly Richard A. Melanson, *Writing History And Making Policy: The Cold War, Vietnam, and Revisionism* (Lanham: University Press Of America, 1983).

2 To get an idea of the intellectual importance of Vietnam for radical analysis of the Cold War see William A. Williams, Thomas McCormick, Lloyd Gardner and Walter LeFeber, *America In Vietnam: A Documentary History* (New York: Anchor Press, 1985). The most detailed radical history of US policy in Vietnam is Gabriel Kolko, *Vietnam: Anatomy of a War: 1940–1975* (London: Allen and Unwin, 1985).

3 In his famous 'Farewell Address To The Nation' on 17 January 1961, Eisenhower warned: 'In the councils of government, we must guard against the acquisition of unwarranted influence, whether sought or unsought, by the military-industrial complex'. Cited in Stephen E. Ambrose and James A. Barber Jr, *The Military And American Society* (New York: The Free Press, 1972), p. 63.

4 Robert W. Tucker goes so far as to suggest that radical revisionism may have been successful even without the Vietnam war. He writes: 'Vietnam must itself be placed against the decline in the sixties of the classic Cold War. This decline could have been expected to give rise to revisionism, including radical revisionism, quite without the war, and the emergence of the radical critique may in fact be traced to the years immediately preceeding Vietnam'. See Tucker, *The Radical Left And American Foreign Policy* (Baltimore: The John Hopkins Press, 1971), p. 154.

5 For a robust critique of the post-revisionist work of John Gaddis see Barton Bernstein, 'Cold War Orthodoxy Restated', *Reviews In American History*, December 1973, pp. 453–62. Daniel Yergin's post-revisionist study on the 'shattered peace' was also attacked by Carolyn Eisenberg in 'Reflections on a Toothless Revisionism', *Diplomatic History*, Summer 1978, pp. 295–305. In a useful debate occasioned by John Gaddis' article, 'The Emerging Post-Revisionist Synthesis on the Origins of the Cold War', *Diplomatic History*, Summer 1983, pp. 171–190, Warren Kimball was to characterise post-revisionism as 'orthodoxy plus archives', in 'Responses to John Lewis Gaddis, The emerging post-revisionist synthesis on the origins of the Cold War', *Diplomatic History*, Summer 1983, p. 198.

6 For a useful guide to the Cold War historiography of the seventies see Richard Melanson, 'Cold War Revisionism Subdued?' in his *Writing History And Making Policy*, pp. 84–120.

7 Radical sensitivity to Carter's human rights strategy is illustrated in Noam Chomsky's *'Human Rights' and American Foreign Policy* (Nottingham: Spokesman Books, 1978).

8 A good index of the right-wing evolution of many former American radicals in the eighties is Peter Collier and David Horowitz's (ed.), *Second Thoughts* (Washington: The National Forum Foundation, 1987).

9 On the unimportance of cruise and Pershing II in the Reagan nuclear programme see Steve Smith, 'The Superpowers And Arms Control in the Era of the "Second" Cold War', in Michael Cox (ed.), *Beyond The Cold War: Superpowers At The Crossroads?* (Lanham: University Press Of America, 1990), pp. 167–84.

10 See Edward Thompson, 'Sources of Exterminism: The Last Stage of Civilization', *New Left Review*, no. 121, May–June 1980, pp. 5–6.

11 For a 'Third Worldist' perspective on the Cold War see Fred Halliday, *The Making Of The Second Cold War* (London: Verso, 1983); and Jeff McMahon, *Reagan and the World: Imperial Policy in the New Cold War* (London: Pluto Press, 1984).

12 See Noam Chomsky, *Towards A New Cold War* (New York: Pantheon Books, 1982); and Mary Kaldor, *The Imaginary War: Was There an East–West Conflict?* (Oxford: Blackwell, 1990). Two American radicals, James Petras and Morriss H. Morley, argued in 1983 that the New Cold War was a US 'attempt to recover economic space by projecting politico-military power'. See their 'The New Cold War: Reagan's Policy Towards Europe and the Third World', *END Papers Four*, Spokesman 42, Winter 1983, p. 86.

13 Halliday, *The Making Of The Second Cold War*, pp. 30–6.

14 For one of the best radical accounts of the collapse of detente in the seventies, see Jerry W. Sanders, *Peddlers Of Crisis: The Committee On The Present Danger* (London: Pluto Press, 1983), pp. 149–316.

15 Even Halliday, who talked of a 'shared but unequal responsibility of East and West for the Second Cold War' in *The Making Of The Second Cold War*, p. 45, still insisted that the most important cause of Cold War II was the 'determination in the USA to reach for a new margin' of nuclear superiority over the USSR, 'and to foster a climate in which such a policy appears legitimate and even defensive', p. 47.

16 See Jonathan Steele, *The Limits Of Soviet Power: The Kremlin's Foreign Policy – Brezhnev To Chernenko* (Harmondsworth: Penguin, 1985).

17 Cited in E. P. Thompson and Dan Smith (ed.), *Protest And Survive* (Harmondsworth: Penguin, 1980), p. 49.

18 See Jim Garrison and Pyare Shivpuri, *The Russian Threat: Its Myths and Realities* (London: Gateway Books, 1983). In a CND publication, it was agreed that 'fear of the "Soviet threat" [was] probably the single most serious obstacle to the aims of the modern peace movement'. See Meg Beresford, 'CND and the Sovet Union', *Sanity*, no. 1, January 1985, pp. 15.

19 See Tom Gervasi's excellent, *The Myth Of Soviet Military Supremacy* (New York: Harper and Row, 1986).

20 On US–Soviet interests in the preservation of the Cold War status quo, see Michael Cox, 'Western Capitalism and the Cold War System' in Martin Shaw (ed.), *War, State And Society* (London: Macmillan, 1984), pp. 136–94; 'The Cold War As a System', *Critique*, no. 17, 1986, pp. 17–82; and 'From The Truman Doctrine To The Second Superpower Detente: The Rise And Fall Of The Cold War', *Journal Of Peace Research*, vol. 27, no. 1, 1990, pp. 25–41.

21 The view that America – as a capitalist power – was aggressive, and the USSR as a non-capitalist power was essentially defensive, informed the different contributions to Edward Thompson et al., *Exterminism And Cold War* (London: Verso: 1982).

22 See, for example, Ed Bottome, *The Balance Of Terror – Nuclear Weapons and the Illusion of Security: 1945–1985* (Boston: Beacon Press, 1986); and Ronald E. Powaski, *March To Armageddon: The United States And The Nuclear Arms Race, 1939 To The Present* (New York: Oxford University Press, 1987).

23 On American nuclear objectives as seen from a radical perspective see, *inter alia*, Paul Joseph, 'From MAD to NUTS: The Growing Danger of Nuclear War', *Socialist Review*, vol. 12, no. 61, January–February 1982, pp. 7–43; Andrew Winnick, 'Rapid Deployment and Nuclear War: Reagan's New Military Strategies', *Socialist Review*, no. 73, January–February 1984, pp. 11–30; and Charles Bright, 'On the Road to War with the Soviet Union: Strategic Consensus for the 1990s', *Socialist Review*, no. 85, January–February 1986. See also the influential studies by Robert Aldridge. *The Counterforce Syndrome* (Washington: Institute for Policy Studies, 1978), and *First Strike!* (London: Pluto Press, 1983).

24 Edward Thompson's most developed attack on the theory of deterrence can be found in his 'Deterrence and Addiction' written in 1981. The full text is in *Zero Option* (London: Merlin Press, 1982), pp. 1–23.

25 Cited in 'The Doomsday Consensus', *New Statesman*, December 1979, reprinted in Edward Thompson, *Writing By Candlelight* (London: Merlin Press, 1980), p. 273.

26 Petras and Morley refer to superpower detente as a mere 'interlude between the political defeat of the late sixties and early 1970s, and the imperial recovery and resurgence at the end of the seventies and in the beginning of the eighties'. James Petras and Morriss H. Morley, 'The New Cold War: Reagan's Policy towards Europe and the Third World', *End Papers Four*, Spokesman 42, Winter 1983, p. 89.

27 On the relationship between the decline of Keynesianism in the seventies and the New Cold War, see Michael Cox, 'From Detente To The New Cold War: The Crisis Of The Cold War System', *Millennium*, vol 13. no. 3, Winter 1984, pp. 265–91.

28 On the role of the 'new right' in the making of US foreign policy in the seventies and eighties see Halliday, *The Making Of The Second Cold War*, pp. 105–33. On the power shift within the US elite see Kirkpatrick Sale, *Power Shift: The Rise Of The Southern Rim And Its Challenge To The Eastern Establishment* (New York: Vintage, 1976).

29 Halliday, *The Making Of The Second Cold War*, p. 264.

30 Cited in his 'The United States: From Greece to El Salvador', in Noam Chomsky et al., *Superpowers In Collision: The New Cold War* (Harmondsworth: Penguin, 1982), p. 26.

31 Sue Cockrill, 'NATO: The Untameable Beast', *Socialist Review*, 17 October–14 November, 1981, pp. 17–19. Others on the left did not go so far as to call for an end to NATO. See, for instance, Dan Smith, 'Fighting for Peace ... inside NATO', *New Socialist*, March–April 1982, pp. 42–4. Mary Kaldor seemed to agree; the primary object she argued, was not to get rid of NATO

as such, but to 'avoid war through lessening the confrontation between the blocs'. Indeed, if Britain were to leave NATO this might actually 'increase tension within and between the blocs'. See her 'Banishing the Fear Factor', *New Socialist*, January–February 1984, p. 13.

32 E. P. Thompson, *Beyond The Cold War* (London: Merlin Press, 1982).

33 Halliday, *The Making Of the Second Cold War*, pp. 261–6.

34 Ernest Mandel, 'The Threat of War and the Struggle for Socialism', *New Left Review*, no. 141, September–October 1983, pp. 23–50.

35 For one of the more vituperative attacks on radical writing on the New Cold War however, see V. Kubalkova and A. A. Cruickshank, 'The "New Cold War" in "Critical International Relations Studies"', *Review on International Studies*, vol. 12, no. 3, 1986, pp. 163–85. For a reply see Fred Halliday, 'Vigilantism in International Relations: Kubalkova, Cruickshank and Marxist Theory', *Review of International Studies*, vol. 13, 1987, pp. 163–75.

36 Bruce D. Porter, *The USSR In Third World Conflicts: Soviet Arms and Diplomacy in Local Wars: 1945–1980* (Cambridge: Cambridge University Press, 1984), p. 1.

37 Even the architects of superpower detente were later forced to concede that their original strategy had collapsed and that US power would have to be rebuilt. See Henry Kissinger, *For The Record: Selected Statements, 1977–1980* (London: Weidenfeld and Nicholson, 1981), pp. 191–230; and Richard Nixon, *The Real War* (London: Sidgwick and Jackson, 1980).

38 This was certainly the perception of the incoming Reagan administration. See *Realism, Strength, Negotiation: Key Foreign Policy Statements of the Reagan Administration* (Washington: USGPO, 1984).

39 See Richard Pipes, *Survival Is Not Enough* (New York: Simon and Schuster, 1984), pp. 110–281.

40 Cited in *Realism, Strength, Negotiation*, p. 78.

41 See Michael Cox, 'Whatever Happened to the "Second" Cold War? Soviet–American Relations: 1980–1988', *Review of International Studies*, vol. 16, 1990, pp. 155–72, for a slightly different assessment of the impact of Reagan's policies upon the USSR.

42 For one of the more lucid critiques of the anti-nuclear movement see Lawrence Freedman, *The Price Of Peace: Living With The Nuclear Dilemma* (London: Firethorn, 1988).

43 See George H. Quester, *The Future Of Nuclear Deterrence* (Lexington, MA: Lexington Books, 1988).

44 Raymond Garthoff, *Detente And Confrontation* (Washington: Brookings, 1985), pp. 849–86. See also his 'The NATO Decision On Theater Nuclear Forces', *Political Science Quarterly*, vol. 98, Summer 1983, pp. 197–214.

45 Michael Howard, *The Causes Of War*, (London: Unwin Paperbacks), pp. 125–6.

46 A point made particularly forcefully in Hans-Henrik Holm and Nikolaj Petersen (ed.), *The European Missiles Crisis: Nuclear Weapons and Security Policy* (London: Frances Pinter, 1983), p. 10.

47 For perhaps the most detailed discussion of the transition from New Cold War to superpower *rapprochement*, see Joseph G. Whelan, *Soviet Diplomacy and Negotiating Behaviour, 1979–88: New Tests for U.S. Diplomacy* (Washington: USGPO, August, 1988).

48 See Michael Pugh and Phil Williams (ed.), *Superpower Politics: Change In the United States And The Soviet Union* (Manchester: Manchester University Press, 1990), for an examination of the new superpower agenda in the latter half of the eighties.

49 Sanders, *Peddlers Of Crisis*, pp. 317–45; Chomsky, *Towards A New Cold War*, pp. 32–4; and Halliday, *The Making Of The Second Cold War*, pp. 242–66.

50 Several of the western contributors to Mary Kaldor, Gerard Holden, Richard Falk (ed.), *The New Detente: Rethinking East–West Relations* (London: Verso, 1989) argue that the peace movement helped bring about the end of the New Cold War. See too Mary Kaldor, 'After The Cold War', *New Left Review*, no. 180, March–April 1990, pp. 33–4, where she makes the same point.

51 Fred Halliday, 'The Ron and Mik Show', *Marxism Today*, June 1988, pp. 16–21.

52 Fred Halliday, *Cold War, Third World* (London: Hutchinson, 1989), p. 1 63.

53 For two thoughtful surveys of the superpower relationship in the seventies see William G. Hyland, *Mortal Rivals; Understanding The Hidden Pattern Of Soviet–American Relations* (New York: Touchstone 1987); and Mike Bowker and Phil Williams, *Superpower Detente: A Reappraisal* (London: Sage, 1988).

54 Although how far the administration was converted to arms control during Reagan's second term is questioned by Steve Smith in his 'The Superpowers And Arms Control In The Era of The "Second" Cold War', in Cox (ed.), *Beyond The Cold War*, pp. 167–84.

55 Two of the most recent and detailed attempts to analyse the Kissinger–Nixon 'grand design' are Robert D. Schulzinger, *Henry Kissinger: Doctor Of Diplomacy* (New York: Columbia University Press, 1989); and Richard C. Thornton, *The Nixon–Kissinger Years: The Reshaping Of American Foreign Policy* (New York: Paragon House, 1989).

56 For a critique of realignment see Austin Ranney (ed.), *The American Elections of 1984* (North Carolina, 1985).

57 See Henry Rowen, 'Central Intelligence Briefing on the Soviet Economy', reprinted in Erik P. Hoffmann and Robbin F. Laird (ed.), *The Soviet Polity In The Modern Era* (New York: Aldine Publishing, 1984), pp. 417–46.

58 For a detailed discussion of Kennan's views on the USSR (and other matters) see Michael Cox, 'Requiem For A Cold War Critic – The Rise And Fall of George F. Kennan: 1946–1950', *Irish Slavonic Studies*, no. 11, 1990/1991, pp. 1–35.

59 See John J. Mearsheimer, 'Back To The Future: Instability in Europe After the Cold War', *International Security*, vol. 15, no. 1, Summer 1990, pp. 5–56; and his 'Why We Will Soon Miss The Cold War', *The Atlantic Monthly*, August 1990, pp. 35–50.

60 See Fred Halliday's attempt to explain the present era in terms of his original theory of the Cold War. 'The Ends Of Cold War', *New Left Review*, no. 180, March–April 1990, pp. 5–24.

61 For a survey of superpower relations in the eighties see Michael Cox 'From Super Power Detente to Entente Cordiale? Soviet–US Relations: 1989–1990', in Bruce George (ed.), *Jane's NATO Handbook: 1990–91* (Surrey: Jane's Information Group, 1990), pp. 277–86.

4 THEORIES OF STABILITY AND THE END OF THE COLD WAR

RICHARD CROCKATT

Introduction

The demise of the political structures which sustained the Cold War in Europe presents international relations theorists no less than practitioners with certain obvious challenges. Discussion of the kind of structures which might develop in their place has become a major industry. There is little point in providing citations since these would embrace a large proportion of the contents of newspapers, periodicals and academic journals for the past two years. Post-mortems on the Cold War have similarly proliferated. It is one of the features of periods of revolutionary change that they open up the past for scrutiny as well as inviting speculation about the future.

More often than not attitudes towards the future are conditioned by stances adopted during the Cold War, and it is noticeable that com-mentators with very different interpretive approaches have at least one thing in common: the attempt to maintain consistency between their readings of the future and the interpretive schemes they brought with them from the period of the *ancien* international regime. Since the events of 1989 were complex and their implications for the future varied, they can be held to confirm a range of positions. Those who had been inclined, for example, to interpret the Cold War system as 'stable', and for that reason to view it as fundamentally benign for all its dangers, have tended to emphasise the dangers of the new and as yet unstructured condition of Eastern and Central Europe. Calling the Cold War 'the long peace,' as John Gaddis did in a widely discussed article of 1986, suggests an ominous prospect for the period following the Cold War.[1] Those, on the other hand, who for a variety of reasons viewed the Cold War as an artificial brake on the global tendency towards interdependence and multipolarity have been more inclined to see the end of the Cold War as an opportunity for some form of new world order to establish itself.

Where debates among international theorists have overlapped with ideological debates within the wider culture, the process of adaptation to the new circumstances has been especially contentious, though this has taken interestingly different forms in the United States and Britain. There is no real equivalent in the United States, for example, of the interplay within the British International Relations community between theorising about the Cold War and the issue of Stalinism. Two of the contributors to this book – Fred Halliday and Michael Cox – illustrate very clearly the connection in Britain between leftist politics and International Relations theory, an issue which will be discussed later in this chapter.

Where in the United States explicit ideological debate has impinged on theorising about the end of the Cold War, it has been provoked by thunder on the right rather than the left, most notably by Francis Fukuyama's essay 'The End of History?'[2] However, his complacent assertion of the triumph of liberal democracy, in particular its American variant, has found relatively little resonance within the social science of International Relations (as opposed to the op-ed pages of the press). This is not because American social scientists lack faith in liberal democracy or even because they doubt that in some sense the West has 'won' the Cold War, but because Fukuyama's Hegelian idealism is patently at odds with the pervasive positivism of American social science.

The political difference between Britain and the United States noted above is part and parcel of the different character of International Relations study in the two countries. In Britain, while American social science has been a crucial influence, the study of International Relations has both retained a closer link with historical study and been more detached from actual policy concerns than is the case in the United States. In the United States, writes Steve Smith, there is 'a very strong commitment to a policy-relevant approach to the subject of International Relations' by comparison with Britain where 'scholarly activity is basically still an individual enterprise, unconnected to the policy community (even shunned by it) and where policy relevance has been, until very recently, a dirty word'.[3] To that extent the 'political' (as opposed to policy-relevant) character of International Relations is frequently more explicit in Britain than in the United States.[4] For all the differences in methodology and assumptions among major American theorists of the international system, these have generally existed within a broad liberal consensus, defined, in the words of a prominent self-proclaimed liberal scholar, by the emphasis on 'the role of human-created institutions ... the importance of changeable political processes rather than simply of immutable structures, and ... a belief in at least the possibility of cumulative progress in human affairs'. This is less a programmatic political agenda than, as the same author puts it, 'a set of guiding principles for contemporary social science'.[5]

Whatever the differences between and within the two countries, analysts of all persuasions have had to contend with the shock to the Cold War system provided by events since 1989. My concern in this chapter is with analyses of superpower relations which have taken stability to be the salient feature of the Cold War system. They are broadly of two sorts: those which employ empirical evidence only to the extent necessary to support a particular theoretical model – and are largely the product of theoreticians – and those which invoke theory only to the extent necessary to support a particular interpretation of the postwar international system. The latter are in the main produced by historians. Indeed one goal of this chapter is to argue for a synthesis of the historical and the theoretical as the best means of understanding the structure of the Cold War and its demise.

Stability in Europe and the Cold War

'Stability', in the well-known definition of Deutsch and Singer, means 'the probability that the system retains all of its essential characteristics; that no single nation becomes dominant; that most of its members continue to survive; and that large-scale war does not occur'.[6] Evidently stability is not synonymous with stasis. Included in the notion of stability is the idea of adaptability to change, though presumably within limits. Establishing where those limits lie – which is to say, how far a system can undergo change before it can be said to have broken down – is one of the chief aims of stability theorists.

The issue arises so sharply, of course, because of the breakdown of the Cold War system, and one's first reaction might be to say that recent events have proved stability theories wrong. Some offered predictions that the system would last at least until the end of the century.[7] Even those who declined to make predictions were impressed by the longevity of the system and implied that it deserved to live on.[8] Broadly speaking, the more tightly organised the arguments for the stability of the system – which is to say, the more dependent the foreign policies of the superpowers have been taken to be upon the Cold War system – the greater the challenge which the breakdown of the Cold War system has posed to those arguments.

However, this is not necessarily a reason for dismissing these views out of hand. Stability is a relative concept and will depend on the continuance of certain vital conditions. The sudden disappearance of those conditions may not cast doubt upon the validity of particular arguments used to explain the system's durability for however long it happened to last. Arguably, in fact, the end of the Cold War has provided confirmation of stability theories, since in establishing those conditions which were necessary to sustain the Cold War, they have also posited certain conditions under which it might collapse. Waltz, DePorte and Gaddis all offer the proviso that unforeseen circumstances could provoke the end of the system they described as stable, the most likely possibility being, in Gaddis' words, 'a substantial decline in the overall influence of either great power'.[9] Those who were wrong about how long the Cold War system would last were thus, it could be claimed, wrong only in the sense that British weather forecasters are wrong when they miscalculate the speed with which particular weather systems move.

Nevertheless, analysts have varied in their interpretations of the basic conditions of stability, and some have proved more successful than others in anticipating the conditions under which the system might collapse. We can therefore usefully distinguish between various interpretations on the basis of the conditions they specify as necessary to the maintenance of stability. Once we have looked at a range of theories we shall consider how they stand up in the light of the end of the Cold War. Attention will be focused on the work of Kenneth Waltz, John Gaddis and Michael Cox: respectively a systems theorist, a historian who has strayed fruitfully into International Relations theory, and a historically minded political scientist drawing on Marxist concepts. The chapter will close with an alternative proposal for conceptualising the Cold War and its relation to the international system. It should be said at this point that no attempt is made to provide a full exposition of the analyses in question, only a reading of their work as it bears on the question of stability. Nor is this paper an exercise in retrospective crowing at failure to anticipate events. The object is to use the opportunity afforded by the events surrounding the end of the Cold War as a means of gaining a fuller understanding of the Cold War itself.

Theories of stability

For Waltz, bipolarity, stemming from the 'preponderant power' of the United States and the Soviet Union, was the stabilising feature of the international system since 1945. He suggested four factors which in combination encouraged the limitation of violence in states. First, 'with only two world powers there are no peripheries'.

Since 'the United States is the obsessing danger for the Soviet Union, and the Soviet Union for us ... any event in the world that involves the fortunes of the Soviet Union or the United States automatically elicits the interest of others'. Superpower relations thus form a zero-sum game in which a loss to one appears as a gain to the other. The result is 'an increasingly solid bipolar balance'. The other three factors flow from this: in a bipolar world 'the range of factors included in the competition is extended as the intensity of competition increases'; 'there is near constant presence of pressure and recurrence of crises'; and, finally, 'the preponderant power of the United States and the Soviet Union' have 'made for a remarkable ability to comprehend and absorb within the bipolar balance the revolutionary political, military, and economic changes that have occurred'.[10]

Each of these factors has been assumed by other analysts and by political leaders to be destabilising, indeed productive of war. This view represented something like a consensus during the early Cold War. Deutsch and Singer, employing the language of quantitative social science, elevated this impressionistic observation to the level of a generalisation. They argued that stability was enhanced as a system moved away from bipolarity towards multipolarity, since it increased the number of interactions in the system. The resulting cross-cutting pressures operated as a restraint on conflict.[11] Waltz, however, considered that the intensity and scope of competition in a bipolar world made for simplicity and clarity of relations. As he put it in a later publication, 'the simplicity of relations in a bipolar world and the strong pressures that are generated make the two great powers conservative'. It evidently struck him as no paradox that it was the Cold War's likeness to war itself which rendered it stable. 'In peacetime', he wrote, 'the bipolar system displays a clarity of relations that is ordinarily found only in war.'[12]

Several further features are entailed by Waltz's approach. (1) Waltz acknowledges the high degree of inequality of power between the superpowers, but because his definition of structure excludes consideration of interaction between the units and of the foreign policies of the units themselves, it also tends to exclude consideration of mechanisms of systemic change, a point to which we shall return in connection with the other stability theories.[13] (2) He does not see nuclear weapons themselves as the basis of stability, since the bipolar structure preceded two-power nuclear competition. Nuclear weapons simply served to reinforce bipolarity.[14] A stronger version of the same argument has been proposed by John Mueller, and arguably both analyses have been justified by the turn of events which has produced

63

system change despite the retention of nuclear arsenals by both super-powers.[15] (3) As late as 1979 Waltz saw bipolarity as still the determining feature of the international system and indeed saw detente as 'the maturation of the bipolar world', not a sign of its passing.[16] To the extent that detente represented largely bilateral arrangements between the superpowers, Waltz's position has much to recommend it. It takes little account, however, of the European dimensions of detente, particularly the role played by German Chancellor Willy Brandt's Ostpolitik. Waltz's perspective also elides the Cold War system and the international system which, as will be argued in the final section of this chapter, obscures a distinction which is important to an understanding of postwar international politics. For the moment it is enough to observe the premium on structural continuity which is entailed by Waltz's systemic approach. (4) Waltz's is a strongly normative argument. Bipolarity, and therefore the Cold War, is taken to be preferable to any other possible arrangement of the international system. (5) His scheme is theory-led, in that the Cold War is taken to be an exemplary case illustrating general characteristics of bipolar systems and their superior capacity over multipolar systems to create stability. They are preferable because the risks are recognisable and foreseeable. By contrast, advocates of the superiority of multipolar systems claim that it is uncertainty about outcomes which creates stability. The advocates of each claim that caution is induced by the preferred conditions.

We can summarise Waltz's position by terming it synchronic and systemic. While the possibility of change in the system is not excluded, Waltz is less concerned with this than with the characteristics of systems in a state of equilibrium. Waltz's systemic approach can be seen as a particularly rigorous elaboration of J. David Singer's insistence that international systems and nation-state levels of analysis are analytically distinct. 'We may', Singer wrote, 'utilize one level here and another there, but we cannot afford to shift our orientation in the midst of a study.'[17]

In the light of Singer's and Waltz's approach to the study of international relations John Gaddis' contribution to the conceptualisation of the Cold War might be viewed as awkwardly hybrid. While he does distinguish clearly between structural and nation-state behavioural factors which have promoted stability in the Cold War system, his central concern with the interaction between them would seem to violate Waltz's assertion that 'one cannot infer the condition of international politics from the internal composition of states, nor can one arrive at an understanding of international politics by summing the foreign policies and external behaviors of states'.[18] Of course, Gaddis' interest lies in the Cold War in and for itself rather than the Cold War as an 'ideal type' designed to promote a generalisable theory of international politics. Gaddis nevertheless does engage in theoretical reflection to a degree which is relatively rare among historians, and there is an element of convergence between his theoretically informed history and the rigours of the Waltzian analysis. They meet at the point where stability is conceived to be the central issue to be explained.

Why, asks Gaddis, 'has this great power peace managed to survive for so long in the face of so much provocation'?[19] He offers a range of structural and behavioural factors to account for the 'long peace' of the postwar period. They can be represented schematically as follows.

Structural: bipolarity, independence, not interdependence, between the superpowers, and a variety of domestic influences which have inclined governments towards prudence.

Behavioural: nuclear weapons, the reconnaissance revolution, which supplemented 'the self-regulating features of deterrence with the assurance that comes from knowing a great deal more than in the past about adversary capabilities; ideological moderation, and mutual adherence to the rules of the superpower game.[20]

Gaddis' inversion of the customary response to the Cold War balance of terror was an interpretive and psychological coup. Because his analysis was so sharply focused upon the dynamics of the Cold War itself and perhaps also because he wrote out of a tradition of humanistic historical scholarship rather than social science, his writing undoubtedly reached a larger audience and resonated more widely in the intellectual community than did the work of Waltz. If anything, the end of the Cold War has intensified scholarly interest in the questions raised by his initial article, as the recent publication of a book devoted to the implications of his work proves.[21]

Gaddis, in short, appears to have lost nothing by being overtaken by events. Indeed his argument for stability stands out in bolder relief with the passing of the conditions which prompted it. While criticism of his interpretation will be dealt with later, it is worth drawing out some of its implications at this point. A striking feature of his analysis is the high degree of symmetry he identifies in the policies of the superpowers and in the structural conditions which underpin them. He does suggest that the greatest challenge to the system might come from a sudden and substantial decline in the power and influence of either superpower, but his main line of argument is premised on the symmetrical roles they perform in the Cold War system, which is to say that the body of his analysis does not establish a dynamic in the relationship which might upset the balance. For a historian his analysis is curiously static. In this respect his argument parallels that of Waltz. Both have difficulty in accounting for possible changes in the system.

The point is all the more significant in the light of Gaddis' sensitive feel for the 'illogic' in many aspects of the superpower relationship:

> One of the most curious features of the Cold War had been the extent to which the superpowers – and their respective clients, who have had little choice in the matter – have tolerated a whole series of awkward, artificial, and, on the surface at least, unstable regional arrangements: the division of Germany is, of course, the most obvious example; others would include the Berlin Wall, the position of West Berlin itself within East Germany, the arbitrary and ritualized partition of the Korean peninsula, the existence of an avowed Soviet satellite some ninety miles off the coast of Florida, and, not least, the continued functioning of an important American naval base within it. There is to all of these arrangements an appearance of wildly illogical improvisation: none of them could conceivably have resulted, it seems, from any rational and premeditated design.[22]

And yet, he suggests, they do have a logic of a kind, based on 'an unwillingness on the part of the superpowers to trade familiarity for unpredictability'.[23] Gaddis is surely right to observe that the lines of geo-political power often run crooked, but surely it is also the case that such anomalies as he cites – in particular the division of Germany and of Berlin – were regular irritants in the superpower relationship and, moreover, were less acceptable to the populations of Germany and Berlin than to the superpowers themselves. If Gaddis' interpretation is a useful corrective to the view that such anomalies put the superpower relationship on a hair trigger basis, it nevertheless also exaggerates the settled character of these arrangements, and correspondingly underestimates the degree to which they were products of and productive of tension. The cost of an emphasis on the theme of stability is, once again, to render mysterious the processes of change.

Michael Cox's main contribution to discussion of the Cold War system, a lengthy article published like Gaddis' in 1986, took the form of a critique of Fred Halliday's *The Making of the Second Cold War*.[24] Cox's chief objection to Halliday's book was its 'specific political purpose' of showing that 'it is America, as the stronger of the two powers, which bears the greatest responsibility for the present crisis [the Second Cold War]'. An impression was created, Cox argues, 'that although the USSR may have contributed to the Cold War, compared to America it is a virtual innocent abroad'. 'The USSR is not exactly whitewashed by Halliday', Cox concludes, 'but it is dealt with kindly compared to the treatment handed out to the USA'.[25] Whether this is an accurate reading of Halliday's book is less important to the present discussion than the fact that both Halliday and Cox inject a specifically political element into their readings of the Cold War. 'Part of the impetus to writing this work,' writes Halliday, 'has come from the peace movement, which has recently pushed the issue of nuclear weapons to the centre of political debate in such a rapid and decisive manner.'[26] For his part, Cox avers that although he will 'tread on a number of political toes,' he will nevertheless argue 'that there can be no alternative to the Cold War system except socialism, but that this will never come about while Stalinism is ascendant in the Soviet bloc'.[27]

We could hardly be further from the detached discourse of American social science. Though on the face of it the sound of political axes grinding would seem to exclude any possibility of objectivity, in fact it is political bias which allows Cox and Halliday to confront certain realities which receive little attention from Waltz and Gaddis. The most important of these is the perception that the Cold War was an unequal contest – at its outset no less than by the mid-1980s when Soviet economic decline was increasingly evident.[28] Since Cox makes most of this point, I shall focus on his work, making side references to Halliday. (Indeed in a recent article Halliday concedes that his chief mistake in *The Making of the Second Cold War* was his failure to see how brittle the overall Soviet position had become by the 1980s.)[29] As before, it must be emphasised that I make no pretence at a full exposition of the writings in question and am concerned simply to draw out those arguments which bear directly on the theme of stability.

Cox's analysis is highly dynamic in form, indeed dialectical. The argument is premised on the supposed saliency of capitalist decline as the main motor of United States policy in the Cold War and, by extension, the main cause of the Cold War: 'I want to suggest that the Cold War was not primarily the expression of some deep irreconcilable socio-economic conflict between the USA and the USSR [the view Cox ascribes to Halliday], but a strategy developed by the American bourgeoisie to rescue a declining capitalism after more than three decades of crisis. The ultimate clue to the Cold War therefore lies in understanding this decline and America's response to it.'[30] What appears to be another case of a leftist argument ascribing blame to the United States subsequently emerges, however, as more even-handed. If, as Cox claims, the Cold War was 'functional' for the United States, to the extent that 'it came to depend upon Stalinism to legitimize its general postwar strategy', it was also functional for the Soviet Union. Since the

US strategy was designed to 'break down Soviet bloc autarchy, the USSR had little option but to place pressure on the West', thus creating the notorious 'Soviet threat' which the United States then exploited in order to promote its goal of domination of the world economic market.[31]

However, and this is an important proviso, lest the Soviet Union be seen merely as reacting to Western pressure (an argument which would seem, like the leftist arguments Cox opposes, to let the Soviet Union off the hook), he observes that 'the Soviet opposition to the *status quo* in the West was not simply a response to America's pursuit of an open world economy after 1945'. It arose from 'some deeper cause,' namely from 'the great weakness of the Soviet economic system and the extraordinary insecurity this created for the Soviet elite'.[32] Soviet policy was thus aimed at actively opposing capitalism resurgent and reinforcing internal discipline and control over the communist movement, especially in Eastern Europe.

The substantial gain offered by this perspective, namely the observation that inequality in superpower resources of power and influence lent a dynamic and potentially unstable character to the US–Soviet relationship, does not relieve it of certain problems. It is curious, indeed paradoxical, that capitalist decline and Soviet weakness should be taken to have produced such manifestly awesome results. It is hard to comprehend from Cox's argument how in an age of capitalist decline the West should have proved so strong. In fact when his argument requires it – that is, when it is necessary to point up Soviet weakness – Cox acknowledges, for example, that by 1947 the Soviet Union faced 'a viable capitalism and a unified West'.[33] It should be noted that questioning Cox's argument about the tight functionality of the Cold War for both powers is not to deny that the United States *feared* a depression in the aftermath of the Second World War. This, however, takes us into the realms of American perceptions of its own power (or weakness) relative to the Soviet Union, a factor which is not easily accommodated by Cox's insistence on the reality of capitalist decline.

Cox's notion of 'system' is unlike that of either Waltz or Gaddis in important respects. Unlike Waltz, who makes a fundamental distinction between structures and processes – the former being characteristics of a 'system' and the latter of the interaction among its units Cox merges the two.[34] In his analysis the internal character and policies of the units are causal factors in producing the system, a view which Waltz would regard as 'reductionist', in the sense that Cox attempts to explain the whole by means of the attributes of the parts.[35] Unlike

Gaddis, who identifies 'a common goal of preserving international order' in superpower behaviour, Cox regards Cold War equilibrium as a product, not of any mutual commitment, explicit or implicit, to maintaining international order but of a functional dialectic arising from deep contradictions in the US–Soviet relationship: 'the Cold War relationship between America and the USSR was highly contradictory in so far as Stalinism both negated and supported the dominant world market economy led by the United States, while in the same way, Western capitalism supported and negated Stalinism'.[36] Furthermore, unlike both Waltz and Gaddis, Cox's analysis is concerned primarily with economic rather than political and strategic aspects of the US–Soviet relationship.

Whether one can accept Cox's notions or not, it seems fair to suggest that the above departures from Waltz and Gaddis enable Cox to be more sensitive to the potential for change in the Cold War system, more so also than Halliday. Rather than, for example, viewing the Second Cold War as a reinforcement of the Cold War system, as Halliday does, Cox regards it as 'the beginning of the end of the cold war as a system,' on the grounds that by comparison with their 'capacity for determining events within their different orbits' during the First Cold War, in the Second neither nation exerted such 'powerful forces of attraction'.[37] This leads Cox to posit the necessary conditions for the end of the Cold War which, he says, must be the introduction of 'real changes' in the East.[38] This as it happens proved to be a prescient remark but it hardly flows from the original premise of the argument, which was that the chief cause of the Cold War was the expansionist strategy of the American bourgeoisie. Of course, it is clear why Cox cannot propose the conclusion which would follow logically from his premise – namely that the end of the Cold War can only come from 'real changes' in the West – because he is enough of a realist to see that this is not likely to happen. Nor does he have any desire to see the continuance of what he somewhat sweepingly calls 'Stalinism'. But precisely because he is primarily concerned to refute what he takes to be pro-Stalinist interpretations of the Cold War, he is left in effect with endorsing the American version of it.

Testing theories of stability

Let us now briefly consider how the Cold War system did collapse and then gauge how well the various theories stand up. Inevitably the present account must be sketchy, merely a few pointers to issues which will be the subject of research and debate for years to come. It will probably be agreed that the vital factor was the demise of Soviet power, its inability and unwillingness any longer to pursue the strategy of denying Western influence in the East while maintaining its own power there and seeking to expand it elsewhere when possible. However, the suddenness of the collapse of the Soviet 'external' empire and of disruption in the internal empire presents huge problems of explanation. The advent of Gorbachev to the leadership of the Soviet Union, representing a generational break with the previous leadership and new departures in domestic and foreign policy, did not immediately herald the collapse of Soviet power in Eastern Europe, nor the complete breakdown of Soviet communism and of the Soviet Union itself in 1991. Paul Dibb in a comprehensive and authoritative analysis of Soviet power published in 1988 concluded that although the Soviet Union was a declining power and faced enormous difficulties both at home and in Eastern Europe, it 'is not now (nor will it be during the next decade) in the throes of a true systemic crisis, for it boasts large unused reserves of political and social stability that are sufficient to endure the most severe foreseeable difficulties'.[39]

Nevertheless, even if the author of this study did not, indeed could not, anticipate the precise course of events, he provided extensive evidence for the weaknesses in the Soviet system which would be more starkly revealed once the events of 1989 themselves were triggered. The main factor in question is indicated by the subtitle of Dibb's book, *The Incomplete Superpower*. The Soviet Union was a superpower mainly by virtue of its military strength. Economically, the Soviet Union was facing 'serious ... difficulties on almost every front. Some sectors of the economy, especially the defence industries, remain impressive but many others, such as agriculture, the consumer sector and welfare, are unbelievably backward.' Furthermore, 'in both the military and civilian spheres of competition with the West, the USSR has most to fear from its technological backwardness,' above all in production and use of computers.[40]

To the economic weakness of the Soviet Union must be added the declining hold of communist ideology within the Eastern bloc, increased access to information about Western culture via the media in those countries able to receive Western television broadcasts, providing means of comparison and contrast between conditions in the West and the Eastern bloc, and chronic economic problems in Eastern Europe, producing social unrest, particularly in Poland, the combined results of which were to undermine the legitimacy of communist ideology and of the Soviet Union's imposition of it.[41] But, as Halliday points out, endogenous factors do not account wholly for the 'final

collapse' of communism. 'What was determinant and what put stagnation into a wholly different light, was the global context, and in
particular the relative record of "communism" compared with its
competitor, advanced capitalism.'[42]

Kenneth Waltz

In the light of the collapse of the Soviet system, each of the
theories of the Cold War system described above contains certain
weaknesses. Waltz's analysis, based as it is on the presumed symmetry
of relations between the United States and the Soviet Union, on
politics and strategy, and on a lack of attention to internal factors,
assumed too much about the ability of politico-military factors to
maintain the balance. Because he lacks curiosity about the origins of
the balance, his scheme is not able to encompass possible reasons for its
demise. Moreover, in banishing unit-level processes as causes of systemic change, it is hard to understand how the structures which constitute the system can change at all.[43] Finally, having, I believe correctly,
observed that the Cold War system possesses many of the characteristics of war itself, he does not press the point to its local conclusion –
namely, that wars have victors and vanquished, and that the process is
subject to a dynamic which can sustain stability only so long as the
units are capable of matching each others' bids for advantage.

John Lewis Gaddis

Gaddis' analysis has comparable weaknesses – those of a
synchronic as opposed to a diachronic analysis. The strength of his
approach – the detailed itemisation of structural and behavioural
factors making for stability – is also its weakness: its inattention to
historical processes which have produced structural changes, both the
relative decline of the superpowers *vis-à-vis* other nations and the
relative decline of the Soviet Union *vis-à-vis* the United States. Gaddis
too, like Waltz, is little concerned with intra-bloc problems, especially
within the Eastern bloc. In an article published in 1990, in which he
considers the post-Cold War world, Gaddis suggests that 'the Cold
War experience, for all its dangers, illogic, and injustice, provided a
valuable opportunity for Europeans to mature, to put away those
irresponsible practices [nationalism] that dragged the continent into
war twice during the first half of this century'.[44] That may apply to
Western Europe, which has been able to move towards unity by a
process of consent (albeit under persistent Cold War pressures), but

surely not to Eastern Europe. Political 'maturity' was precisely what the citizens of Eastern Europe were denied in the effective suppression of civil society throughout the period of the Cold War. Gaddis' scheme comprehends only the view from the top. Most damagingly, it discounts a key weakness in the reach of Soviet power and one which was germane to its collapse.

Michael Cox

Cox's case is more complex. The main problem lies in his notion of the functional character of the Cold War for each side. It will not be denied that each side made use of the threat of the other to legitimise its goals. It is not clear, however, that 'without the Soviet Union the rehabilitation of bourgeois rule on a global scale would have been impossible in the postwar period' or that Stalinism was 'a necessary condition for bourgeois hegemony'.[45] For one thing, the necessary condition for American absolute and relative economic strength in the postwar world was supplied by the Second World War itself: the combination of the boost which the war gave to the American economy and the temporary destruction of its competitors. This is not to say that the emerging Cold War did not sharpen the edge of American expansionism or even influence the shape it took, but it is to say that the United States was not entirely dependent upon the goad of the Soviet Union to achieve it. Secondly, and closely related to the last point, Cox writes, like so many Cold War theorists, as if the superpowers were the only significant actors on the international scene. But surely the revival of capitalism after the war owed much to the internal dynamism of West European and Japanese capitalism and the presence of a developed industrial infrastructure. The Marshall Plan would scarcely have succeeded if this had not been the case. (The lack of such an infrastructure in the Soviet Union is now commonly given as the chief reason for not mounting a new Marshall Plan for the Soviet Union.)

An alternative interpretation

The broader response to the arguments of Cox, Waltz and Gaddis is best placed within an alternative interpretation of the postwar international system. Inevitably this must take only outline form and is presented as an agenda for discussion rather than a definitive scheme. It addresses what I take to be the chief implications of the collapse of the Cold War system for an understanding of postwar international politics. These can be reduced to two main points: (1) an adequate understanding of the postwar international system must be able to account for the forces of change as well as the forces making for stability; (2) in the light of the collapse of Soviet power, account must be taken of the differences in the status and roles performed by the United States and the Soviet Union in the international system. It is the link between these two points which provides the key to the structure of the Cold War system and its demise.

Asymmetries in American and Soviet power are, as Cox says, of vital significance, but it is not simply a case of a face-off between a 'viable capitalism' and an economically weak Soviet Union. It is important to distinguish between different levels of power and the means of exercising it. The general proposition is that the United States and the Soviet Union possessed different strengths and weaknesses. In the initial phase of the Cold War American economic power was preeminent, and despite its relative decline this has continued to be the case. However, the Soviet Union's relative weakness in economic power was counterbalanced by its conventional military strength and later its growing nuclear power, its geographical proximity to the major theatre of potential conflict, and (as Gaddis and others have pointed out) its autarkic economic development which rendered it effectively immune, at least until the early 1970s, to American economic pressure. In the early postwar years, in Joseph Nye's apt summary, the balance of power 'was based on asymmetrical resources: US economic power, nuclear force, and liberal ideology versus Soviet conventional forces, geographical location, and Communist ideology and institutions'.[46] Even in the early postwar period the United States could hardly be termed a true 'hegemonic power', if by that is meant a capacity to exert decisive control over the destinies of other nations, and for that reason it is hard to accept hegemonic stability theories as an adequate explanation for the durability of the Cold War system. 'Most versions of hegemonic stability theory,' writes Jack Levy, 'define hegemony in terms of dominance in economic production, finance and/or trade, while the role of military power is generally ignored or de-emphasized.'[47]

Soviet 'hard' power, represented by its conventional and nuclear forces and its geographical advantage, and its 'soft' power, represented by the attractive force of communist ideology especially in the crucial period from 1945 to 1960, enabled the Soviet Union to compensate for its relative weakness in economic power. However, it is worth recalling that in the first two decades of the Cold War the Soviet economy appeared anything but weak. While there are doubts among

Western observers about the validity of Soviet economic statistics,[48] nominally Soviet GNP grew at an annual rate of 6.7 per cent between 1953 and 1958, exceeding the rates of all other nations except Japan and Germany, slowing to 5.2 per cent between 1958 and 1965.[49] The comparable American rates are 3.2 per cent during the 1950s and 4.3 per cent in the 1960s.[50] Despite all the qualifications one must make regarding the low base from which the Soviet Union was working, slow rates of technological innovation in the non-military sector, poor productivity, the chronic weakness of agriculture, and the disproportionate growth of heavy industry as compared to consumer goods, the American (and indeed the Soviet) perception was of increasing momentum in Soviet economic growth. And of course in the military and aerospace fields the Soviet Union showed itself capable of striking advances, as manifested in the launch of Sputnik in 1957.

These developments were sufficiently alarming to the Eisenhower administration for the president to observe as early as 1955 that the Soviets had apparently abandoned the Stalinist tactic of using force to achieve their objectives and had turned instead to economics, so that 'it would appear that we are being challenged in the area of our greatest strength'.[51] Six years later in his speech to the Twenty-Second Congress of the Soviet Communist Party, Khrushchev invoked Lenin's formula, 'communism is Soviet power plus electrification', and went on to predict that 'in the current decade (1961–70) the Soviet Union, in creating the material and technical basis for communism, will surpass the strongest and richest capitalist country, the USA, in production per head of population'.[52] Given our knowledge of the stagnation of the Soviet economy in the 1970s and 1980s and its catastrophic decline in the 1990s, it takes an effort of imagination to reconstruct the circumstances of the 1950s and early 1960s when communism appeared as a genuine competitor to Western capitalism. The communist bloc did not at that time seem to suffer unduly from its virtual detachment from the global capitalist system. On the contrary, the Soviet bloc's capacity to generate its own economic dynamic apparently rendered it immune from Western economic pressure.

Autarky was ultimately unsustainable not merely because of the long-term structural problems of the Soviet economy but because of differential rates of growth within the Soviet Union and the West. Much attention has been focused recently upon American relative economic decline, but from the point of view of East–West relations as a whole Soviet relative economic decline was arguably more important, since it took place in the context of substantial overall growth, above all in trade, within the world capitalist system.[53] The Soviet

74

share of world manufactures and of world trade fell in the 1970s (and had been falling for some time before that).[54] Moreover, this occurred at a time when the volume of East–West trade was increasing as a result of the detente policies. One reason for the disparity in the figures is that the fastest growing trading nations were among the newly industrialised countries, not the Eastern bloc. Another reason is that most East–West trade was one way. In all categories of East–West trade, except Soviet oil, Eastern bloc exports fell while imports rose. The gap was covered by borrowing from the West, which gave rise in the course of the 1970s 'to the build-up of heavy debt to the industrial West'.[55] Not only did autarky have its limits, but efforts to overcome it tended to increase rather than reduce the Eastern bloc's vulnerability to external and internal pressures.

Soviet economic problems had important repercussions in its relations both with the West and with Eastern Europe. In the former case rising defence expenditures were coupled with economic growth rates moving in the opposite direction. Of course the Soviet Union has always sustained a higher level of military spending in relation to GNP than the United States (variously estimated at between 12 per cent and 14 per cent or as high as 17 per cent in the mid-1980s as compared to the United States' 7 per cent).[56] However, the pressure to match the increased defence expenditures of the Reagan administration came at a time when there were equally powerful pressures to introduce major and expensive economic and social reforms.

As far as Eastern Europe is concerned, a striking index of the strains in Soviet–Eastern bloc relations which antedates the events of 1989 was a substantial and damaging shift in the Soviet supply of energy (oil and gas) to Eastern Europe. The Soviet Union had always sold energy products to Eastern Europe at prices well below the world market price, its surplus being sold on the world market for hard currency. However, when the world price dropped dramatically in the early 1980s the Soviet Union announced in 1982 an immediate 10 per cent cut in planned energy deliveries to Eastern Europe, the intention being to recoup its losses of hard currency by increasing the volume of its exports to the world market. As John Kramer observes, 'this action provided a harbinger of the even greater problems that awaited Eastern Europe after Mikhail Gorbachev assumed power in the USSR in March 1985'.[57] The costs of empire had always been a drain on the Soviet Union. The effort to cut them exacerbated the difficulties which the Eastern European economies were experiencing, most notably Poland which in the mid-1980s was in a state of uneasy calm following the crisis of 1980–1.

These circumstances provide an economic backdrop to the more familiar story of the political and ideological collapse of communism after 1989. The concern here is not with the details of that story but with the implications of the Soviet Union's economic travails for an understanding of its position within the international system. If the above account can be accepted, then it seems plausible to argue that what is at issue in US–Soviet relations is not one system but two overlapping but distinct systems: (1) a Cold War system defined by the geo-political division of Europe and its extension to parts of the Third World, the existence of nuclear weapons, and ideological conflict, and (2) a world capitalist system which was defined by the expansion of production and trade, growing economic interdependence, and the establishment of international 'regimes' for the management of various transnational processes.[58] The development of international relations theory mirrors this bifurcation. Realism, with its source in the early Cold War but continued and developed by such neo-realists as Waltz, stresses inter*state* relations, the political and military dominance of the United States and the Soviet Union within a bipolar international system, and the notion of the balance of power as the operational force making for system stability. Pluralist theories, with roots in the increasingly multipolar world of the 1970s, stress the growing importance of transnational processes, especially economic, the declining saliency of the US–Soviet bilateral relationship and of military/national security concerns associated with it,[59] and interdependence as the chief systemic force. 'Interdependence,' it has been well said, 'is to many pluralists what balance of power is to realists.'[60]

Arguably both approaches are justified within the terms of the realities they set out to explain, but neither on its own seems capable of accommodating the full reality, which is that, while the Soviet Union's capacity to sustain itself was limited to and by the Cold War system, the United States was never so constrained, since it had access to the resources of the world system. Stability did indeed exist within the Cold War system so long as the Soviet Union's economic resources were sufficient to maintain military and political control over its own domain. Once that came into doubt, however, the costs of its isolation were starkly revealed and no more so than when the effort was made to surmount it by increasing imports and borrowing from the West. Integration with the Western economies could never be more than partial, given the incompatibility between Western market economies and the command economies of the Eastern bloc, the inconvertibility of their currencies, and the generally low quality of the goods they had to trade. The United States has never been limited to the Cold War system and that, despite its economic problems since the mid-1970s, was a major source of its power *vis-à-vis* the Soviet Union. The United States could, so to speak, afford to fight the Cold War with one hand while making money with the other. Put differently, we could say that the Soviet system, born in war, developed by Stalin as a military command system with power centred in the state, tempered further by the Second World (or 'Great Patriotic') War, and steeled by the Cold War, was above all a society permanently mobilised as if for war. Arguably that is the real meaning of totalitarianism, of Hitler's Reich no less than of Soviet communism. Significant as the military-industrial complex was and is within American society, it has never been the all-encompassing reality in either its internal or external affairs.

Viewed in this light, the Cold War system has been subject to a dynamic – the growth of the world capitalist system – which was tangential to the Cold War itself. The Cold War system has not so much collapsed as been bypassed, and to that extent it is an example of system change without war. This is no guarantee that war is now impossible between the United States and the successor states of the Soviet Union. The continued existence of vast nuclear arsenals, the ever-present possibility of nuclear accidents, and the chance that a militarist regime might take power in the Soviet Union could concei-vably trigger off crises with global consequences. Far less can we speak of the end of history, even if one accepts that Fukuyama meant by this only the end of a certain kind of history, one characterised by conflict between major ideologies. Hegel, Fukuyama's guiding light, made the same claim about the consequences of the French Revo-lution, as did Marx about the consequences of the coming socialist revolution. It is a strangely unhistorical reading of the historical process to believe that human beings are now permanently released from fundamental ideological conflicts. All one can say is that one particular phase of history, characterised by a particular arrangement of the international system, is now over. What its outcome will be is as yet unclear. It appears likely that while the costs of Cold War 'stability' have been greater to the Soviet Union than to the United States, the United States will bear a large burden of responsibility for reshaping a new world order. Ironically, because the costs of the Cold War have weighed less on the United States, it has less reason than the new states of the former Soviet Union for abandoning the assumptions which underpinned its policies during the Cold War period.

77

Conclusion

International Relations theorists rightly seek to develop theories which are internally consistent and are, as far as possible, consistent with known facts about the behaviour of states and the structures within which they exist. Any theory is in a literal sense an abstraction from reality much in the way that a map is an abstraction from geographical features, an important difference being that in the case of international relations not all the facts can be known. Nor can the tendencies of events be easily interpreted, even those which have already taken place, not only because they are always in motion but because the range of variables is so immense that the ascription of particular causes to particular events can never be certain. Needless to say these cautionary remarks apply also to the scheme outlined above. The events of recent years, however, offer new triangulation points from which to gauge the changes over the whole postwar period. From this perspective it is possible to view the postwar period as one of an interplay between two distinct but intersecting systems, the Cold War system possessing a political and military dynamic of its own, and a globalising capitalist system whose growth progressively undermined the stability of the Cold War system. In that sense, the end of the Cold War, which was a structure made possible by the geopolitical shock delivered by the Second World War to the international system, represents the belated settlement which never took place in 1945. Only now can we begin to dispense with the term 'postwar' to refer to our present reality.

Two final conclusions suggest themselves. Firstly, re-envisioning the Cold War as the 'long peace' is clearly of great value in understanding the pattern of relations between the United States and the Soviet Union, particularly its nuclear and geo-political elements. The most common criticism of this view – that in concentrating on superpower stability it ignores the chronic instability which has characterised events in the Third World over the past four decades[61] – is not the only or even perhaps the most important qualification to be made. There is also the problem that abstraction of the Cold War system from its global economic context distracts attention from a key factor making for change within the Cold War system. A theory of the Cold War system must in some sense be a theory of change. The second conclusion flows from this. For a system level explanation to work – that is, for it to be able to account for change as well as stability – some elements must be included in the explanation which are not restricted to the system level itself. *Pace* Waltz, that explanation must be able to accommodate aspects of both nation state behaviour and *processes* as opposed simply to structures. To adhere too strictly to one or another level of analysis – that of the system of states or that of nation-states – is to cut oneself off from an explanatory tool without which the historical process is rendered mysterious. Historians and international relations theorists have much to learn from each other.

Notes

1 J. L. Gaddis, 'The Long Peace: Elements of Stability in the Postwar International System', *International Security*, vol. 10, no. 3, pp. 99–142; and J. L. Gaddis, 'Beyond the Triumph of Liberty', *The Guardian*, 1 June 1990, p. 19.
2 F. Fukuyama, 'The End of History?' *The National Interest*, vol. 16, Summer 1989, pp. 3–16.
3 S. Smith, 'Paradigm Dominance in International Relations: The Development of International Relations as a Social Science', *Millennium*, vol. 16, no. 2, 1980, p. 197.
4 By contrast, American historical writing on the Cold War has been profoundly political, leading a British historian to remark somewhat intemperately that 'American historiography of the Cold War tells us very little of the Cold War, much of American intellectual history in the 1960s and 1970s.' (D. C. Watt, 'Rethinking the Cold War: A Letter to a British Historian', *Political Quarterly*, vol. 49, 1978, p. 447.) Only recently have historiography and International Relations scholarship come to feed productively off each other, a development which owes much to the work of John Gaddis.
5 R. O. Keohane, *International Institutions and State Power: Essays in International Relations Theory* (Boulder: Westview Press, 1989), p. 10.
6 K. W. Deutsch and J. D. Singer, 'Multipolar Systems and International Stability', *World Politics*, vol. 16, no. 3, April 1964, p. 390.
7 K. Waltz, 'The Stability of the Bipolar World', *Daedalus*, vol. 13, Summer 1964, pp. 898–9; and A. W. DePorte, *Europe Between the Superpowers: The Enduring Balance* (New Haven: Yale University Press, 1986), p. xv.
8 Gaddis, 'The Long Peace'.
9 *Ibid.*, p. 141.
10 Waltz, 'The Stability of a Bipolar World', pp. 882, 883 and 886.
11 Deutsch and Singer, 'Multipolar Systems', p. 390 and *passim*.
12 K. N. Waltz, *Theory of International Politics* (Reading, Mass: Addison-Wesley, 1979), p. 174; and Waltz, 'The Stability in a Bipolar World', p. 901.
13 Waltz, *Theory of International Politics*, p. 64.
14 Waltz, 'The Stability of a Bipolar World', p. 886; and Waltz, *Theory of International Politics*, pp. 180–2.
15 J. Mueller, 'The Essential Irrelevance of Nuclear Weapons: Stability in the Postwar World', *International Security*, vol. 13, no. 2, 1980, pp. 55–79. However, it is interesting to note that since 1979 Waltz has become much more convinced of the role of nuclear weapons as distinct from geopolitical bipolarity in maintaining the 'long peace' since 1945. See Kenneth Waltz, 'Nuclear Myths and Political Realities', *American Political Science Review*, vol. 84, September 1990, pp. 743–4.

16 Waltz, *Theory of International Politics*, p. 204.
17 J. D. Singer, 'The Level of Analysis Problem in International Relations', in J. Rosenau (ed.), *International Politics and Foreign Policy* (New York: Free Press, 1961), p. 28.
18 Waltz, *Theory of International Politics*, p. 64.
19 Gaddis, 'Long Peace', p. 100.
20 *Ibid.*, p. 123.
21 C. Kegley (ed.), *The Long Postwar Peace: Contending Explanations and Projections* (New York: Harper Collins, 1991).
22 Gaddis, 'The Long Peace', p. 138.
23 *Ibid.*
24 F. Halliday, *The Making of The Second Cold War* (London: Verso, 1983).
25 M. Cox, 'The Cold War and Stalinism in the Age of Capitalist Decline', *Critique*, 1986, p. 20.
26 Halliday, *The Making of the Second Cold War*, Preface.
27 Cox, 'The Cold War', pp. 19–20.
28 Halliday, *The Making of the Second Cold War*, pp. 36–9, and 263; and Cox, 'The Cold War', pp. 27–30.
29 F. Halliday, 'The Ends of Cold War', *New Left Review*, vol. 180, March–April 1990, p. 15.
30 Cox, 'The Cold War', p. 29.
31 *Ibid.*, pp. 26–7.
32 *Ibid.*, pp. 27–8.
33 *Ibid.*, p. 28.
34 Waltz, *The Theory of International Politics*, p. 114.
35 *Ibid.*, ch. 2.
36 Gaddis, 'The Long Peace', p. 127; and Cox, 'The Cold War', p. 19.
37 Cox, 'The Cold War', p. 64.
38 *Ibid.*, p. 66.
39 P. Dibb, *The Soviet Union: The Incomplete Superpower* (London: International Institute for Strategic Studies/Macmillan, 1988), p. 260.
40 *Ibid.*, pp. 80 and 266.
41 G. Schopflin, 'The End of Communism in Eastern Europe', *International Affairs*, vol. 66, no. 1, 1990, pp. 3–16.
42 Halliday, 'The Ends of the Cold War', p. 117.
43 See the analysis by J. G. Ruggie, 'Continuity and Transformation in the World Polity: Toward a Neo-realist Synthesis', in R. O. Keohane (ed.), *Neorealism and Its Critics* (New York: Columbia University Press, 1986), pp. 152–3.
44 Gaddis, 'Beyond the Triumph of Liberty', p. 19.
45 Cox, 'The Cold War', p. 36.
46 J. S. Nye Jr, *Bound to Lead: The Changing Nature of American Power* (New York: Basic Books, 1990), p. 71.
47 J. Levy, 'Long Cycles, Hegemonic Transitions, and the Long Peace', in Kegley (ed.), *The Long Postwar Peace*, p. 149; and Nye, *Bound to Lead*, pp. 87–90.
48 Nye, *Bound to Lead*, pp. 119–20.
49 R. Munting, *The Economic Development of the USSR* (London: Macmillan, 1982), pp. 132 and 137.

50 H. Van der Wee, *Prosperity and Upheaval: The World Economy, 1945–1980* (Harmondsworth: Penguin, 1987), p. 50.

51 S. E. Ambrose, *Eisenhower the President* (London: George Allen and Unwin, 1984), p. 283.

52 R. V. Daniels (ed.), *A Documentary History of Communism*, I, *Communism in Russia* (London: I. B. Tauris, 1985), p. 339.

53 P. M. Kennedy, *The Rise and Fall of Great Powers: Economic Change and Military Conflict from 1500 to 2,000* (London: Unwin Hyman, 1988), pp. 430–32.

54 *Ibid.*, p. 436; and Van der Wee, *Prosperity and Upheaval*, pp. 262–3.

55 Van der Wee, *Prosperity and Upheaval*, pp. 398–9.

56 A. Marshall, 'Sources of Soviet Power: The Military Potential in the 1980s', in C. Bertram (ed.), *Prospects of Soviet Power in the 1980s* (Hamden Court: Archon Books, 1980), p. 64; and US Government, *Soviet Military Power 1987* (Washington DC: US Government Printing Office, 1987), p. 108; and Kennedy, *The Rise and Fall of Great Powers*, p. 532.

57 J. Kramer, 'Eastern Europe and the "Energy Shock" of 1990', paper delivered to the Conference of the British International Studies Association, Newcastle-upon-Tyne, December 1990, p. 4; and Z. Medvedev, *Gorbachev* (Oxford: Basil Blackwell, 1987), pp. 227–38.

58 R. O. Keohane and J. Nye, *Power and Interdependence: World Politics in Transition* (Boston: Little Brown, 1977), chs. 3 and 4.

59 *Ibid.*, p. 47.

60 P. R. Viotti and M. V. Kauppi, *International Relations Theory: Realism, Pluralism, Globalism* (New York, Macmillan, 1987), p. 209.

61 M. Brecher and J. Wilkenfeld, 'International Crises and Global Instability: The Myth of the "Long peace"', in Kegley (ed.), *The Long Postwar Peace*, pp. 85–104.

5 EXPLAINING SOVIET FOREIGN POLICY BEHAVIOUR IN THE 1980s

MIKE BOWKER

Introduction

The aims of this chapter are essentially four-fold. Firstly, the chapter outlines the different analyses of Soviet foreign policy behaviour in the pre-Gorbachev era. This is important because one's judgement on the significance of the changes since 1985 are largely dependent on one's original conception of Soviet foreign policy behaviour. The second section takes up this issue and discusses the substance and importance of reform under Gorbachev. Thirdly, and at the heart of this chapter, is an attempt to explain why Gorbachev embarked on such a radical policy as new political thinking. Finally, a very brief review will be made on the likely consequences of contemporary Soviet foreign policy on the West.

Before proceeding, however, it should be noted here that this chapter makes no great claims to definitive statements on any of the issues above. It is perhaps too early to seek to do that. Instead, it attempts only to outline the general trends in the current debate on Gorbachev, both in the West and the Soviet Union. This, in itself, is an ambitious task, given the volume and diversity of writing on the subject.

Traditional theories on Soviet foreign policy behaviour

Before Gorbachev came to power in March 1985, explanations of Soviet foreign policy tended to fall into two basic categories. The first stated that the USSR should be treated as an 'exceptionalist' state. To use Zbigniew Brzezinski's phrase, the Soviet Union was a world power of a 'new type'.[1] The second, disputed this claim and suggested the USSR was, on the contrary, a 'normal' state. Irrespective of its political culture, ideology or totalitarian structures, the USSR, according to this view, acted in the international system much like any other state. By way of an introduction, these two contrasting explanations will be discussed below.

The exceptionalist state model

Marxist–Leninist ideology

For the majority of adherents to the exceptionalist model, Marxist–Leninist ideology was central to an understanding of Soviet foreign policy behaviour.[2] Proponents of this view, such as George Kennan and Zbigniew Brzezinski, always stressed the long-term communist goal of destroying the international capitalist system. In the short term, Moscow's policies were aimed at undermining basic Western interests, such as free enterprise and free trade. As a result, the USSR was perceived in the West, at a minimum, as a highly destabilising power. Soviet ideology appeared to leave little room for the subtle arts of diplomacy, negotiation and compromise. The West feared that any such attempt could easily lead to some form of appeasement. President Reagan rejected superpower detente on these grounds, declaring that the only responsible way to deal with Moscow was through a policy of strength – especially military strength.

This explanation was given greater credibility because the Moscow leadership readily accepted the accusation that Marxism–Leninism was the driving force behind Soviet foreign policy behaviour. The only difference being, of course, that the Kremlin saw this in a wholly positive light. Moscow promoted the downfall of capitalism because it was believed to be inherently aggressive and expansionist as it searched for ever more markets and higher profit margins. The communist decision to embark on a policy of autarky and obstruction to Western economic penetration around the world was a direct threat to international capitalism. As the stakes were so high, Moscow believed the West was always ready to use force to overthrow communism. Therefore, the only way to secure peace and protect the Soviet state was through the destruction of capitalism and its eventual replacement by international communism.

Countless speeches were delivered, countless articles and books were published in the Soviet Union expounding global politics in these terms. Andrei Gromyko was at the centre of Soviet foreign policy making as foreign minister from 1957 to 1985. In his memoirs, he chose to stress the pivotal role of ideology to his political thinking: 'In the course of historical development, one social order is inevitably replaced by another. Certainly we take the view that the capitalist order will be replaced by the socialist order – we believe this in the way people believe the sun will rise tomorrow morning . . .'[3]

Thus, the long-serving Soviet foreign minister, Gromyko, and President Carter's National Security Adviser, Brzezinski, from different ends of the political spectrum, were able to agree on one central fact – namely, the long-term goal of Soviet foreign policy was the elimination of international capitalism. However, it was less easy, as Kennan and Brzezinski were always ready to acknowledge, to explain every short-term policy decision in terms of ideology. Stalin's changing attitude towards Hitler in the 1930s and 1940s, and the Sino–Soviet split were just two of the most obvious examples when national interest seemed to take precedence over ideological concerns.

The totalitarian model

Other exceptionalist thinkers have stressed the totalitarian structures of the Soviet Union as a primary source of its expansionist tendencies.[4] This view did not necessarily conflict with those emphasising the importance of ideology. Indeed, it was usually argued that the two reinforced each other. It was certainly true that all models of totalitarianism had the concept of a militant ideology at their core. Nevertheless, there could be a difference of emphasis. The totalitarianists suggested that it was the domestic political structures that were of primary importance rather than the nature of the ideology itself. In other words, the ideology – be it of the left or right – was less important than the fact that the government ruled repressively and without the consent of the people. Central to this view was the idea that a dictatorship had to justify its monopoly position through the existence (real, imagined or manufactured) of militant enemies determined to overthrow the state. For the USSR, Western capitalism provided just such an enemy image.

Before glasnost, any notion that dictatorships were more prone to fight wars than liberal democracies was dismissed in the USSR as bourgeois propaganda.[5] Nowadays, new political thinking is based on the idea of a link between peace and democracy. The Russian foreign minister, Andrei Kozyrev, has been quite explicit on this point. He has written that totalitarianism in the Soviet Union 'helped the system to justify its strengthening at home and expansionism abroad'. He continued, 'It has been confirmed that developed countries of pluralistic democracy and a free market economy are now more inclined to safeguard international law than authoritarian dictatorships.'[6] However, this notion is far from universally accepted, even in the West. For example, the American, John Mearsheimer, has rejected the claim that democratic states do not fight each other. In his article in *International Security*, Mearsheimer stated that the democracies have gone to war as often as any other form of state.[7] Moreover, countries such as the United States have attacked freely elected governments in

84

the Third World, and he continued, only an uncharitable definition of Wilhelmine Germany as a dictatorship prevents World War One from being a war among democracies.

Russian political culture

The third and final view within the exceptionalist framework derived from a more historical perspective. This view claimed that the Kremlin's policies could best be explained by reference, not to Marxist–Leninist ideology, but to Russian political culture. There were two main elements to this explanation: the Slavophile and the geostrategic. The Slavophile explanation suggested that Russia had a culture quite different from the West. After the Mongol conquest of the thirteenth century, Russia was said to have become an oriental rather than a Western power. This historical development led to a more collectivist political culture and a far greater tolerance of authoritarian forms of government. This separateness also fed a messianic strand in Russian thinking which helped to legitimise the tsarist, and later the Leninist, land-based empire. However, there have been many critics of this view. For example, Jerry Hough suggested that the notion of separateness could be exaggerated. The Slavophiles did not always dominate Russian political culture to the extent often implied. In fact, Westernisers were not uncommon in the tsarist household. Peter the Great was a famous Westerniser, Catherine the Great was born in Germany, and French was the language of the royal court until the eighteenth century.[8] Although Hough would disagree, Lenin too could be described as a Westerniser. He based most of his political ideas on Western philosophers, not least the German Karl Marx, and sought the salvation of Russia through its integration into the hoped-for socialist Europe.

The second explanation claimed that Russia's supposed expansionist tendencies were due to strategic insecurities. Lacking clear natural borders, Russia always felt vulnerable to attack. As a result, the Russian empire was pushed ever outwards from its heartland. Yet this process only served to further overstretch its military resources. As Brzezinski wrote: 'A relentless historical cycle was thus set in motion: insecurity generated expansionism; expansionism bred insecurity.'[9]

Many adherents to the Russian political culture model would not necessarily see it as being in conflict with any of the ideas on ideology or totalitarianism outlined above. Indeed, a number, including Brzezinski and Kennan, perceived them all as complementary, with the messianic strands of Marxism–Leninism easily subsumed by Russian political culture. Helmut Schmidt, the former West German

Chancellor, would agree: 'Three fourths of the strategy hatched in Moscow was traditionally Russian, while one fourth was communist.'[10]

Critics of the geo-strategic explanation have included the academic, Michael MccGwire of the Brookings Institution. He doubts the claim that Russia was more expansionist than any other imperialist power. Furthermore, he has effectively argued that communist Russia had rejected the expansionist idea of revolutionary war by 1921.[11] The CPSU, for its part, always denied any link between tsarist and Soviet policy. The party consistently emphasised the fissure in Russian history caused by the Bolshevik Revolution of 1917.

The normal state model

This model was opposed to the idea of Russian or Soviet exceptionalism, and could itself be divided into two main categories. The first concentrated on the domestic; the second on the international.

The domestic critique

Proponents of this view might accept the importance of domestic factors in determining foreign policy, but they would reject the claim that the nature of the Soviet system set it apart in any fundamental way from the Western liberal democracies. Such analysts embraced one or more of the following claims. Firstly, the role of Marxist–Leninist ideology should be downplayed as a factor in decision-making. Secondly, the totalitarian model had ceased to be relevant in the post-Stalinist USSR. Thirdly, a general scepticism was required in dealing with the concept of Russian political culture.[12]

Supporters of the normal state model did not deny the existence of differences between capitalist and communist states, but they would make the central claim that general theories about political behaviour could be applied to the Soviet Union just as much as to any liberal democratic state. In other words, it was possible to study the USSR in the mainstream of political science. This view had won many adherents by the 1970s among Western academics specialising in domestic Soviet politics. However, it was far easier to dismantle the totalitarian model than construct an acceptable replacement. Both interest group and bureaucratic decison-making models have been severely criticised when applied to the Soviet Union.[13] Furthermore, foreign policy specialists have been far less willing than their domestic policy counterparts to abandon the exceptionalist model.

International systems theory

The second group of scholars adhering to the normal state model have perceived the internal workings of a state as peripheral to an understanding of foreign policy behaviour. As John Mearsheimer has written: 'The key to war and peace lies more in the structure of the international system than in the nature of the individual states.'[14] Mearsheimer puts forward the case of the Realist school which states that the root cause of conflict is the anarchical nature of the international system. For such analysts, the state – even the Soviet state, although this is not always made explicit – is essentially a 'black box' or, according to metaphorical preference, a 'billiard ball'.

Thus, the Soviet Union, like any other state in an anarchical international system, will seek to further its national interests, as the political leadership perceives them. Realists have described these interests as ranging from the minimum desire – the preservation of the state, to the maximum desire – world domination. The ability to fulfil such desires is dependent on a nation's power in relation to other states in the international system. Therefore, according to this view, the best explanation of Soviet foreign policy behaviour is the level of Soviet power (measured in military, and to a lesser extent, economic terms) and its position in the international system. Since the USSR emerged after the Second World War as one of only two acknowledged military superpowers, Realists saw an expansion of Soviet interests around the world as virtually inevitable. This expansion would inevitably bring it into conflict with the other superpower, the United States. The only way this East–West conflict could be prevented would be through a change in the balance of power, which would be brought about by the emergence of new power centres or the collapse of an existing pole. Usually these changes come about through war. In this model, at its extreme application, no knowledge of domestic policy is required to explain Soviet foreign policy.

Realism is a persuasive explanation for the behaviour of states. Despite concerted criticism since the 1970s in particular, Realism has remained the dominant model in International Relations theory. Undeniably, it has considerable explanatory power in the case of the Soviet Union too. However, the type of Realism described above is less useful in studying the reasons for the collapse of the Soviet pole, which is the question at the heart of this chapter.

A synthesis

There may be objections to the implication of the above that there is any inherent tension between the so-called exceptionalist and the normal state models. In some ways, it is simply a repeat of the familiar argument over the primacy of ideology or national interest in the making of Soviet foreign policy. In the West, a growing number came to the view that it was eminently possible for Moscow to further both its Marxist–Leninist ideals and its national interests simultaneously. Robert Miller, in his recent book, *Soviet Foreign Policy Today*, was only the latest to agree with this general proposition. He wrote that the impact of Marxist–Leninist ideology 'has more often than not been indirect rather than direct. That is, instead of directly prescribing policies, it has acted to shape the frame of reference and expectations of Soviet decision-makers, as well as their perceptions of such non-ideological considerations as "security", "defence" and the conditions for "peace".'[15]

Miller's analysis may be correct. However, there are at least two reasons for outlining in this chapter the division between the exceptionalist and normal state models. First, there is no consensus on this issue in academic or official circles; and secondly, the two models have different implications for Western policy. Exceptionalists would always remain sceptical of conducting normal relations with Moscow unless the Soviet Union dismantled its domestic political structures and abandoned the ideology underpinning them. Even then, Russia's strategic position and political culture may impel the West to take a constantly cautious attitude. On the other hand, analysts who perceived the Soviet Union as a more normal state would always be more open to the possibility of cooperation. Such analysts would not necessarily see the USSR as any less threatening than the exceptionalists. The Realists, for example, saw competition between the USA and the USSR as almost inevitable after the war. However, for the Realist there was no *a priori* need for the Soviet Union to abandon its communist beliefs, totalitarian structure or political culture before some kind of alliance could be formed with Moscow. All that was required was a substantial shift in the balance of power in the international system.

The nature of change in the USSR since 1985

From 1985, Gorbachev embarked on a policy of radical reform in both domestic and foreign policy. At home, in the early stages of his administration he introduced the terms *glasnost* and *demokratizatsiya*.

Under these headings, Gorbachev sponsored unparalleled critical debate, multi-candidate elections, and an end to the CPSU's constitutional right to rule. In the aftermath of the failed coup, radical reform has been dumped in favour of revolution, as Gorbachev agreed to the suspension of the party and the break-up of the centralised Soviet Union.

In foreign policy, which is the focus of this chapter, the results were no less radical. By the time of the Twenty-Seventh CPSU Congress in 1986, Gorbachev's new political programme had been unveiled which abandoned the international class struggle as the centrepiece of Soviet foreign policy. As a result, Moscow adopted a more positive attitude towards the West. No longer were Western economies routinely dismissed as being in terminal decline. Instead, it was officially acknowledged that international capitalism had proved far more durable than Moscow had ever expected. Moreover, capitalism was no longer perceived to be inherently expansionist. The cases of Japan and West Germany were often cited as examples where capitalist economies were thriving without excessive defence spending or aggressive foreign policies. Thus, Gorbachev in his book, *Perestroika*, was able to openly express the view that the West did not pose a military threat to the Soviet Union.[16]

From these basic precepts, most of Gorbachev's new political thinking flowed. If the military threat from the West had been radically reduced, it was no longer necessary to base Soviet defence policy purely on military power. Therefore, arms cuts – even unilateral and asymmetrical cuts – would not necessarily jeopardise Soviet security. Political and collective security could replace the old ideas of military parity and balance of power politics. Gorbachev spoke regularly of the need to improve East–West understanding and build up trust on both sides. As capitalism was no longer perceived to be the prime cause of war there was no need to base Soviet foreign policy on undermining Western interests. Military and regional confrontation could be discarded. The urgency to gain new allies at the expense of the West dissipated. Equally, the loss of existing allies, whilst not perhaps anticipated, could nevertheless be tolerated. As a result, Gorbachev was able to adopt a much more flexible attitude towards his allies in Eastern Europe and the Third World. With the abandonment of the international class struggle, the possibility arose that East and West need not be in conflict on every issue. The zero-sum concepts of the Cold War became redundant. New political thinking stated that East and West had some basic interests in common. The most obvious of these was human survival, which was directly or indirectly threatened by modern weaponry, the arms race, pollution and poverty. Such problems, Gorbachev argued could best be settled through East–West cooperation, using such organisations as the UN and the CSCE process. According to new thinking, they could never be solved by one country in isolation, or by the old politics of power blocs and class struggle.

It was clear that Gorbachev had introduced reforms which had initiated changes in the international system. However, at least up to the failed coup of August 1991, there was considerable debate over the nature and importance of these reforms. One school of thought perceived perestroika to be superficial and, therefore, easily reversible. A second school believed the reforms to be more substantial and deep-rooted. This chapter will now consider these two views with the main focus on the pre-coup period.

The pessimistic view

Even before the coup, the notion that Gorbachev's reforms were superficial or a fraud was a minority view. However, it did command support in some quarters on the right in America, and amongst many sectors of leading Soviet opinion. Sakharov, Kagarlitsky, Solzhenitsyn and Yeltsin, from very different reformist wings in the USSR, have all gone on record at one time or another to condemn the lack of substance to the reforms. All these figures warned before the coup failed that it was premature to declare communism dead. Solzhenitsyn went so far as to claim in an article in *Literaturnaya gazeta* that the sole purpose of perestroika was to prevent the Communist Party losing power.[17] Certainly, up until the failed coup of August 1991, the Stalinist political structures of Soviet society remained in place. The party had lost some influence before the putsch, but it remained the most powerful institution in the Soviet Union. It retained its influence in most local and central government structures and was the overlord of the KGB and military. Undoubtedly, the party, together with the central institutions of repression represented a formidable force favouring the status quo. Gorbachev was a radical reformer, but as a self-proclaimed Leninist, he always seemed reluctant to move against these forces of reaction and irrevocably break up the totalitarian structures of the Soviet state. Even after the coup, he had to be forced by Yeltsin to take these revolutionary steps. For that reason, Gorbachev has met with considerable suspicion over his real motives for instigating reform.[18]

Such doubts led to a similar mistrust over his foreign policy initiatives. Western commentators on the right pointed out the limited impact of arms control on Soviet military procurement. The cuts were not aimed, in this view, at weakening the power of the Soviet military, but to 'cut the fat' and to allow the military to re-emerge a leaner, meaner, and more modern and efficient outfit.[19] There were some establishment figures in the Soviet Union who accepted the burden of this argument. Georgy Arbatov, for example, said that whilst political detente had developed rapidly and deeply since 1985, progress on military detente, even after the START Treaty of July 1991, had been negligible.[20] Some cynics even described the Soviet withdrawals from Afghanistan and Eastern Europe as tactical. For example, Michael Scammell in the *International Herald Tribune* wrote that 'jettisoning Eastern Europe was ... but a means of preserving the Soviet Union and its socialist form of society'.[21] Whilst according to his fellow columnist, William Safire, Gorbachev's new thinking was devised to give Moscow a breathing-space before relaunching its anti-Western campaign.[22]

The pessimists were right to urge caution. The coup attempt of August 1991 showed up the limited nature of Gorbachev's reforms up to that date. However, this view can have little relevance in the aftermath of the failed putsch. For the collapse of the coup only hastened the death of Marxism–Leninism and the final destruction of the Soviet Union as a centralised state. The CPSU has been suspended, state institutions have been 'departified' and the KGB is in the process of reorganisation. The return of a Marxist–Leninist dictatorship is no longer an option. Nevertheless, some commentators fear that democracy may still be overthrown, not by communists but by the new nationalist forces in the USSR. Historians point to precedents in recent Russian history when sudden bursts of reform were followed by long periods of reaction: for example, the emancipation of the serfs in 1861; the 1905 Revolution; the 1917 Bolshevik Revolution; and the thaw under Khrushchev after the Secret Speech of 1956. There is foreboding that history could repeat itself. Economic and ethnic crisis is gathering pace. The new leaders confront enormous difficulties in restoring any kind of stability to the country. In the circumstances, authoritarian measures may be perceived as an increasingly attractive option. Viktor Alksnis, the so-called Black Colonel and prominent member of the conservative group, Soyuz, may be right when he predicted that even the reformers will be compelled to use tanks to quell future food riots.[23] As central and republican leaders are operating with few institutional constraints, the temptation in the current situation to accumulate ever greater power may be overwhelming. Democracy is new to the Soviet Union. Its structures and organisation are weak and untested. In the absence of strong institutions, strong individuals invariably arise. Some republics may be better equipped than others to endure the birth-pains of democracy. The Caucasus and Central Asia look particularly vulnerable. In fact, under the nationalist leadership of Gamsakhurdia, it appears that Georgia is already sliding into dictatorship, with civil war a growing menace.

The measures currently underway to de-Stalinise Soviet society and decentralise power to the republics make a repeat of the August 1991 coup both less likely and more difficult to organise. However, many powerful people have lost careers, status and privileges in the revolutionary aftermath of the coup. They have watched the collapse of communism and the union with horror. Such was the disillusionment of Gorbachev's military adviser, Akhromeev, that he committed suicide. A large number of communists have been silenced by the coup, but they still harbour considerable resentment towards the new regime. There is certainly no guarantee that they will all seek a similar solution to Akhromeev. Indeed, Shevardnadze has not been alone in warning of the possibility of another military coup. 'The threat from the right is still there and it could intensify. In view of the aggravation of the social and economic situation in the country, the worsening of material conditions and also the degree of political heat, the right-wingers could gain a certain degree of popular support.'[24] The return of some form of authoritarianism remains a plausible future scenario. Any theorist who believes domestic factors are important in determining foreign policy must view this prospect with some concern.

The optimistic view

This group of scholars believed that the reform programme which Gorbachev set in motion back in 1985 would prove durable. In this view, new thinking was usually seen as the culmination of a long-term process of social and intellectual change which began long before and quite independently of Gorbachev.[25] Therefore, these analysts believed the reforms had a relatively strong base and were less reliant than sometimes supposed on just a handful of leading personalities.

Thus, whilst the political structures had remained static for so long after Stalin's death, social forces had changed radically. In 1945, approximately 56 million lived in cities, by 1987 this figure had risen to 180 million or 66 per cent of the Soviet population. Furthermore, over the period 1950–85, the number of Soviet citizens with a higher degree had increased ten-fold.[26] Thus, a large group of highly educated, urbanised professionals had emerged in the USSR after the war. This group fitted uneasily into the ethos of working-class politics and Marxist–Leninist dogma. Such disaffection was said to stretch even to the higher reaches of the Communist Party itself. According to Alexander Yakovlev, Gorbachev's political adviser, a group of influential reformers had always existed inside the party after Khrushchev's fall from power in 1964.[27] Disaffection inside and outside the party related to such issues as poor economic performance, political repression and personal frustrations, which will be considered in detail later in the chapter.

Western Sovietologists have also shown that a policy debate of sorts was taking place in the Soviet Union for much of the Brezhnev era. The debate was limited to the Soviet elite, and was frequently obfuscated by pro-government propaganda. However, Western writers were frequently able to detect some discordant voices and, occasionally, oblique criticism of party policy.[28] Much of the reformist element of this debate was later taken up by Gorbachev and absorbed into his new political thinking. Furthermore, a large number of these reformist writers, such as Yevgenii Primakov, Tatayana Zaslavskaya, Fedor Burlatsky and Georgi Shakhnazarov, have since risen to greater prominence under the Gorbachev administration. Clearly, there is a danger in placing too much emphasis on reformist writing when the vast majority of academic literature slavishly followed the party line. Nevertheless, this kind of Sovietology was better placed to explain the origins of perestroika than any strict reading of totalitarianism was able to do.

A synthesis

At the extremes, the pessimistic and optimistic views may be incompatible. However, it is still true to say that some of the differences of opinion outlined above may be less great than sometimes appears to be the case. Differences can often relate to the issue area or time period being referred to. For example, in the sphere of economics, reforms always remained tentative, whilst the reform process in other areas only began to radicalise in late 1988.

Prior to 1988, much of Gorbachev's perestroika could legitimately be dismissed as changes more of style than substance. Nina Andreeva's famous letter of 13 March 1988 published in *Sovetskaya Rossiya* calling for a return to Stalinist principles showed, amongst other things, the weakness of glasnost at that time. The letter was published whilst Gorbachev was away in Yugoslavia, and it was widely believed to have the support of Ligachev, the then number two in the Politburo. The letter was interpreted by publishers and public alike to mean that a new wave of repression was underway. Glasnost was halted in its tracks. It was only when the Andreeva letter was repudiated a few weeks later in a *Pravda* article written by Yakovlev that the momentum of reform was regained.[29] The affair showed graphically that up to that time in early 1988, perestroika was a process controlled and managed by the party. The occasional confusion over policy was due mainly to splits at the top which occurred with far greater regularity than before. Thereafter, Gorbachev decided to reduce the power of the party leadership which he saw as frustrating his reform programme.

Therefore, the General Secretary persuaded the Nineteenth CPSU Conference, which took place in June 1988, to permit nationwide, multi-candidate elections and to shift more decision-making powers to directly elected state bodies. In the subsequent elections of March 1989, approximately 20 per cent of candidates officially supported by the Communist Party failed to win an absolute majority of votes. As a result, a small contingent of perhaps 400 radical deputies was elected to the new Congress of People's Deputies, the most famous being Andrei Sakharov and Boris Yeltsin. Thus, the process of creating a civil society had begun.

At the same time, the process of democratisation and glasnost unleashed nationalist forces. The Baltic Republics began a radical but peaceful campaign for independence. Elsewhere, notably in the Caucasus, nationalist awakening was accompanied by an explosion of ethnic violence. Nevertheless, nationalism too represented a vital part of the revolution from below which began to wrest power from Gorbachev and the centre.

In sum, radical change had occurred in the political processes of the Soviet Union by 1989. This was less obvious, however, in the field of economics. The main reform to date remains the self-accounting experiment (*khozraschet*), which was introduced in January 1988. However, it soon subsided under the combined weight of its 'internal contradictions' and bureaucratic opposition. As soon as *khozraschet* was launched, the economy began its downward spiral from which it shows little sign of recovery. According to official statistics, the USSR suffered negative growth rates for the years 1989 and 1990, and its output for the first quarter of 1991 was 10 per cent lower than a year before. Labour productivity fell 3 per cent in 1990, the trade deficit trebled in the same year and had reached $65 billion by 1991 with $40 billion due for repayment by 1992. For the tax year April 1990 to April

1991 inflation was officially recorded to be 90 per cent, but it had risen to 300 per cent in the four months up to August 1991. In May 1991, 2.5 million were estimated unemployed and 90 million were officially registered as living below the poverty line.[30] The disintegration of the economy after January 1988 has been a central reason why the party leadership lost control of the country.

In foreign policy, on the other hand, Gorbachev had been both more active and more successful. In the first two years of his administration, he was able to rebuild East–West relations after the troubles of the Second Cold War. The INF Treaty was signed in December 1987, but it was once again only in 1988 that radical change set in. In April 1988, the Geneva accords were signed and Moscow agreed to withdraw its troops from Afghanistan. Then in December of the same year, Gorbachev gave an important speech at the UN in which he announced a change in military doctrine to one based on reasonable sufficiency and defensive defence. The change in military doctrine was given practical realisation through a commitment to unilateral cuts of half a million troops in Europe and Asia.

The momentous year of 1989 followed. Moscow finally withdrew from Afghanistan in February, and by the end of the year all the Brezhnev elites in Warsaw Pact countries had been overthrown. Moscow did not use force to prevent their overthrow, and on occasion even seemed to encourage the East European revolutions. The most recent evidence of the radical nature of Gorbachev's foreign policy reforms was the reaction to the Iraqi annexation of Kuwait in 1990. Moscow condemned the invasion, and despite some wavering shortly before the UN attack on Iraq, the USSR supported all the UN revolutions against its former ally.

The Cold War was over and this was welcomed in most quarters inside the Soviet Union. However, at the Twenty-Eighth CPSU Congress Shevarnadze's foreign policy came under severe attack from hardliners. A series of military men stood up and accused the foreign minister of having sacrificed Soviet security in Eastern Europe, and of having allowed the United States to reassert its dominance globally. Both the abandonment of Saddam Hussein in Iraq and the abandonment of the Brezhnev doctrine in Europe were depicted by the military as having seriously undermined the USSR's status as a world power, as well as damaging the credibility of international communism. Without wishing to give succour to the hardliners in any way, it is plain that their arguments had some force. Why did the Moscow leadership allow these events to happen? This important question is the focus of the rest of the chapter.

Explaining the changes in Soviet foreign policy

This discussion will be divided into two parts. The first will consider the internal pressures, the second the external pressures for reform. Can we best explain Gorbachev's new political thinking in terms of internal factors, such as public discontent and economic problems? Or in terms of external pressures generated by the Western policy of containment?

Internal pressures

Under this heading we will consider the pressures for change from the public, the dissident movement, the political elite and the failings of the economy. Most emphasis at this juncture will be placed on the period 1985–88 when the leadership made the key decisions in favour of radical reform.

Public discontent

In a speech defending perestroika, Gorbachev said that Soviet society was in turmoil in the early 1980s and there had been no alternative to a programme of radical reform.[31] This may have been so, but there was relatively little sign of overt public pressure for change when Gorbachev came to power in March 1985. Hedrick Smith in his book, *The New Russians*, said that the Soviet public was less docile in this period compared to the 1970s. As evidence he notes that there was an outbreak of wildcat strikes in the early 1980s.[32] However, these strikes were put down with little obvious strain on the political structures of Soviet society. Public demonstrations were also rare, and dealt with by the authorities with hard-headed brutality. It is true that social problems were on the rise throughout the Brezhnev period. But problems of alcoholism, drugs and crime were ignored by the media, and certainly never reached the levels of the West.

Some commentators suggest, however, that the passivity of the Soviet population could not hide an underlying desire for change. This desire, so the argument ran, was fed by an increasing awareness of the gap between living standards in the Soviet Union and the West.[33] After the eruption of glasnost this was true. Back in 1985, however, the evidence was more ambiguous. In the big cities, like Moscow and Leningrad, especially among the more educated groups, knowledge of the West was fairly extensive. For the rest of the population, there must be doubts. Throughout the 1970s, the management of information was strictly controlled by the centre, and there is little to suggest that the people had become more aware by the time Gorbachev was elected General Secretary. It has been claimed that the CSCE process which began with the Helsinki Final Act in 1975 had some impact in opening up the country to Western ideas. If there was a change in policy towards the issue of human rights after 1975 it was minimal. There was little change in the rights of Soviet citizens to emigrate or express dissident opinion. The number of Soviet people arrested for political crimes did decline marginally after the Helsinki Final Act was signed, but the CSCE process could do nothing to prevent the renewed clampdown after the Soviet invasion of Afghanistan in 1979.[34]

Moscow also tightly controlled the right of Soviet citizens to visit Western countries. As a result, the number of Soviets visiting the West remained low and scarcely rose in the period 1975–85; 695,000 Soviet citizens visited Western countries in 1985 compared to 589,000 in 1975.[35] Only those approved by the party were able to obtain exit visas. Thus, for the vast majority of Soviet people their knowledge of the West was reliant, not on personal experience, but state information or gossip. Western radio provided a channel of alternative information which attracted many listeners. At times of crisis, however, Western radio was frequently jammed.

Intellectual dissent

In the pre-Gorbachev era, the bulk of opposition to the system came, not from the masses, but the intellectual dissidents. This group received extensive publicity in the West, but there is little evidence to suggest that they were in a position in the mid-1980s to *force* their opinions on the political elite. It is certainly possible that some of their ideas, especially from such prominent figures as Sakharov, influenced Gorbachev's new political thinking. Indeed, Gorbachev has said as much.[36] Moreover, in the period of glasnost, Sakharov, Roy Medvedev and Solzhenitsyn have all, to a greater or lesser extent, participated in the political debate in the USSR. But to say the dissidents may have influenced new thinking is not to say they were important in a political sense. In fact, the pressure the dissidents placed on the Soviet leadership in the early to mid-1980s was minimal. By this time, the dissident movement in the Soviet Union had been politically defeated. The repression of the dissident movement undoubtedly damaged the image of the Soviet Union abroad, it may even have corrupted the body politic, but it is also true to say that the policy had been very effective in silencing the opposition to the party. For the dissident movement had been losing support throughout the 1970s. At its peak in the late 1960s, Roy Medvedev reported there to be several thousand active dissidents, but, he said, by the late 1970s that figure had dropped to several dozen.[37]

Even the dissidents themselves had come to the conclusion in the early 1980s that they were essentially whistling in the wind.[38] The Soviet public appeared completely uninterested, and various reasons were put forward for this. Firstly, a lack of democratic culture; secondly, the dissidents were members of the intelligentsia and were unable to communicate their ideas to the masses; thirdly, the views of the dissidents were not known fully due to censorship; and finally, the people believed the dissidents would have little impact on policy, and were, therefore, unwilling to risk their freedom, jobs and families in a lost cause.

Mary Kaldor, however, has suggested that the unofficial peace movement in the Soviet Union may have had some impact on policy. She claims that Gorbachev's disarmament proposals were inspired by the Western peace movement, which sought links with unofficial groups in the USSR. She goes on to say that the peace movement shook the status quo in Western Europe, and points out that the demonstrations were often as large as those in Eastern Europe in 1989.[39] However, by the time Gorbachev came to power in 1985, the peace movement in the West was in decline. Western governments remained intact and the deployment of cruise and Pershing had gone ahead, usually with the majority support of the public. The position in some East European countries may have been different, but as far as the Soviet Union is concerned, the independent peace groups had little impact on policy. The so-called Moscow Trust Group, which was the centre of the peace movement in the USSR, was very small, with a core of activists numbering no more than thirteen. Only sixty people signed its inaugural statement in June 1982.[40] Furthermore, the independent peace movement, such as it was, had been effectively silenced before Gorbachev became general secretary, with its leaders arrested or exiled abroad. Inside the Soviet Union, the group could be ignored or dismissed as irrelevant. An academic, Orel, said these groups were 'often in the aid of Western governments', and suggested they were 'created' by the West for propaganda purposes.[41] In 1987, the Moscow Trust Group admitted it was not structured in any way, lacking both a formal organisation and any leaders.[42]

Overall, there is little evidence that political pressure from below had much impact on Soviet policy in the mid-1980s. At the same time, Western analysts, with a few notable exceptions, perceived the Soviet Union as stable and believed the Cold War system would remain in place for the foreseeable future. Both Yeltsin and Sakharov have acknowledged that back in 1985 there was little direct public pressure on Gorbachev to reform.[43] Indeed, Gorbachev, in apparent contradiction to some of his other statements, declared in his Nobel Lecture of 1991 that 'to a casual observer the country seemed to present a picture of relative well-being, stability and order. The misinformed society under the spell of propaganda was hardly aware of what was going on ... the slightest manifestations of protest were suppressed.'[44] Why then the change?

Economic problems

Gorbachev himself has said that a driving force for change was the poor performance of the Soviet economy. During the latter years of the Brezhnev administration, a number of academics began to debate the issue of economic reform. This became apparent when such secret surveys as Tatyana Zaslavskaya's Novosibirsk Report was leaked to the West.[45] Even some elements of the traditionally hardline military establishment, like Ogarkov, came to favour economic reform. Such people believed that only a revived and more dynamic economy could maintain the Soviet Union's position as a military superpower.[46] Gorbachev, for his part was aware of the problems of the economy when he came to power and quickly made his concerns known.[47] He had always been a proponent of experimentation during his time as party secretary in Stavropol and as the Central Committee secretary in charge of agriculture.

What was the evidence of crisis? The Soviet economy had always lagged behind the West, however, it was suggested that the USSR entered a period of terminal decline in the 1970s. Growth rates, according to CIA statistics, had continued to fall from an average of 5 per cent annually in the period 1966–70 to 1.8 per cent during 1980–85.[48] Living standards for most Soviet people had risen during Brezhnev's time in office. Nevertheless, consumer goods and services were neglected in favour of heavy industry and defence. Productivity levels remained low, the quality of most goods was poor, and there were persistent shortages for even the most basic commodities, such as food, clothes and housing. Of particular concern to the military, although rather less to the general public, was the growing gap in technical innovation between the West and the socialist economies, epitomised by SDI. It has been estimated that Soviet computer technology is anything up to fifteen years behind the West.[49] Telecommunications are in a similar state of backwardness. Geron, in a recent study, found that it was possible to make only sixty-eight simultaneous telephone calls, including faxes, between the Soviet Union and the United Kingdom; the figure for the USA and the USSR was even lower – thirty-two.[50]

Another important factor in the USSR's poor performance related to its isolation from the rest of the world. It has long been established that there is a link between trade and economic performance. Since the war, the volume of international trade has grown massively, with the trade in manufactured goods exceeding primary products. Yet the Soviet Union was hardly touched by this global phenomenon. In fact, its share of world trade dropped in the 1970s, and its total volume of trade is still below that of the Netherlands.[51] Its pattern of trade is similar to that of a Third World country rather than a superpower, with the vast majority of exports being primary products, especially oil and gas.

Thus, there was pressure on the leadership to introduce economic reform and open the USSR more to international competition. There was no pressure in 1985, however, to embark on the current rush to embrace the market. On the contrary, the hope was to strengthen the socialist system, not overthrow it, with the reforms in China under Deng Xiaoping or in Hungary under Kadar more likely models than American free enterprise or Willy Brandt's style of social democracy.

Disillusionment amongst the Soviet elite

A major source of internal pressure for reform in 1985 came from the Soviet elite itself. A significant number had become disillusioned with the Brezhnev regime, not only because of its unimaginative economic policy, but often for personal reasons as well. Brezhnev's policy of 'stability of cadres' had resulted in inertia at the top of the political structure. In 1981, 90 per cent of the 1976 Central Committee had been re-elected, creating a so-called gerontocracy at the highest level of the Soviet political system by the end of the decade. The average age of the Central Committee had risen from 56 in 1966 to 63 by 1982. In the Council of Ministers, the average age rose in the same period from 58 to 65, whilst in the politburo in 1982, no less than eight were 70 years old or more. Gorbachev, the youngest, was the only member in his fifties. The situation was the same in the foreign policy establishment. By 1985, the leading officials had been in office a minimum of seventeen years. Gromyko, the foreign minister, and Patolichev, the minister of trade, were both appointed in 1957. Ponamarev, the head of the International Department was appointed two years earlier, whilst his deputy, Rusakov, who dealt with other communist states, was a comparative novice, having been appointed only in 1968. The average age of this foreign policy cohort was 75.[52] These leading officials could certainly claim experience, but at the expense of frustrated ambition below them, and at most levels of the system. Many reformers also felt frustrated because they believed their political superiors to be their intellectual inferiors. Burlatsky, for example, in various articles has consistently revealed his contempt for the Brezhnev cohort, regarding them as ill-educated, unimaginative and corrupt.[53] Even Gromyko joined in the condemnation of his former boss after Brezhnev's death in 1982.[54] The long-time foreign minister declared in an interview that Brezhnev had no deep understanding of problems and was indecisive. Undoubtedly, the resentment towards the Brezhnev cohort rose over time as it aged collectively and became more complacent and corrupt.

The Communist Party in the post-Stalinist era was never quite the monolith of totalitarian myth. A reformist wing, the disillusioned Khrushchev generation, as stated earlier, existed throughout the Brezhnev administration. In the 1970s, many reform-minded communists centred around the unlikely figure of Yuri Andropov, head of the KGB from 1967. At one time or another, Andropov could count among his entourage personalities such as Burlatsky, Arbatov, Bogomolov, Shakhnazarov and Bovin. *The World Marxist Review*, edited by Rumyantsev, a friend of the KGB chief, was also a journal known for its reformist ideas.[55] It may be misleading to portray these reformers as comprising a group within the party. Zaslavskaya, for one, has said she knew of reformers in the party, indeed they often met to discuss issues, but she denied the existence of any organisation in the formal sense.[56] Such a faction within the CPSU would have contravened Lenin's rules on party unity.

Nevertheless, it was through Andropov, and his control of the KGB, that Brezhnev came under the most concerted attack of his administration. The KGB in the late 1970s launched an anti-corruption drive which came to include many of Brezhnev's closest colleagues, friends and even relatives. The impotence of the general secretary in his twilight years was starkly revealed when he was unable to protect them. It seemed the KGB's net, which was already tightening around the Brezhnev family, might even seek to entrap the general secretary himself. He died, however, before he had to face any such ignominy.

Under Andropov, and later under Gorbachev, the old Brezhnevites were quickly eased or forced out of office. In the first two years, Gorbachev got rid of as many as 200,000 officials. He promoted younger people, who were generally better educated and had often pursued, like his first prime minister, Ryzhkov, a technocratic career. The intellectuals, who had felt themselves undervalued and underpaid as a group, found their status dramatically raised under Gorbachev.[57] Academics, like Aganbegyan, Shakhnazarov and Primakov, suddenly shot to world prominence as top policy-makers in the new Gorbachev administration. The rise of the intelligentsia was perceived in some quarters to be at the expense of the old guard. Perhaps a majority of party *apparatchiki*, ministers, KGB and military officials opposed the more radical elements of the reform programme and provided formidable opposition to the intellectuals.

To conclude, there were growing economic pressures for change, but it was the Soviet elite rather than the masses or the intellectual dissidents who were the instigators of change.

External pressures

This view essentially claims that Kennan's containment policy was successful. It took forty-five years, but Western economic, political and military pressure finally forced the Soviet Union to reform at home and abandon the Cold War. The extraordinary achievement for the West was the fact that all its goals were achieved without having to resort to war. An array of Soviet writers have rejected this assessment, but it has won widespread support in the West.[58] More controversial is the role of the Reagan administration, which supporters claim was the reason the Cold War ended when it did.

Reagan and arms control

According to this view, the West, was essentially correct to build up its military power in the early 1980s to deter Soviet expansionism. The relative strength of the Western economies always meant that an equal commitment to defence on Moscow's part would lead to unequal sacrifices by the Soviet consumers. Reagan threatened to arm the USSR to death, and, it could be argued, this is exactly what he did. Crucial to this analysis is the American development of SDI. The Soviet leadership realised, so it was said, that Star-Wars represented a further twist to the arms race, but the Soviet Union could no longer compete in the high-technological age.[59]

There can be little doubt that the costs of the arms race forced Gorbachev to reassess his defence policy; 20–25 per cent of Soviet GNP was devoted to defence, and according to CIA estimates the percentage had risen by 3 per cent in real terms over the period, 1965–85.[60] Nevertheless, there are reasons to suppose the cost of the arms race was not an overwhelming factor in Gorbachev's thinking. Firstly, the defence budget continued to rise under Gorbachev with a projected plan for 1986–90 to increase defence spending by 40 per cent.[61] It was only in 1989 that cuts in defence expenditure of about 14 per cent began to filter through. Even then, shortly before the 1991 coup, it was reported that this process would be reversed with an increase in defence spending of over 25 per cent for the fiscal year 1991–92.[62]

Secondly, the importance of SDI in Soviet thinking can be contested. Soviet leaders, from Andropov to Gorbachev, made the abandonment of SDI a central bargaining issue. A radical plan to abolish all strategic nuclear weapons floundered at the Reykjavik summit over Reagan's commitment to Star Wars. Yet there were grounds for suggesting the Soviet opposition was less substantive than sometimes seemed the case. Jerry Hough believed it was a useful propaganda lever for Gorbachev, whilst Fred Halliday has emphasised the inoperability of Reagan's original scheme.[63] As many Western analysts pointed out, SDI could be circumvented fairly cheaply, for example through the deployment of more ICBMs. Supporters of the SDI theory, however, usually place more stress on the innovatory technological aspects of the system rather than its military viability. Star Wars simply brought home to the Soviet leaders their lag in technical expertise. The Soviet Union had always been behind in the arms race and the effort to keep up was becoming increasingly difficult and costly. No doubt, some Soviet analysts feared the complexity of computer and laser technology would be beyond the Soviet science community. The fear was that the attempt would bankrupt the Soviet economy. Nevertheless, similar arguments had been expressed in the past, and yet Moscow had developed its own atomic bomb in 1949, hydrogen bomb in 1953 and MIRVing system in the 1970s. Few in the United States were confident that the USSR would never be able to develop its own SDI system sometime in the future. Furthermore, the fact that Moscow never got any commitment from Washington to halt or reduce its investment in Star Wars (even though SDI has been downgraded as a priority in practice) suggests that the system may not have been the pivotal reason for Gorbachev's reassessment of foreign and defence policy.

It seems that the key to understanding Gorbachev's new political thinking was the reappraisal of defence policy in 1987 which led to the Soviet leadership minimising the threat of war from the West. The Soviet population had borne a heavy defence burden throughout its history and it would have continued to do so if Moscow believed a security threat existed. In the absence of such a threat, however, the main danger to peace became 'accidental war' and the arms race.[64] Therefore, from 1987, Gorbachev determined to reduce those risks through a stronger commitment to arms cuts, confidence building measures and transparency. Michael MccGwire, in his study, suggests that this shift in Soviet military thinking had been underway before Gorbachev came to power. He, therefore, claims that Reagan's tough policies slowed down that process rather than speeded it up.[65]

MccGwire's analysis may well be correct. However, the negative impact of Reagan's invigorated containment was short, and there are grounds for suspecting that his Soviet policy crystallised some of the fears and frustrations of many Soviet analysts, not least Moscow's persistent technological lag. As a result, the changes were both more radical and rapid than might otherwise have been expected.

Containment and the Third World

Reagan stated that Moscow had taken advantage of America's goodwill during the detente period of the 1970s to expand its influence around the world. The Reagan doctrine demanded a military challenge to the USSR in the Third World to roll back communism. As the Cold War came to an end, the Reagan administration claimed this policy had been an overwhelming success. In February 1989 the USSR withdrew its troops from Afghanistan, and began to cut back its support for a number of other Third World allies, such as Cuba, Vietnam and Nicaragua. Moscow has pressed for political solutions to long-standing regional crises in Central America, Africa, Indo-China and the Middle East.

The main challenge to Soviet Third World penetration came in Afghanistan. The standard Western view is that the American support for the *mujahidin* played the decisive role in the Soviet withdrawal. The transfer of Stinger anti-aircraft missiles in 1986 is frequently cited as the turning point in the war. Mark Urban has suggested that this may be a simplistic account of events. The evidence shows that the decision to withdraw from Afghanistan took place before the deployment of Stingers. A decision seems to have been taken at the time of the Twenty-Seventh CPSU Congress in February 1986 when Gorbachev described the Afghan War as a 'bleeding wound'. In any case, as Urban points out, the Stingers were far less deadly than is sometimes made out. The Soviet Union was still able to use helicopters after the arrival of the Stingers, and Moscow was still in control of the major cities and roads.[66] There were no public demonstrations at home in the USSR against the war despite growing public unease. Soviet casualties at approximately 13,000 remained relatively low, especially in comparison to the 50,000 Americans who lost their lives in Vietnam. The Afghan War had long since been stalemated, but there was little direct pressure on Gorbachev to withdraw. After all, previous leaders had believed the prestige of the USSR demanded a continued military commitment to Afghanistan.

It is even more difficult to perceive military containment as a primary cause behind the more general Soviet withdrawal from the Third World. For example, the support of Cuba and the Sandinistas was a relatively cheap way of embarrassing the United States. Moreover, Moscow had little to gain too from its support of the UN in the Gulf War of 1991. Moscow was humiliated, at least indirectly, by the poor military performance of Iraq, its ally, and the United States took the opportunity to become the dominant force in an area of vital strategic importance to the Soviet Union. Only if Gorbachev was eager to improve relations with the West and uphold international law did Gorbachev's Gulf policy make much sense. There is, therefore, some evidence to support Urban's contention that 'the West did not win the 20th Century Great Game – Gorbachev simply decided he was not playing any more – not with Soviet soldiers at least'.[67]

It is also apparent that the Soviet leadership came to the view that 'the costs of empire' were simply too burdensome. A Rand survey in 1980 found that the costs had risen from 1 per cent of GNP in 1971 to 3 per cent in 1980.[68] An Izvestiya report said that the developing world owed the USSR 85,000 million roubles, whilst the Afghan War cost 60 billion roubles from invasion to pull-out.[69] The returns to the USSR for this outlay were not obvious. Soviet activity in the Third World won Moscow few friends, and was in part to blame for the deteriorating relations with China and the West. Moreover, the Soviet Union's closest allies were all impoverished and frequently at war. States like Vietnam and Ethiopia hardly provided a good image for Marxist–Leninist ideology. By the late 1970s, many Soviet academics had come to the conclusion that Soviet Third World policy was a failure.[70] In one sense this is a harsh view. At the core of Soviet foreign policy was a commitment to destroy Western imperialism. By the end of the 1970s Western colonialism had, indeed, been defeated. Soviet writers on the Third World could, therefore, talk of the 1980s as the post-imperialist era. There was no need any longer to challenge the Western states in the developing world. All of which suggests that the change in Soviet Third World policy is not a temporary retreat. The USSR is not yet seeking isolationism. In fact, it has increased its ties with a number of countries, but the basis of those ties is no longer anti-imperialism but the promotion, more openly, of economic and security interests.

Containment and Eastern Europe

The most dramatic changes in policy came in Eastern Europe. The Brezhnev doctrine was abandoned and the old regimes fell without armed intervention from Moscow. Why did the Soviet Union allow this to happen? Only in the vaguest terms could this be attributed to Western containment policy. In effect, Soviet dominance of the region had been accepted by the West, officially since the Helsinki Final Act in 1975, unofficially long before that. On occasion, the West had used the rhetoric of roll-back, but in practice it supported the status quo in Europe. There was no question of military action after the Soviet invasion of Hungary in 1956 or Czechoslovakia in 1968. In fact, no sanctions of any kind were imposed on Moscow after the suppression of the Prague Spring, which was in stark contrast to Western policy after the invasion of Afghanistan in 1979. Western academics, as well as their Soviet counterparts, wrote at length about the essential stability and the likely longevity of a divided Europe.[71]

Unlike in the USSR, in Eastern Europe much pressure for change came from the people. Poland was at the forefront of this process, with the country in almost constant upheaval from the 1970s. The Poles never accepted the suppression of Solidarity with the same passive resignation as the Czechs after 1968. By the 1980s, there was a real feeling, however, that passive resignation was about the best any East European government could hope for. Much of the region seemed to be limping along from one crisis to the next. There are two basic reasons why the Soviet bloc was so unstable internally. Firstly, the domination of the USSR was crucial.[72] The USSR was perceived by most East Europeans as an occupying force imposing its will like an imperialist power. In the post-imperialist era, the governments of the region had great difficulty in gaining any public legitimacy without cutting their dependency on Moscow. Prior to Gorbachev this was not possible. Secondly, there was a general crisis of communism in the 1980s. This related in particular to an economic decline throughout the region. Various programmes of economic reform had been tried since the war. By the early 1980s, all were perceived to have failed. As Soviet writers have noted, capitalism has not been successful everywhere, but communism has not been successful anywhere. East Germany appeared to be the most affluent of the East European states. Yet even here, the success was a chimera. Former East German officials have since revealed that the country faced bankruptcy by the time of the 1989 revolution.[73] Therefore, as the people of the region expressed their dissatisfaction under the freer climate of perestroika, the governing elites, barren of new ideas and with no new models to follow, lost the will to rule.

The key to the timing of the collapse of communism, however, lay with Moscow's unwillingness to maintain control of the region through force. How much was Gorbachev simply accepting the inevitable in allowing Eastern Europe self-determination? In contrast to the case of the Third World, little published in the USSR was critical of Moscow's East European policy prior to glasnost.[74] The region was perceived to be of vital interest to the Soviet Union, and therefore little change in policy was expected. However, under Gorbachev, some commentators began to be more critical of the rigidity of past policies. Yet, right up to the time of the revolutions of 1989, few Soviet analysts were willing to accept the proposition that communism had been imposed on the area against the will of the local people. Gorbachev's own position was often unclear. In *Perestroika* he wrote that socialism was not to blame for the problems of the area.[75] He was also slow to condemn the Warsaw Pact invasion of Czechoslovakia in 1968, and changed his mind frequently over the issue of a reunified Germany.

Yet, with the benefit of hindsight, Moscow's policy towards Eastern Europe seems surprisingly consistent, especially considering its radical nature. In the circumstances, some hesitancy and doubt were only to be expected. The apparent, short-term inconsistencies were due in large part to power politics in the Kremlin, and on occasion to Moscow showing deference to the leaders of Eastern Europe. It was difficult, for example, for the USSR to condemn the suppression of the Prague Spring if the Czech leadership objected. However, by the time of the Twenty-Seventh CPSU Congress in 1986, Gorbachev had revealed a willingness to reform Soviet policy in Eastern Europe despite opposition from some states, especially East Germany and Czechoslovakia. Gorbachev declared his wish to break down the military blocs and create a Common European Home. Although such statements contained elements of propaganda, subsequent actions helped realise these general aims. In a series of speeches in 1988, Gorbachev clearly distanced himself from the more imperialist aspects of the Brezhnev doctrine.[76] Despite considerable unease in much of the region, the following year on its twenty-first anniversary, August 1989, Izvestiya condemned the Warsaw Pact invasion of Czechoslovakia.[77] The denunciation was of even greater moment given the earlier withdrawal from Afghanistan and the collapse of Stalinism in Poland. Nevertheless, it was the Presidential spokesman, Gennadi Gerasimov, who publicly fired the starting pistol for radical reform in Eastern Europe. In October 1989, Gerasimov formally declared that the Brezhnev Doctrine was dead, and said it had been replaced by the

Sinatra Doctrine. In other words, the people of Eastern Europe were free to leave the Soviet embrace and do things their way.

The most remarkable case in the revolutions of 1989 was East Germany. Shevardnadze has gone on record as saying that he had accepted the impracticalities of maintaining a divided Germany in the longer term as early as 1986.[78] However, to most observers of the time, East Germany seemed the most stable state in the region, the most important strategically, and Moscow's staunchest ally inside the Warsaw Pact. If East Germany fell, therefore, other states in Eastern Europe were likely to follow. Despite this possibility, evidence suggests that Moscow intervened directly to undermine Honecker's hardline regime. Firstly, Gorbachev personally attacked Honecker at an SED meeting, shortly after having shown his distaste for the military aspects to the fortieth anniversary celebrations of the East German state.[79] Secondly, Moscow told the SED that it would not support the violent suppression of the East German demonstrators, and ordered the Soviet troops to remain in barracks throughout the crisis. Moscow's influence on events in East Germany was just as great as back in 1953 when Soviet tanks crushed the Berlin uprising. On this occasion, however, Moscow favoured reform and self-determination for the citizens of the GDR. Gorbachev could often be accused of naivety in his foreign policy dealings, but even he must have been aware that his actions in Berlin would not only have momentous implications for East Germany and the whole region, but for the postwar international system itself. In effect, Gorbachev abandoned Eastern Europe in 1989.

Why did the president decide to do this? Jerry Hough has written that in terms of security and economic interests, it was a wholly rational policy.[80] In the age of long-range missiles, the region had lost its former stragtegic importance. Secondly, as mentioned earlier, the Soviet leadership no longer saw an attack from the West as a likely scenario. Thirdly, the economic benefits from withdrawal would be great. Fourthly, the abandonment of the Brezhnev Doctrine would improve East–West relations, and therefore increase the likelihood of more Western aid. Finally, the policy followed the logic of Gorbachev's new thinking. Slogans, such as the Common European Home, often sounded like idle rhetoric or simple propaganda. Nevertheless, Europe has been reunited, albeit in a way very different from Gorbachev's original conception.

Conclusion

The reason for the sudden and radical change in Soviet foreign policy will remain a matter of great controversy for some time. However, from the evidence above, a number of interim conclusions can be drawn. Firstly, direct pressure on the Kremlin in 1985 to embark on a programme of radical reform was generally rather weak. The masses were quiescent and the dissident movement was largely ineffectual. Perestroika started life very much as a revolution from above to benefit the elite and the burgeoning professional groups in the Soviet Union. Secondly, the pressure for change was the culmination of long-standing problems, which included economic difficulties, long-term disaffection in Eastern Europe and Western containment. Thus, the poor performance of the economy over a protracted period, and especially in the light of unsuccessful reforms in the USSR and elsewhere in the socialist world, demanded a radical review of policy. In the case of Eastern Europe, in contrast to the USSR, economic and other deep-seated problems led to sporadic outbursts of rebellion against the system and the Soviet domination of the region. The patient, long-term policy of Western containment may also have played a part in undermining the Soviet economy and overstretching Moscow's foreign policy. Ronald Reagan's part in America's postwar containment strategy should not be lightly dismissed. However, it is easy to exaggerate the importance of certain policy initiatives, such as the SDI programme. Thirdly, this chapter has found that internal factors dominate, containment policy notwithstanding, in understanding the changes in Soviet foreign policy.

What of the future? Many 'exceptionalist' thinkers could be expected to be reasonably optimistic. Marxism–Leninism has been abandoned by Moscow and the totalitarian structures of state are in the process of being dismantled. Moreover, as the USSR disintegrates and the Soviet army withdraws from Eastern Europe and from other positions around the world, the theory on the expansionist tendencies of the Russian state seems less relevant than ever. Optimists suggest that the Soviet Union, however it is constituted in the future will adopt a foreign policy stance that is more 'normal', more status quo and more pro-Western. Both George Bush and Mikhail Gorbachev have expressed the hope that the changes underway in the USSR will lead to greater US–Soviet cooperation and a new world order.

Many, however, remain sceptical, and fear that the world has become a more dangerous place since the collapse of communism. An unofficial KGB report which was leaked in the autumn of 1991 outlined many of these fears. Firstly, it stated that although most supporters of the coup had been dismissed from top positions, many remained in place at the regional level. Secondly, in the absence of a legitimate central authority and with the economy out of control, crime, terrorism and nationalism were rampant. As a result, there was a strong possibility of populist or even fascist leaders emerging in some of the republics. The break-up of the USSR had foreign policy implications too. The central authorities could lose control over Soviet nuclear weapons, violations of international agreements were more likely, and further instability in the international system highly probable. In these circumstances, the prospect of new nuclear powers rising from the ashes of the former Soviet Union was one that would cause great consternation, not only in Moscow, but throughout the world.

In conclusion, a number of Western academic theorists have also expressed concern over the break-up of the bipolar international system. Scholars, such as Kenneth Waltz, have argued that the Cold War bipolar structure was far more stable than any other option. Fears are rising of nuclear proliferation, which may be more difficult to control in the complex post-Cold War world. Others, like Robert Gilpin, emphasise the dangers of change in an international system, and fear the destabilising effects of a declining hegemonic power. Such theorists imply, therefore, that nuclear war is more likely now than at any time during the Cold War.

Nevertheless, so far at least, the dire warnings of some of the pessimists have not been borne out by events. In fact, the radical shift in the international system has been achieved with surprisingly little turmoil, the problems in Eastern Europe and the Gulf notwithstanding. Legitimate doubts remain, however, over whether this can continue.

Notes

I would like to thank Caroline Kennedy of Leeds University for her detailed comments on a first draft of this chapter. I also benefited greatly from a conversation with David Miller at the Foreign Office Research Department. Neither, of course, bear any responsibility for the views expressed in the chapter.

1 Zbigniew Brzezinski, 'The Soviet Union: Her Aims, Problems and Challenges to the West', in Robbin F. Laird and Erik P. Hoffmann (eds.), *Soviet Foreign Policy in a Changing World* (New York: Aldine Publishing Co., 1986), p. 7.
2 For the exceptionalist case, much has been taken from, Brzezinski, 'The Soviet Union'; and Zbigniew Brzezinski, 'Communist Ideology and International Affairs', *Journal of Conflict Resolution*, vol. 4, September 1960,

pp. 266–90; and George Kennan [X], 'The Sources of Soviet Conduct', *Foreign Affairs*, vol. 25, July 1947, pp. 566–82.

3 Andrei Gromyko, *Memoirs* (London: Hutchinson, 1989), p. 305.

4 For a more recent exposition of this position, see Michael Doyle, 'Liberalism and World Politics', *American Political Science Review*, vol. 80, no. 4, Dec. 1986.

5 Mikhail S. Gorbachev, Speech to the UN, *Pravda*, 8 December 1988; see too, Eduard Shevardnadze, *Soviet Weekly*, 22 April 1989, p. 15.

6 Andrei Kozyrev, *New Times*, 15, 1991, p. 26.

7 John J. Mearsheimer, 'Back to the Future: Instability in Europe after the Cold War', *International Security*, vol. 15, no. 1, Summer 1990, pp. 5–56.

8 Jerry Hough, *Russia and the West: Gorbachev and the Politics of Reform* (New York: Simon and Shuster, 1988), pp. 44–6.

9 Brzezinski, 'The Soviet Union', p. 4.

10 Helmut Schmidt, *Men and Power: A Political Retrospective* (London: Cape, 1990), p. 11.

11 Michael MccGwire, *Perestroika and Soviet National Security* (Washington: Brookings Institution, 1991), p. 401, see also pp. 388–401.

12 For excellent writing within this general framework, see, e.g. Jerry Hough and Merle Fainsod, *How the Soviet Union is Governed* (Cambridge, MA: Harvard University Press, 1980); and Mary McAuley, *Politics and the Soviet Union* (Harmondsworth: Penguin, 1977).

13 For a good discussion of different models of the Soviet political system, see A. H. Brown, *Soviet Politics and Political Science* (London: Macmillan, 1974)

14 Mearsheimer, 'Back to the Future', p. 12.

15 Robert Miller, *Soviet Foreign Policy Today: Gorbachev's New Political Thinking* (London: Unwin and Hyman, 1991), p. 2.

16 Mikhail Gorbachev, *Perestroika: New Thinking for our Country and the World* (London: Fontana, Collins, 1987), pp. 11–12.

17 Alexander Solzhenitsyn, *Literaturnaya gazeta*, 18 September 1990.

18 For a withering attack on Gorbachev, not uncommon in the USSR, see Tatyana Tolstaya, *Guardian*, 5 September 1991, p. 23.

19 For good coverage of this position, see, Christoph Bluth, *New Thinking in Soviet Military Doctrine* (London: RIIA, Pinter, 1990); see too, MccGwire, *Perstroika*, p. 395.

20 Georgi Arbatov, *Soviet Weekly*, 8 August 1990, p. 6. For a similar view, see, Kortunov, *Moscow News*, 23 April 1989, p. 3.

21 Michael Scammell, *International Herald Tribune*, 26–7 January 1991, p. 6.

22 William Safire, *International Herald Tribune*, 15 February 1991, p. 4.

23 Viktor Alksnis, *Guardian*, 27 August 1991, p. 2.

24 Shevardnadze, *International Herald Tribune*, 23 September 1991, p. 2. See also the comments of the then foreign minister, F. M. Pankin, *The Observer*, 1 September 1991, p. 21.

25 For an example of this view, see Roger E. Kanet, 'Gorbachev and the End of the Cold War: An Interim Assessment of Gorbachev's Impact on World Affairs', *Union sovietique*, vol. 16, nos. 2–3, 1989.

26 Blair A. Ruble, 'Stepping off the Treadmill of Failed Reforms', in Harley D. Balzer (ed.), *Five Years That Shook the World: Gorbachev's Unfinished Revolution* (Boulder: Westview Press, 1991), p. 17.

27 Alexander Yakovlev in Stephen F. Cohen and Katrina vanden Heuvel, *Voices of Glasnost: Interviews with Gorbachev's Reformers* (New York: Norton, 1989), p. 41.

28 See, for example, Jerry Hough, *The Struggles for the Third World: Soviet Debates and American Options* (Washington: Brookings Institution, 1986); Neil Malcolm, *Soviet Political Scientists and American Politics* (London: Macmillan, 1984); Raymond L. Garthoff, *Deterrence and the Revolution in Soviet Military Doctrine* (Washington: Brookings Institution, 1990); and Allen Lynch, *The Soviet Study of International Relations* (Cambridge: Cambridge University Press, 1989).

29 Nina Andreeva, *Sovetskaya Rossiya*, 13 March 1988; *Pravda*, (editorial), 5 April 1980. For a general review of the episode, see, *Moscow News*, 17, 1988, p. 8.

30 *Times*, 15 July 1991 p. 2: *International Herald Tribune*, 14 August 1991, p. 2; and *New Times*, 39, 1991, p. 17.

31 Gorbachev's speech to the Central Committee, 25–6 July 1991, reported in *Soviet Weekly*, 8 August 1991, p. 7.

32 Hedrick Smith, *The New Russians* (London: Hutchinson, 1990), p. 19. Strikes were rare in the past, but did happen, see a report in *New Times*, 15, 1991, pp. 8–9.

33 See, for example, Fred Halliday, 'A Singular Collapse: the Soviet Union, Market Pressure and Inter-State Competition', *Contention* (Los Angeles), vol. 1, no. 2, Fall 1991.

34 The Polish academic and official thought CSCE was important in improving conditions in Eastern Europe for dissidents, *Guardian*, 28 December 1990, p. 10; Vladimir Bukovsky, the famous Soviet dissident, thought the opposite, see *New Times*, 14, 1991, p. 33. For the numbers arrested during the period, see Peter Reddaway's statistics quoted in Dilys M. Hill (ed.), *Human Rights and Foreign Policy: Principles and Practice* (London: Macmillan, 1989), p. 103.

35 *Ekonomika i zhizn'*, no. 32, 1989, pp. 84–85. (Thanks to *Soviet Weekly* for the reference.)

36 See, for example, Gorbachev's comments reported in *Moscow News*, 46, 1988, p. 9.

37 Roy Medvedev, *On Soviet Dissent* (New York: Columbia, 1980), p. 146. See also: Albert Szymanski, *Human Rights in the Soviet Union* (London: Zed Books, 1984), p. 273.

38 Medvedev, *On Soviet Dissent*, and Boris Kagarlitsky, *The Thinking Reed* (London: Verso, 1988), p. 352.

39 Mary Kaldor, 'Avoiding a New Division in Europe', *World Policy Journal*, vol. 8, no. 1, Winter 1990–1, p. 181.

40 Paul Mercer, *Peace of the Dead* (London: Policy Research Publications, 1986), p. 54.

41 V. Orel, *Kommunist*, no. 12, 1984, p. 96.

42 New Statesman, 24 July 1987, p. 4.

43 Sakharov quoted in *Soviet Weekly*, 9 May 1991, p. 14; and Boris Yeltsin, *Against the Grain* (London: Cape, 1990), p. 113.

44 Gorbachev, *Pravda*, 14 June 1991.

45 Tatyana Zaslavskaya, *The Novosibirsk Report* (with an introduction by Philip Hanson), *Survey*, Spring, 1984.

46 G. Weickhardt, 'Ustinov versus Ogarkov', *Problems of Communism*, January–February, vol. 34, 1985, pp. 77–82.

47 Smith, *The New Russians*, pp. 69–71.

48 CIA statistics, reported in David Armstrong and Erik Goldstein (eds.), *The End of the Cold War* (London: Cass, 1990), p. 88.

49 Armstrong and Goldstein, *The End of the Cold War*, p. 89.

50 Leonard Geron, *Soviet Foreign Economic Policy under Perestroika* (London: RIIA, Pinter, 1990), p. 67.

51 *Ibid.*, p. 28. See, for similar statistics, Paul Kennedy, *The Rise and Fall of Great Powers* (London: Unwin/Hyman, 1988), p. 513.

52 Jerry Hough, *Russia and the West*, p. 223.

53 Fyodor M. Burlatsky, 'Khrushchev, Andropov, Brezhnev: The Issue of Political Leadership', in Alexander Yakovlev (ed.), *Perestroika Annual*, I, (London: Futura, 1988), pp. 210–12. See too a damning article on Brezhnev by Roy Medvedev, *Moscow News*, 11 September 1988, p. 8.

54 Andrei Gromyko interview in *The Observer*, 2 April 1989, p. 23.

55 For evidence of Andropov's reformist credentials, see Burlatsky, pp. 176–7; and Arbatov, pp. 309–10 in Cohen and vanden Heuvel, *Voices of Glasnost*. See too, Vladimir Tismaneanu, 'The Neo-Leninist Temptation: Gorbachevism and the Party Intelligentsia', in Alfred J. Rieber and Alvin Z. Rubinstein (eds.), *Perestroika at the Crossroads* (New York: M. E. Sharpe, Ind, 1991), pp. 38–9.

56 Zaslavskaya in Cohen and vanden Heuvel, *Voices of Glasnost*, p. 122.

57 Smirnov in Cohen and vanden Heuvel, *Voices of Glasnost*, p. 84, see too, Andrei Sakharov, *Trevoga i nadezhda* (Moscow; Inter-Verso, 1990), p. 242.

58 For a Western view suggesting containment worked, see, e.g. Fred Halliday, 'A Singular Collapse'. For an East European view which agrees, see Geremek, *Guardian*, 28 December 1990, p. 10. For a Soviet view which rejects this line, see Yurii Zhukov, *SSSR–SShA: Doroga dlinoyu v sem'desyat let* (Moscow: Idatel'stvo Politicheskoi Literatury, 1988), chs. 7–8.

59 See, for example, Naomi Koizumi, 'Perestroika in the Soviet Military', in Tsuyoshi Hasegawa and Alex Pravda (eds.), *Perestroika: Soviet Domestic and Foreign Policies* (London: RIIA, Sage, 1990), p. 156; Geremek, *The Guardian*, 28 December, 1990), p. 10.

60 Armstrong and Goldstein, *The End of the Cold War*, p. 91.

61 MccGwire, *Perestroika and Soviet National Security*, p. 383.

62 *International Herald Tribune*, 13 August 1991, p. 4.

63 Jerry Hough, *Russia and the West*, see, e.g. p. 238; and Fred Halliday, 'A Singular Collapse'.

64 MccGwire, *Perestroika and Soviet National Security*, p. 392.

65 *Ibid.*, p. 382.

66 Mark Urban, *War in Afghanistan* (London: Verso, 1989), p. 45.

67 Urban, *War in Afghanistan*, p. 304.

68 Armstrong and Goldstein, *The End of the Cold War*, p. 90.

69 *Izvestiya*, 30 March 1990; and on costs of war in Afghanistan, see report in *Izvestiya*, 17 October 1990.

70 On Brezhnev's Third World policy failures, see e.g. Andrei Kozyrev quoted in J. Feffer, *Beyond Detente: New Options on East–West Relations*

(London: I. B. Tauris, 1990), p. 85; and Vyacheslav Dashichev, *Literaturnaya gazeta*, 18 May 1988. For a slightly different view, see A. Vasilev, *Soviet News*, 22 February 1989, p. 60.

71 See Richard Crockatt's chapter in this volume for a detailed survey of this point.

72 George Schopflin, 'The End of Communism in Eastern Europe', *International Affairs*, vol. 66, no. 1, January 1990, pp. 3–16.

73 See Gunther Mittag interview reported in the *Guardian*, 10 September 1991, p. 7.

74 See, for example, Roundtable, 'East–West Relations and Eastern Europe: A Soviet–American Dialogue', *Problems of Communism*, May–August 1988, pp. 55–70.

75 Gorbachev, *Perestroika*, p. 165.

76 Gorbachev made a speech explicitly accepting the equal status of all social states, *Pravda*, 23 May 1988. He also condemned any interference in the domestic affairs of socialist states, see, *Pravda*, 23 May 1988 and *Pravda*, 24 February 1989.

77 The invasion of Czechoslovakia was condemned in a number of Soviet publications, including, *Izvestiya*, 20 August 1989; and Dashichev in *International Affairs* (Moscow), August 1989, p. 128.

78 Shevardnadze, *Soviet Weekly*, 2 May 1990, p. 6.

79 Miller, *Soviet Foreign Policy Today*, p. 119.

80 Jerry Hough, 'Lessons for Theories of International Security', in Balzar (ed.), *Five Years That Shook the World*, pp. 181–99.

6 FEMINIST THEORY AND INTERNATIONAL RELATIONS

MARYSIA ZALEWSKI

Introduction

Feminist theory has made rather a late arrival on to the scene of the International Relations academic agenda. Surely, International Relation's most established academics claim, the business of wars, superpower relations and inter-state behaviour are in no need of a theory of gender? What's the problem? Perhaps there should be more women teaching International Relations or in foreign policy decision-making communities (but would they push the button?) but surely that is about the extent of the problem?

International Relations has been reluctant to open its doors to the challenge posed by feminism and theories of gender. Long after other social sciences had at least given marginal attention to the presumed gender neutrality of their subjects, International Relations remained stubbornly convinced that gender was a variable which could be ignored. However, the mid-1980s provided a window of opportunity for feminist critical voices to get on the agenda. It is often claimed that the academic study of International Relations is dominated by the United States and this is reflected in the way the discipline develops. That this is the case is evidenced by the dominance of the realist/positivist paradigm which recent critical voices have pitted themselves against. Recent literature on feminist theory and International Relations, at least that emanating from the United States, has tended to assume, almost unchallenged, the dominance of Realism, its positivist credentials being the target of increasing attack since the mid-1980s with post-modernist voices taking a leading role in that attack. It is not surprising, therefore, that many feminists have been drawn towards post-modernism, seeing potential for developing a post-modern feminism, when the only other alternative seems to be Positivism and Realism. There is however a major tension in the acceptance of the tenets of post-modernism into feminist thought, a point which I will return to later.

Given the title of this volume, the fundamental question is, 'what does feminist theory have to say about International Relations in general and the changes in world politics in the 1980s in particular?' In order to address this question I want to take a few steps backwards. This chapter originated as a paper at the 1990 British International Studies Conference in Newcastle. Prior to writing the paper I was given to understand that, despite the expertise and experience of the majority of the audience with regard to International Relations, the level of understanding and awareness with regard to feminist theory was somewhat limited (this assumption turned out to be, in the main, correct). Because of this, the paper was structured in such a way as to introduce the uninitiated to feminist theory and its recent arrival on the International Relations academic agenda. In a similar way, I see a major task of this chapter as offering some background to the rising interest in feminist theory and International Relations. The richness and diversity of feminist thought is difficult to overestimate and problems often arise when those uneducated in matters of feminism try to understand the implications of feminist critiques of their subject. In an attempt to go some way to redress the problem of the paucity of feminist knowledge this chapter will introduce the reader to a variety of feminist perspectives presented firstly as a chronological/political typology, highlighting the main strands, and secondly as an epistemological typology.[1] I will then outline and discuss some of the literature on feminist critiques of International Relations. Finally, I will offer an assessment on the impact of feminist theory on International Relations focusing on the main debates; I will then make some concluding remarks regarding what feminist theory has to say about the changes in world politics in the 1980s speculating on the future direction of the feminist critique of International Relations.

Feminist thought

Liberal feminism

Liberal feminism is perhaps the most longstanding and easily understood and acceptable version of feminism. It is the 'add women and stir' variety of feminist thought. As its name suggests liberal feminism takes its philosophical roots from liberalism placing much importance on the primary importance of the individual and the necessity for individual freedom and autonomy. However, as many feminist critics of liberal political and democratic theory have pointed out, traditional theory either does not include women or prescribes

116

women a specific and subordinate role in society.[2] The individual referred to in traditional theory was implicitly and explicitly a male individual. For standard liberal feminism the exclusion of women is an error based on erroneous and misogynist beliefs about women. But this error can be redressed by bringing women back in. Eighteenth and nineteenth-century liberal feminists, such as Mary Wollstonecraft, J. S. Mill and Harriet Taylor Mill, campaigned for rights to equal education and entry into public life as well as the abolition of laws which gave men ownership of their wives. Twentieth-century liberal feminism has carried on the campaign for equal rights with, for example, the suffragette's and suffragist's plea for formal political equality via the vote in the early part of the century, and the Sex Discrimination and the Equal Pay Acts of the mid to late twentieth century. Liberal feminism is currently alive and well and much effort is put into getting women included, especially in traditionally male dominated institutions such as the House of Parliament, the scientific community and institutions of higher education.

Marxist and socialist feminism

These two forms of feminist thought are interlinked as they share the same roots – a Marxist materialist analysis; it is material forces which shape and structure social life and individual lives within society, not individuals as separate units. From a traditional Marxist perspective the cause of women's oppression is to be found in the exploitative economic system. What is needed is the elimination of capitalism to liberate women – and of course men. With the demise of capitalism there will be no need for women to sell themselves and their services to maintain their livelihood. A major criticism of this Marxist analysis of women's oppression is that it does not explain the oppression of women in pre-capitalist or socialist societies. It is primarily for this reason that many Marxist feminists have expanded the scope of explanations for women's oppression to include more than capitalism and exploitative class relations. They attempt to synthesise various explanations for women's oppression using many of the insights of other strands of feminist thought, particularly radical feminism. We can call this strand of feminism socialist feminism.

Socialist feminism makes an explicit commitment to the abolition of both class and gender. Socialist feminists argue that we need to transform not only the ownership of the means of production but also the social system which is dominated by patriarchy. Socialist feminists share the Marxist conception of human nature – people are only really

117

free and fulfilled if there is free productive activity. For Marxists, productive activity is limited to labour and usually that is labour which is paid for in the public sphere. But socialist feminists include other forms of productive activity, specifically the procreative and sexual work done by women in the home. Sexuality and procreation are human activities which are no more biologically determined than any other and are thus capable of social development. Socialist feminism draws upon the insights of the radical feminist analysis of the male control of women's sexuality and reproductive capacities claiming that women's sexuality is developed for men's enjoyment rather than women's. This control of women's sexuality, fertility and reproduction finds expression in patriarchal laws, policies and practices throughout the world which limit women's own control within these areas.

Marxist feminists see class as the primary oppressor. Women are exploited both economically and sexually but until the capitalist system is abolished the sexual system of domination will continue as it is necessary to furnish capitalism's needs. Socialist feminists see a worldwide web of domination and oppression but are attempting not to fall into the exclusive universalising tendencies of either Marxist or radical feminism.

Radical feminism

Radical feminism emerged alongside the left wing, civil and human rights type movements of the 1960s and 1970s and does not easily fit into pre-existing philosophical frameworks. Because radical feminism is so wide-ranging and constantly emerging I am going to list four of the basic tenets of radical feminist thought and practice just to give an insight into radical feminist ideas.

Firstly, radical feminism takes women as its chief concern and for radical feminism there is a common and universal oppression of women. Obviously, women of different races, classes and colours will have enormously different experiences of life, but for radical feminism the systematic existence of patriarchy is fundamental, all pervasive and the root of all other oppressions.

Secondly, male domination and control is not limited to unjust legislation or unequal treatment at school, for example, but it permeates every aspect of life – economic, social, psychological, sexual, political and personal. Radical feminism asserts that women's lives are not only dominated by men and masculine values at a physical level but also in the way we learn to understand about ourselves, our role and status in society, how we should act, how we should live and what counts as 'normal' behaviour. Even what counts as acceptable know-ledge and ways of explaining events in the world and life generally are shot through with masculine values. Radical feminists claim that masculine ideals and ideas have taken supremacy in the world and have divided the world into categories of good and bad, us and them, superior and inferior. This categorisation or bifurcation exists at all levels, and women and 'female' characteristics occupy the subordinate position at every stage. For example, the practice of science and its promising student – social science – is premised on objectivity, reason, rationality, non-emotiveness, coolness – all identified by radical femin-ists (and others) as typical 'masculine' values and attributes which hold a higher place in the hierarchy than do the characteristically 'female' opposing traits of subjectivity, emotiveness and intuition. Radical feminists challenge both this bifurcation and also the inferior value of traditional female characteristics. Radical feminists typically eulogise the traditional womanly virtues such as nurturing and caring and envisage the promotion of a womanculture which encourages and validates these characteristics.

A third distinctive tenet of radical feminism is the aim to redescribe reality – to use different criteria to judge importance, to use a different value system and to ask different questions. Women's real lives and subjective experiences are to be taken seriously and are to have a high status. A fourth point, common to radical and socialist feminism, is that the personal is the political (and for Enloe the personal is inter-national).[3] The notions that the personal is the political brings into focus that it is not just political and judicial institutions which have oppressed women but private lives and relationships are also oppress-ive and they should not remain hidden and secret. Separating public and private worlds is another example of the false bifurcation or dichotomy characteristic of male dominated society. In reality, public and private worlds are inextricably linked, and for radical feminism the power that exists in the relationship between men and women, or more specifically between husbands and wives, is the best example of a relationship characterised by dominance and control. Radical femin-ism is sceptical of existing political theory and practice as it is ineluc-tably shot through with patriarchal ideology. Radical feminists want to redescribe the world from a woman's perspective, ask different ques-tions about the world and use different methods of gaining knowledge and understanding of the world.[4]

Liberal, socialist, Marxist and radical feminism are the most common and basic strands of feminist thought but a typology emerging from a more fundamentally epistemological level is being taken up by contemporary feminist theorists of International Relations, especially those in the United States. This way of discussing feminist critiques stems from a fundamental concern about the validity of feminist claims. The recurring hostility and dismissal of many of the claims made by feminists has led to a concern over the epistemological status of feminist theories. From the early 1980s, onwards, many feminist scholars have been involved in comparing feminist epistemologies in an attempt to produce the epistemological basis appropriate for feminist theory. The epistemological typology most commonly used is the three-fold categorisation delineated by Sandra Harding.[5] Harding discusses three feminist approaches to traditional theorising; feminist *empiricism*, feminist *standpoint* and feminist *post-modernism*.

Feminist empiricism

The feminist method allows for the tendency for human knowers to fall prey to cognitive dissonance. The feminist empiricist is a realist (in philosophical, not International Relations terms) – there is a world out there which (a) can be apprehended and understood using the correct methods correctly and (b) which exists independently of either our senses or our creation of knowledge about it. In short, there is a world out there which we can uncover if we *correctly* use the existing methodological tools inherited from the Enlightenment, i.e. reason, logic, non-contradiction, observation, controlled measuring – all of these being 'neutral' procedures. The difference between standard empiricism, or positivism, and feminist empiricism is that the latter claims that there has been an *androcentric* (male centred) bias in conventional empiricism. The standard empiricist researcher would have us believe that the social identity of the inquirer is irrelevant as the scientific method works via falsification and verification. If a researcher is biased in one way or another this will show up when her or his work is tested by another researcher. However the feminist empiricist will discount the latter in two ways. Firstly, it is claimed that the gender of researchers does matter, not necessarily on an individual level but on a larger scale. It is argued that women as a *social group* are more likely to notice androcentric bias than men, as a social group, and are therefore more likely to produce unbiased and objective results.[6] Secondly, the feminist empiricist would claim that it is not just at the level of the social identity of the researcher that androcentrism exists but also in the selection of problems to investigate. A powerful form of social control and androcentric bias exists at the level of the identification and definition of what issues to look at. For the feminist empiricist the scientific method is not at fault; it is simply that its methods are used incorrectly. The eradication of androcentric bias is a necessary measure to achieve the goal of objective knowledge, the goal of apprehending the truth about the world.

Feminist standpoint

The feminist empiricist claim that past knowledge suffers from an androcentric bias does not fit easily with the empiricist belief in the possibility of an unmediated apprehension of the real world. Feminist standpoint theorists provide a way of incorporating this belief as they reject the possibility of an unmediated truth. Instead they rely on a more materialist understanding of social being and consciousness, claiming that knowledge will be affected, and constructed, by the prevailing social, political, ideological and historical setting. However, the concept of truth is not rejected altogether. Indeed, just as the proletariat is able to gain more understanding about the oppressive nature of the capitalist system once a revolutionary consciousness has developed, so can the woman, from a feminist standpoint perspective, see and understand the world more clearly once a feminist consciousness has been developed. Men's dominant position in social life has produced only a partial understanding of life. Women, as the oppressed group, can pierce through these distorted views and develop a more adequate understanding of the world.

Feminist post-modernism

Post-modernists reject the idea that there is a real world out there waiting to be discovered. Knowledge and reality are social constructs and any attempt to discipline the world into an homogeneous straitjacket is both futile and a reflection of power structures which will continue to define what is 'good' and 'right'. Post-modernism is the subject of much debate and consternation not least because of its ability to shock, be explosive and difficult to grasp hold of (precisely its adherent's intention). Jane Flax claims that 'post-modernists share at least one common object of attack – the Enlightenment' and that despite their many differences post-modernist discourses are all deconstructive and seek to distance us from and make us 'skeptical about the ideas concerning truth, knowledge, power, history, self and language that are often taken for granted within and serve as legitimations for contemporary Western culture'.[7]

Post-modernists revel in denying privilege (the architect, the philosopher, the author, the composer) and eulogise the nature of differ-ence and plurality. Rather than searching for coherent epistemologies post-modernists engage in rhetoric and conversation. Post-modern feminists typically share the post-modern critique of grand, universa-lising narratives and are intent on creating a standpointed, decon-structive but non-prescriptive discourse.

Feminist critiques of International Relations

Feminist critiques of International Relations are ever increas-ing, indeed it is difficult to know what to include. There has already been a great deal of research on related issues of women and war, women and peace and women and development but my main concern here is to give a brief introduction to the impact of feminist *theory* on the discipline of International Relations, and its nascent development in the British and North American academic communities. As I work within the former, perhaps a fitting place to start is with some of the contributions in the special issue of *Millennium* published in the winter of 1988 as a result of a one-day symposium on *Women and International Relations* held at the London School of Economics in June 1988.

Fred Halliday

Halliday makes use of Sheila Rowbotham's concept of the invisibilisation or silencing of women in history and claims that this is also the case in International Relations.[8] He isolates an important point by highlighting the accepted assumption that international processes are gender neutral. If gender as an issue is going to be given serious consideration then two specific challenges have to be considered. Firstly, to look at how gender issues and values do and could play a role within international relations and secondly, an analysis of the gender specific consequences of international processes whether they are military, economic, political or ideological.

Halliday then looks at what issues are involved in the emerging concern of gender, starting with some of the central concepts used in International Relations such as power, security, rights and the national interest. What is the significance of the symbolisation of power in gender terms and could these basic concepts be interpreted differently from a 'woman's' perspective? He broadens the issue to human rights. If gender is now to be included does this mean that the International Relations community now has to look more closely at the roles of states and other actors in promoting or denying rights to women?

This links to Halliday's second concern; the extent to which inter-national policies and processes play an important role in determining and structuring women's place in society. Economics is a key culprit here. He discusses briefly the mass recruitment of women into high technology industries in the new industrialising countries and also the specific gender consequences of the structural adjustment policies by a number of Third World governments which frequently force women out to work in low paid jobs.

Halliday then looks more closely at two specific issues; women and nationalism and the place of women's rights in the formulation of inter-state relations. Investigation of these issues leads Halliday to what he terms *unacceptable conclusions*.[9] For Halliday this alone suggests that the questions they pose are of *some* importance. For me it is a striking revelation which *necessitates* further and thorough investigation. Take, for example, his comments on nationalism. Nationalism is a buzz word in both International Relations theory and practice. In practice it mobilises and unites groups and is generally perceived to be a useful force in societies exalting traditional culture and practices. But, as Halliday so trenchantly points out, nationalist movements tend to subordinate women to traditional subservient roles in society. In the name of nationalism, male dominated states continue to control the lives of women.

The case is similar with regard to human rights issues. States often impose or threaten sanctions on other states which do not fulfil expectations with regard to human rights. Such moral indignations are often hypocritical (for example the United States admonishing the Soviet Union) but the question of specific violations of women's human rights is seen to be almost irrelevant or indeed a 'private' matter. The fact that it would be, in conventional terms, preposterous that questions of gender play such an important role in the relations between sovereign states is itself indicative of how international processes buttress the continued devaluation and control of women's lives. Halliday then goes on to conclude that 'it is not as if consideration of gender will alter the teaching and research of International Relations as a whole' but is willing to concede that it will do more than just add another subject to the list of topics already covered.[10] He ends with a warning, however, against what he calls 'precipitate totalisation'; the tendency to see all events or practices as the expression of a single mechanism.[11] His concern is that once the connections between gender and the processes and practices of international relations are made obvious it will be tempting to claim that gender issues constitute *the* core of international relations or indeed that all aspects of women's experience can be derived from the international. Despite this reservation Halliday expresses a commitment to the continuation of investigation into the issue of gender and International Relations and that such issues become an established part of the teaching agenda.

Halliday presents a thoughtful and wide-ranging preliminary analysis of the effects the incorporation of gender would have on the discipline of International Relations. He moves from questioning the presumed gender neutrality of the subject to a discussion of the gendered effects of specific international policies and processes. His political and epistemological positions are not explicitly stated, although one could hazard a guess that the former lies somewhere in the socialist/Marxist camp. As to epistemology, he seems to be veering towards a standpoint position (which would be compatible with a Marxist/socialist feminism), specifically when considering the interpretation of key International Relations concepts such as security and the national interest from a woman's perspective. There are a number of problems with this approach which I will return to when discussing J. Ann Tickner's article. Finally, in my view Halliday ultimately shies away from the more radical implications of his comments, particularly his observation that investigations of gender might lead to unacceptable conclusions; I will return to this issue later.

J. Ann Tickner

Tickner's article, the second in the special issue of *Millennium*, is entitled 'Hans Morgenthau's Principles of Political Realism: A Feminist Reformulation'.[12] In her article, Tickner focuses on the inherent nature of the discipline of International Relations and is concerned to address the question of why it continues to appear inhospitable to women. Tickner intends to analyse Morgenthau's six principles in order to shed light on her claim that the discipline of International Relations is based on a masculine world view. She outlines his six principles arguing that his portrayal of the international system is only a partial one based on assumptions about human nature which are partial and which privilege masculinity. She discusses the concepts of masculinity and femininity describing them as socially constructed facets of humans rather than biological determinants. However the dichotomy exists and there are clearly identifiable masculine and feminine characteristics.

Tickner argues that Morgenthau, in his search for a science of international politics based on objective laws which have their roots in human nature, constructed an abstraction which he calls political man – 'a beast completely lacking in moral restraints'.[13] Survival depends on the maximisation of power and the willingness to fight. Any state which does not adhere to this maxim will lose. Tickner, referring to Carol Gilligan's work on moral development argues that Morgenthau's conception of morality is a partial one and is premised on a masculine conception of human nature and morality, based on dog eat dog.[14] In a world with nuclear weapons this moral base is becoming little more than a recipe for disaster.

Tickner goes on to reformulate the concepts of power and security from a feminist perspective. Power is redefined in a multidimensional sense to incorporate notions of mutual reciprocity, cooperation and enablement rather than Morgenthauian notions of control of man over man. Similarly we would be better served if the concept of national security were widened to include economic and environmental security in interdependent terms rather than just military security in an isolationist manner. Tickner refers to Sara Ruddick's use of 'maternal thinking' which focuses on the preservation and growth of life, not its destruction.[15] Conflict resolution in a nuclear world seems to be a more realistic prospect if one can view 'the other side' in a nurturant rather than a hostile light. The consequences of perceiving the enemy as inhuman, less worthy of life than oneself leads to horrific consequences as the Nazi extermination of Jews shows us. The practice of delineating sub-species of humans is a persistent one.

Tickner concludes her article with a feminist reformulation of Morgenthau's principles of political realism which I will summarise briefly.

1 Objectivity is associated with masculinity and thus any objective laws are necessarily partial.
2 National interest is multidimensional and therefore cannot be defined solely in terms of power.
3 Power defined as domination and control is a limited and masculine definition.
4 It is impossible and inadvisable to separate morality from political actions.
5 A goal is to focus on commonalities in human aspirations with a view to decreasing conflict and fostering a communitarian spirit.
6 The public sphere is not autonomous, and claiming that it is necessarily excludes the concerns and contributions of women.

J. Ann Tickner takes a clear 'feminist standpoint' position in her approach. For her the adoption of feminist principles into the discipline of International Relations is necessary in order to redress the masculine imbalance that we have inherited. She ends her article with the statement that 'this ungendered or human discourse becomes possible only when women are adequately represented in the discipline and when there is equal respect for the contributions of both women and men alike'.[16] The reformulation of principles she described is an interesting one and one which gains the attention of a number of mainstream International Relations scholars, for example, Robert Keohane.[17] However, there are two main problems with this approach. Firstly, she too easily conflates *feminist* principles with *feminine* traits – the latter resting upon stereotypical characteristics. Although she claims that feminists on the whole regard masculinity and femininity as socially constructed, her identification of feminine and feminist values with women, and her assumption that things will only change when women are adequately represented in the discipline, serves to reify the notion of inherent differences between men and women which has for so long served to justify differential and unequal treatment. This is not a plea for androgeny but a plea for the recognition of the fact that notions of sexual difference, based on patriarchal stereotypes, are fraught with problems for feminist praxis. This leads to the identification of a *second* problem with this type of approach. The acceptance of 'feminine' values stems from radical and standpoint feminist beliefs in the possibility of redescribing reality (or at the very least completing the picture) using women's perspectives as well as men's. The assumption is that women see and experience the world differently to men and thus women's description and understanding of social life would present a different picture of reality than that presented, hitherto, by men. The ensuing *implication* that there are different and separate male and female routes to knowledge is problematic as it invites a return to notions of innate male and female capabilities on a par with biological determinist theories. The acceptance and reification of masculine and feminine formulations will do nothing to change the hierarchical positioning of these traits. The reformulation of the basic concepts used in International Relations is well overdue but this does not necessarily have to be done from a feminist perspective as there is nothing exclusively feminist about the reworking of such concepts. Indeed the very notion that there is something about this approach which is better done by women because of their femininity or femaleness (whether socially constructed or not) will foster the current trend to marginalise feminist investigation and leave the established (mostly male) academics comfortable in the belief that feminism isn't really anything to do with them.

Sarah Brown

The last article I want to look at from the special issue of *Millennium* is Sarah Brown's robust paper entitled 'Feminism, International Theory and International Relations of Gender Inequality'.[18] Brown objects strongly to the way feminist discourse is being 'added on' to existing International Relations theory. She claims that the liberal feminist concern to simply 'add women and stir' will do nothing to alter the mainstream belief that the proper objects of inquiry are states and citizens. She argues that by including women into the theory and practice of International Relations we will be led to the erroneous conclusion that this is synonymous with the removal of gender inequality. This ignores the fact that one of the prerequisites of citizenship and the societal ordering of states is the subordination of women. Liberal feminism, accepting the existence of the public/private split, has the goal of full incorporation of women into public life. Addressing the issue of gender within International Relations would then simply imply the inclusion of women into public/international life.

However, Brown claims that women have *long* been involved in activities relevant to International Relations. So instead of bringing women *in* we need to investigate why women's activities in the international arena have been deemed unimportant or invisible. Brown wants to reconstruct the starting point for International Relations enquiry to be 'the identification of the constraints upon the capacity of the discipline of International Relations to theorise effectively about the international relations of gender inequality'.[19] To try and incorporate feminism into International Relations is the wrong way round and is indeed dangerous for two main reasons. Firstly, it leads feminists to uncritically adopt mainstream methods, objects of enquiry and concepts which are based upon the subordination of women. Secondly, there is a danger in an uncritical acceptance of the very possibility of *gender equality*. Brown claims that the term *gender equality* is somewhat of an oxymoron. Gender is a social construct predicated on notions of difference and inequality whereas equality implies sameness and equal worth. The pursuance of such a goal within the confines of mainstream theorising is an impossible task as the latter is infected with the acceptance of gender as a natural construct.

For Brown, feminist analysis must take gender as its starting point but must not take it as a given. She claims 'that a feminist critical theory of International Relations is fundamentally a political act of

127

commitment to understanding the world from the perspective of the socially subjugated'.[20] Thus a feminist analysis of International Relations would not consist of an addition to the subject but instead a commitment to the transcendence of gender (inequality) through its elimination. The proper object and purpose of a feminist International Relations must be to explain how gender has been constructed and maintained in International Relations and if and how it can be removed. Although Brown calls her approach a feminist critical theory her suggestion that the study of International Relations should be reformulated to explain gender inequality from the position of the socially subjugated is more accurately placed in the radical/standpoint camp.

Sarah Brown's paper is somewhat esoteric but nevertheless she makes a crucially important point about the oxymoronic nature of the phrase gender equality. However, I am unsure as to how Sarah Brown thinks International Relations scholars would be convinced to change the focus of the discipline from war, peace and interstate behaviour and turn their attention *solely* to issues of gender – thereby reconstructing the starting point of International Relations enquiry. The type of feminist analysis that Brown puts forward already exists in many forms. It is, of course, still marginalised, as those of us who work in academic institutions are well aware, but it is on the agenda. Brown's insistence that the proper object and purpose of a feminist International Relations must be to explain how gender has been constructed and maintained is probably what Fred Halliday has in mind when he talks about *precipitate totalisation* – tending to lead towards the claim that gender issues constitute the core of International Relations. The current discipline of International Relations will probably not change to become a feminist International Relations in this sense; but the study of feminist theory internationally is a different thing and is part of what feminists are working towards.

Sandra Whitworth

In her article Sandra Whitworth attempts to theorise about gender using existing International Relations paradigms.[21] Like Sarah Brown she is not concerned with 'bringing women in' to International Relations, as we are already there, but to investigate why the theory and history of International Relations continues to sustain the mythical absence of women. Gender is a social construct which rests on inequality between men and women. In order to find a space to theorise about gender, thus identified, within conventional International Relations, Whitworth claims that there are three criteria which should be satisfied. Firstly, whether it permits discussion of the social construction of meaning, secondly, whether it permits the discussion of historical variability, and thirdly, whether it is possible to discuss power on wider terms than just as an overt expression of force. Whitworth then goes on to discuss these issues trying to place gender within the three paradigms of Realism, pluralism and critical theory.

Identifying Realism as the central traditions of International Relations theory she initially claims that there is unlikely to be any theoretical room here to discuss gender. She paraphrases Morgenthau – International Relations that are not concerned with the pursuit of power are simply not about international politics. Thus, by definition, gender would not find a place (although this is questionable – for many feminists the existence of gender only continues via the use of power). However, Whitworth claims that using the classical tenets of Realism, specifically those outlined by Morgenthau, there is space to theorise about gender. The concentration on the *practice* of international relations (although narrowly defined by Morgenthau as diplomatic behaviour), and the recognition that concepts are only given meaning within an historical context via those practices, creates the space for the first two criteria outlined by Whitworth – namely the acknowledgement of the social construction of meaning and the historical variability of such meanings. There is therefore epistemological space for theorising about gender, but Whitworth concludes that realism's ontological commitment to states and states*men* ultimately precludes analysis of gender.

For her discussion of pluralism and gender Whitworth concentrates on the 'world as a cobweb' perspective put forward by John Burton. Briefly, all conflictual relationships ranging from war to drug abuse and racial conflict are all interlinked and can be traced to the denial of human needs. We need to discover the source of these conflicts and eradicate them. Thus, at first glance, this expansion of the sphere of International Relations seems to open up space for gender. However, she argues that pluralism opens up less spaces for theorising about gender as a social construct as pluralism is inherently liberal in nature and thus tends to ignore the possibility of structural causes of oppression.

Critical theory, it is claimed, holds out the greatest promise for incorporating gendered analysis into International Relations. Instead of just problem solving, critical theory asks how the order came about which created those problems. The problem is that critical theory perspectives on International Relations are on the periphery of the subject just as feminist theory is. But for Sandra Whitworth the next stage for International Relations theory is one which should be both *critical* and *feminist*. This is an interesting paper and one which, I suspect, will appeal to the more established academics in the field as it refers to the existing paradigms. Her discussion of the epistemological spaces within classical realism is novel and is worth pursuing but I suspect she is correct in her conclusion that Realism's steadfast adherence to states, states*men* and the pursuance of power will mitigate strongly against any serious consideration of gender at more than the liberal feminist level. However, there is surely more to pluralism than the work of John Burton, although I would again agree with Whitworth's conclusion that pluralism does not allow space for a more than superficial investigation into the effects of the social construction of gender.

Critical theory and (most) feminist theory share in common a deconstructive and an emancipatory discourse. They also share the experience of being marginalised. What they do not apparently share (as pointed out by Whitworth) is any agreement on which aspect of the social construction of reality to concentrate on and what path emancipation should take. Emancipation for feminists would imply the eradication of the oppression of women. But what is emancipation for a critical theorist? That the two paths might be different does not automatically mean that there is no possibility of a critical feminist theory, but the possible consequences of different emancipatory paths is something that needs further thought.

Cynthia Enloe

Cynthia Enloe's enlivening book *Bananas, Beaches and Bases* is aimed at making feminist sense of international politics. She rightly claims that, so far, feminist analysis has had little impact on international politics. 'Women's roles in creating and sustaining international politics have been treated as if they were "natural" and thus not worthy of investigation'.[22] Enloe adopts a clear feminist standpoint position in which she aims to redefine what the important questions and issues are and also to provide an impetus to change the existing structure. She wants to take women's experiences seriously in order to gain a more realistic understanding of how international politics works. Enloe makes it clear, however, that a feminist analysis of International Relations would not indicate an eschewal of issues such as arms dealing, crisis behaviour and the president's men but claims that *only* looking at such issues would be inadequate for an understanding of how the international political system works.

130

Enloe takes on conventional categories of International Relations and reworks them to take women's real lives into account. Categories such as *nationalism*, *diplomacy*, *the military* and *international debt* are discussed, looking at what they mean for women. Nationalism, for example, is often seen as a way for countries to regain their independence and revive their own cultural practices. In reality, however, this often means a return to traditional female roles of servitude to the family. When looking at the art of diplomacy in Enloe's terms, we can concentrate on the role played by diplomatic *wives* who, in the main, do not follow a career of their own but follow their husbands around the world acting the role of hostess. As Enloe points out, diplomacy runs smoothly when there is trust and confidence between officials representing governments which usually have different if not conflicting interests. That trust and confidence tends to be fostered in the diplomat's homes rather than their offices and it is in the home, the site of numerous dinner parties, that diplomatic wives play such an important role in the continuation of foreign policy.

Enloe claims that the international system works via the construction and continual reconstruction of masculinity and femininity with women, for example, fulfilling the female/feminine role as loyal wife, prostitute, diplomatic wife etc. She describes such roles as part of the building blocks of the international political system without which the whole system would collapse. She deploys the radical feminist slogan 'the personal is the political' and enlarges it to 'the personal is the international' – a phrase which is used by Halliday but Enloe takes it to its logical conclusion. For Enloe the international is also the personal, which implies that governments depend on certain kinds of allegedly private relationships in order to conduct their foreign affairs and to operate in the international area. Conventional analysis of international politics is incomplete as whole areas of reality are excluded. What we need to look at is how states depend on particular constructions of the domestic and private spheres to foster smoother relationships at the public and international level.

Enloe claims that women will be in a better position than men to carry out such a realistic investigation of international relations because we are more used to asking questions about gender. She makes a crucial point about *power*. This is such a central concept in International Relations and it is thus one of the concepts being looked at for the purposes of reconceptualisation. However, unlike Keohane and Tickner, Enloe does not concentrate on the more empowering rather than coercive capacities of power; instead she exposes just how much more coercive power is wielded in the international system than conventional analyses would have us believe. In her words 'an exploration of agribusiness prostitution, foreign service sexism and attempts to tame outspoken nationalist women with homophobic taunts all reveal that in reality it takes much *more* power to construct and perpetuate international political relations than we have been led to believe'.[23]

Enloe's book draws attention to the implications of the assumption that private lives are not importantly linked to public activity. It may seem initially preposterous to claim that the roles performed by disparate groupings of women, such as diplomats' wives, army wives and base prostitutes, serve the purposes of the conventionally defined international political system, but Enloe's point it that without such putatively private gendered arrangements, conventional international relations would be in danger of complete collapse.

Christine Sylvester

Finally, I will look at the work of Christine Sylvester, spending some time outlining her work because she raises some fundamental issues, most notably those to do with the question of what counts as feminist knowledge. This will enable me to say something about the strengths and weaknesses of each of Harding's three epistemological categories outlined above. Christine Sylvester works within the mainstream International Relations community but attempts to deconstruct that discipline. She has presented a number of papers at ISA panels most recently putting forward a feminist post-modernist perspective on International Relations. She is currently working on a book about feminist post-modernism and International Relations. For the purposes of this chapter I will look at a chapter she has written entitled 'The Emperors' Theories and Transformations: Looking at the Field Through Feminist Lenses'. In this chapter Sylvester claims that mainstream International Relations and political economy do not consider questions about gender, labouring under the assumption that international processes are gender neutral. On the contrary, claims Sylvester, 'there is a hidden gender to the field and it affects how we think about empirical International Relations and political economy'.[24] She then proceeds to look at neo-Realism and world systems theory through feminist lenses using the epistemological typology outlined by Sandra Harding.

Sylvester claims that the debate between Neo-Realists and transnationalists is rich and varied but there is a near silence regarding the issue of male hegemony in the system they discuss. She wants to raise the question, 'is the absence of women empirically and theoretically warranted?'[25] There are many silences regarding gender but, as Sarah

Brown astutely points out silences are not vacancies and as such require investigation.[25] Using the Harding typology outlined earlier in this chapter (empiricist, standpoint and post-modern), Sylvester states that none of these approaches poses a direct and theoretically complete challenge to conventional understandings of International Relations and political economy but instead adds a further dimension by identifying deceptions and distortions which ultimately skew the knowledge created.

Feminist empiricists claim that the work of researchers is not objective but is unknowingly influenced by prevailing views about the proper roles for men and women. She claims that standard androcentric research, as exemplified by neo-Realism, is biased towards rationality, an understanding of the world as a single (male) society, a preoccupation with the world system's functional purpose (for continuing that 'male' world order) and with an emphasis on objective knowledge collection. For Sylvester, rationality has a double edged androcentric bias. Firstly, because it is historically associated with the masculine and not the feminine; secondly, rationality pervades important social structures, such as states, and as such they become implicitly gendered. This implies that as long as women are not part of the decision-making hierarchy, in anything but small numbers, the perception of rationality will not change (e.g. the emotional aspect of decision making will continue to be underplayed) and politics will continue to be seen as a male preserve. Similarly, feminist empiricists suspect that women and men occupy quite separate societies which have to be researched and validated much more systematically rather than accept the assumption that a unitary system exists. Mainstream theorists may see different world systems when taking other criteria into account, but not when looking (or not looking) at gender. Additionally, when considering the functional nature of societies the feminist empiricist will ask whether a society is functional for women as well as for men.

Social science, taking as its role model the scientific method (objective, logical, subject to testing and ultimately falsifiable, thereby 'proving' its verifiability), aspires to be as free from bias as possible. However, feminist empiricists would claim that both the actors and processes which create the systems in which we live are centrally involved in structuring women and their activities out of official significance. Sylvester supplies the examples of (a) midwifery – once a respected and profitable profession, outlawed as witchcraft with the advent of the age of science; (b) the market system rewarding only exchangeable commodities, leaving women's procreative and nurturing work external to the economic realm of significance.

133

Feminist standpoint theorists claim that women, who for so long have been excluded and marginalised, have a less distorted perception of social issues 'which more insightfully reveal the true structures and actors of the world than do theories spun by representatives of the dominant group'.[27] Sylvester uses the work of Mary Daly as the archetypal example of a theorist intent on recovering the true story of womanhood.[28] Our world and thus our reality has been created by patriarchy. The task is to abandon that patriarchal world and restore a world in which women's ways and activities regain credibility. Women, from their vantage point on the periphery, will be the central actors in the transformation of the world from patriarchy to post-patriarchy. Sylvester draws on psychonanalytic versions of feminist thought to expand on this theme. Our gender identities are central to our understanding of ourselves and others. Girls and boys have markedly different socialising experiences which leave them with a differing set of skills, values and beliefs – many of which are oppositional. In simple terms, boys grow up internalising the values of 'masculinity' which is defined (partially) in terms of unconnectedness, distance from the subject, control and order. On the other hand, girls grow up valuing connectedness, continuity and fluidity of relations, emotions and intellectual endeavour. Women learn to become women which by definition is a group with inferior status to men. Does this imply that we cannot be effective as system challengers?

Feminist post-modernists, like other feminists, start with considerations of gender. However, there is a distrust of any attempt to find 'one true story'. Women have a wide variety of differing experiences and realities and for Sylvester it is 'theoretically preferable to accept the notion of permanent partiality and to explore intersecting, contradictory and simultaneous realities within a pro-women framework'.[29] She also points out that feminist post-modernism stands alone in seeking to deconstruct more than it prescribes. Sylvester uses Jean Bethke Elshtain's book *Women and War* claiming that Elshtain demonstrates one post-modernist approach.[30] In this book Elshtain explores the political claims and social identities deemed to us through war stories. Elshtain questions the notion that real war is deemed to 'belong' to men with women fading into the background. Women have been 'in' wars and have the capacity to 'want' war just as much as men. The feminist post-modernist perspective urges us to resist the temptation to accept 'one true story' which invites excessive conformity; instead we should realise that there are multiple realities. We should concentrate our efforts on revealing what stories we have accepted which have denied the agency of women.

Sylvester concludes her chapter by summarising the various feminist positions without discussing which, if any, she thinks would be the most effective approach. This is not surprising, however, as her leanings towards post-modernism would draw her away from any one coherent framework of understanding. However, I am not altogether sure if Sylvester is writing about the different feminist approaches in an historical sense or if she is implying that there are separate groups of feminists chipping away at mainstream International Relations from each of the different perspectives. I would presume the latter although in another paper written by Sylvester she talks about feminist post-modernism being the 'third wave of contemporary feminist theorising'.[31]

Her discussion of feminist empiricism leaves me with the impression that there is much more to empiricism that one would have suspected. But is this correct? Feminist empiricists believe in doing science properly. Up to now this has not been done because of the inherent androcentric bias at the level of initial selection of worthy issues to investigate and the bias of male researchers as a social group. However these errors can be corrected. I am not clear if this would lead a feminist empiricist to question the use of rationality as a methodological tool. Empiricists of all persuasions are keen to do good science properly with the aim of discovering knowledge about the world. Rationality is a key tool in this endeavour. Thus I think the discussion of rationality as bias is a little misplaced in the feminist empiricist camp. It would seem more appropriate coming from either radical or standpoint feminists.

In a similar vein, the considerations she believes feminist empiricists would raise seem overly radical. If such feminists are empiricists then a major aim is *discovery* of the world and problem solving in that world. Sylvester's discussion of structures seems again misplaced in the feminist empiricist camp. However these are obviously not simple issues and one has to be wary of slipping into deep philosophical waters. The whole question of feminist empiricism, as pointed out by Sandra Harding, is paradoxical as the notion that the scientific method has been practised with a large amount of bias is deeply subversive to empiricism itself.[32]

The section of feminist standpoint is much more straightforward at the epistemological level. This perspective is illuminating in the sense that it draws attention to the value of women's reality and the fact that such realities are seemingly invisible when it comes to the accepted canons of academia. The work of radical feminists in particular is responsible for this reclaiming of women's voices and is to be applauded for this achievement. However, the concept of feminist as transformer is problematic as it tends to fall back on notions of inherent differences between the sexes which can only facilitate the impression that feminist work is for women only, which will continue its marginalisation. When discussing women's standpoint on International Relations and the international political economy, surely it is better to investigate the specific effects of such policies on women's lives rather than relying on notions of separate women's ways of understanding and seeing the world? Within feminist theorising the very concept of women's standpoint has come under attack. How is it possible to talk about a woman's standpoint when there are so many different types of women in the world. Does the experience of white Western women become the norm/standpoint?

Feminist post-modernism is the subject of much debate within mainstream feminist theorising and also within the International Relations feminist community. There is not the space here to do justice to the various debates regarding the utility of post-modernism for feminist discourse; what I will do is briefly mention two of the major challenges to the appropriation of the tenets of post-modernism into feminism. Firstly, one of the basic tenets of post-modernist thought is the problematisation of the centrality of the subject, both as the exemplar of an ahistorical, transcendental category and as privileged owners of knowledge and authoritative statements about the world. The decentring of the subject has led some critics of post-modernism to argue that this makes any feminist politics impossible as the category of 'women' becomes decentred into non-existence. As Linda Alcoff claims, for many contemporary feminist theorists, the concept of woman has become a problem.[33] Alcoff argues that this is a problem of primary significance for feminist theory as the concept and category of 'woman' has been the necessary point of departure for any feminist theory and feminist politics. The post-modern distaste for subject-centred enquiry and subject-based politics propels post-modernism into gender blindness. Take for example the special issue of *International Studies Quarterly* on 'Speaking the Language of Exile: Dissidence in International Studies'. The editorship of this mainstream North American International Relations journal was temporarily taken over by two post-modern writers, Richard K. Ashley and R. B. J. Walker. The purpose of the issue was to give a platform to the critical and dissident voices in contemporary International Relations. Not one of the articles in this issue represented feminist concerns. It might be suggested that these 'exiles on mainstreet' are as gender insensitive as their neo-Realist colleagues.[34]

This leads on to a second major problem with the conflation of post-modernism and feminism. The post-modernist intention to challenge the power of dominant discourses in an attempt to lead those discourses into disarray is at first glance appealing but we have to ask what will the replacement be? If we are to believe that all is contingent and we have no base on to which we can ground claims to truth, then 'power alone will determine the outcome of competing truth claims'.[35] Post-modernist discourse does not offer any criteria for choosing among competing explanations and thus has a tendency to lead towards nihilism – an accusation often levelled at the purveyors of post-modernism and to which they seem unable to provide any answer, except perhaps in the words of one post-modernist scholar 'what's wrong with nihilism'?[36] Feminists drawn towards the post-positivist nature of post-modernism, but repelled by its gender insensitivity, have been tempted to adopt an eclectic approach, selecting the admirable qualities of post-modernist thought and rejecting the undesirable. However, this 'pick 'n' mix' approach misunderstands the epistemological incompatibilities of post-modernism and feminism. Post-modernism is essentially an anti-epistemological and apolitical collection of interpretations whereas feminism is grounded in an emancipatory politics which necessitates some semblance of an epistemological foundation. Feminists within the International Relations community seem to be in a quandary, having to choose between either positivist or post-modern discourse. This, however, is not the only choice, a point to which I will return later.

Conclusions

Feminist critiques have been included as part of the 'third debate' or the 'post-positivist' challenge to International Relations.[37] Along with critical theory and post-modernism, feminist theory is seen to be part of the challenge to the hegemony of realist, positivist discourse. A useful way to analyse the current directions and trends within the arena of feminist theory and International Relations is to highlight some of the common themes and questions that have emerged.

(a) Reworking of core concepts: can we use existing concepts and theories? Is there theoretical space to 'bring women in'?
(b) Would it make any difference if women were equally represented in the International Relations community?
(c) Does it matter that women and men (to a large extent) inhabit different worlds in terms of experience and expectations?

137

(d) Why is it that women's experience is marginalised and does not appear to be really significant? Why don't women count?

(e) Should we concentrate on how international policies and processes vary in their effects on women and men? And perhaps more crucially what are the implications of such an investigation?

(f) Are International Relations theories inherently 'male biased'?

(g) Should feminist discourse be added on to International Relations or should International Relations accommodate itself to the demands of feminism?

These are some of the questions being raised by feminists within International Relations. That these questions are given some thought, and that this essay is included in this volume, indicates that issues of feminism and gender are having some impact on mainstream International Relations, although it still remains very much at the margins. However, I should make it clear that it is not an easy task to apply one disparate and large body of theory to another. For example, there is a tendency to be asked to give a 'feminist' answer to, or perspective on, an issue already outlined and defined as worthy of investigation by the existing creators of the discipline. This is like asking a committed Marxist to run a factory more successfully than its capitalist owner. Both would have completely differing views as to what constitutes success. It is of course possible at some level to supply a number of feminist perspectives to issues already identified as important by the discipline such as defence of national sovereignty. But this is more complicated than it sounds, as it entails taking into account a whole area conventionally defined as invisible or as part of the private realm and therefore out of the scope of conventional political analysis. A key task of feminist analysis is to extend the scope of the agenda rather than answering questions about what is already on the agenda.

What does feminist theory do to International Relations? If I were to conform to a conventional understanding of the changes in world politics in the 1980s, what would feminist theory have to offer?[38] Liberal feminism has much to offer by highlighting the neglect of women in traditional theory and practice and redressing that error. International Relations hardly deserves its self-appointed label of international if women are left out. But the liberal emphasis on 'including women in' tends to accept the traditionally defined agenda, which imposes a veto on what is and what is not a legitimate area of study for scholars of International Relations. Radical and socialist/Marxist feminism, particularly if utilising a specifically standpoint epistemology, provides a basis for extending the existing agenda. From these perspectives the assertion is made that women's voices and lives *are* important and not secondary. If we recall Halliday's comment that taking gender into consideration might lead in conventional terms to 'unacceptable conclusions' this should lead us to ask, 'what are these unacceptable conclusions and why would they be unacceptable'?[39] Halliday discusses women and nationalism and the place of women's rights in the formulation of inter-state relations. National independence is a key concept in International Relations theory and a key value on the international agenda. Given the value put on independence and the murky history of imperialism, the concept is accepted, if not totally uncritically, as a 'good thing'. But what are the specific effects on women? Often nationalism signals a return to traditional subordinate roles for women, maintaining male control over women's lives, hardly a gender neutral effect. Similarly, in the case of women's human rights it does not seem to matter that Western governments continue to support regimes in which women are relegated to the status of a sub-species without even formal political equality. Similarly, we take no notice that the international spread of prenatal diagnostic technology is being abused in countries such as China and India to abort female foetuses on the grounds that they are the 'wrong' sex. We in the West are very insistent that our distaste of racial apartheid is known about but gender apartheid is too easily accepted as either a private or cultural affair. If the implications of considering issues of gender lead to unacceptable conclusions, if the cost appears to be too high, we must ask ourselves the questions, 'how much do we care about the injustices of gender?' and 'how much do women count?'

However, we should be very wary of uncritically adopting the notion of reworking core concepts from a 'feminist' perspective. It is of vital importance that concepts, or, more accurately, defending concepts such as sovereignity and nationalism, should be analysed in detail with regards to the differing effects they have on men and women. Similarly, we should stop and ask ourselves the question 'if we are so concerned about human rights why do violations of women appear to be a private or a cultural issue?' An obvious example is the genital mutilation of approximately 80 million women worldwide. However, we should take care when reconceptualisation implies using stereotypical feminine traits. This concentration on women's ways of knowing, whether deemed to be socially constructed or not, skirts dangerously close to essentialism and probably also serves to retain the perception that feminism is for women only. Instead it is much more illuminating to widen the perception of power in the way Cynthia

139

Enloe does. The use of power to smooth the workings of international politics is much more widespread than conventional International Relations analyses would have us believe.

The contribution of post-modern feminism is harder to gauge. Post-modernism is the subject of much debate in feminist circles both inside and outside the International Relations community. I was a discussant (along with V. Spike Peterson) on a feminist theory panel at the 1991 International Studies Association Conference in Vancouver, commenting on papers given by Christine Sylvester and Geeta Chowdry. One of my abiding memories from that panel, and the other feminist/ gender panels (apart from them being paradigmatic examples of interesting and stimulating conference sessions), was the overwhelming desire to maintain and create a distance from the intellectual straitjacket of Realist discourse. It is hard to convey to those outside the discipline of International Relations just how dominant Realism is. Indeed, its critics, as well as it purveyors, tend to reify Realism, adding to its hegemonic status.[40] The urgent need to displace realist, positivist discourse has led many feminists to climb aboard the post-modernist bandwagon with its alleged commitment to the rebuttal of tyrannical truth claims. Indeed, given the choice between positivist realism and the promise of a reflexive, anti-foundationalist post-modernism, I confess I too would probably veer towards the latter. However, it is not as simple, or as clear, as that.

The dichotomy between positivist and post-modernist discourse gives the impression that there are only two alternatives. I would suggest that critical theory, following Sandra Whitworth and Mark Hoffman, offers the possibility of a third alternative.[41] There is not the space here to develop this perspective in any detail but I will outline some basic features. A feminist critical theory would regard the problematisation of gender as its starting point. It is not committed to the discovery of one single truth and its political stance is emancipatory and normative but not prescriptive. This model makes a specific connection between knowledge and interests and thus crucial initial questions to be asked are: 'whose interests are served by defining the study and practice of International Relations in certain ways?' 'Whose interests are consistently served by accepting the claim that private lives are not the proper sites of academic research? A critical feminism would examine the silences in International Relations, and ferret out the implicit and explicit assumptions about women and their 'nature' and 'roles'. Research into the gendered implications of these findings would call into question the 'givenness' or 'naturalness' of the world International Relations is trying to explain.

A critical feminist theory would look at the changes in world politics in the 1980s and come up with some interesting conclusions. The 'democratisation' of Eastern Europe has been seen by many in the West and the East as a change for the better. Of course this is a somewhat simplistic understanding of the enormous changes that are occurring but nevertheless there is some consensus that democratisation is at least better than that which existed before. But if we look more closely at the gender specific effects of democratisation we are left with a different picture. Romania may now have relaxed its draconian abortion and contraception laws but in the 1990 Romanian election campaign there was a move away from suggesting women should be given political responsibility. Women now hold only 3.5 per cent of parliamentary seats. In Czechoslovakia the figure is 6 per cent and in Hungary 7 per cent. The East is indeed following the example of the West, but is this necessarily a good thing as far as women are concerned?

The changes in Eastern Europe have also opened the way for the importation of traditionally Western styles of entertainment for men. The use of women as sex objects, particularly via pornography and beauty contests, is finding a large market in the East. The American monthly *Playboy* sold out its first Hungarian language edition within days and Poland's news stands are full of pornographic material. Poland's acceptance of the use of women as objects of sexual desire sits uneasily next to Lech Walesa's current moves to ban abortion completely. And in both Czechoslovakia and Poland there is a growing (male) consensus that one way to solve the economic plight of working men is to send women home. A feminist may well turn round and look at the changes in Eastern Europe and comment 'the more things change, the more they stay the same, at least for women'.

There are many feminist critiques of International Relations, each with varying weaknesses and strengths. Liberal feminist attempts to 'include women in' and Marxist/socialist attempts to make us aware of the gendered consequences of the policies and practices of a capitalist, racist and patriarchal world system are invaluable counters to the partial perspective of current International Relations research. The radical feminist insistence that women's real lives and experiences are of vital importance is also a necessary antidote to an International Relations heavily concerned with the activities of men. It might be regarded as somewhat churlish to imply that certain feminist perspectives are more useful than others, as each perspective has valuable contributions to make. However, the importance of the political imperatives of feminism urges me to suggest that a critical feminist

141

theory will provide even further insights into the gender blindness of International Relations.

Critical feminism does not ask us to include women and their issues on the agenda because we are already there. This perspective will not take the existing agenda as a given but will ask what is left out by defining the agenda in such a way. A critical feminist perspective will endeavour not to fall into the trap of prescribing what is important in women's lives or to women but will draw attention to policies and practices which exploit women or which limit their autonomy. A critical feminist approach will illuminate the connections between interests served and knowledge created by International Relations research, but without falling into the functionalist trap of equating interests served with first and final causes. This critical feminist approach will take the problematisation of gender insensitive credentials of other critical approaches. This perspective makes us question the very gender neutrality of the subject, its assumptions and approaches, the crucial point being that the gendered assumptions embedded within International Relations produced distorted and partial knowledge. This should make us think long and hard about what International Relations is and especially about the version of it that we define as the subject of International Relations. Disciplines create boundaries, and these boundaries have powerful effects on what a subject defines as its agenda. In International Relations, these boundaries, like those in all the other social sciences, have long ignored gender questions: raising these questions now may appear political or biased, or simply as against common sense. The problem for International Relations is that it is one of the last social sciences to face up to the possibility that its cherished concepts and agenda may not be gender neutral. This silence is now so loud that it screams. We should not be afraid to acknowledge that feminism is a subversive strategy as implied by Anne Sisson Runyan and V. Spike Peterson. However, when the notion of subversion is stripped to its derisory connotations, applied to it by defenders of the status quo, subversive strategies provide a foundation from which to emancipate and liberate.

Notes

I would like to thank Steve Smith for providing immeasurable support and advice.
  1 For those working within feminism, such a brief outline of feminist thought might be perceived as doing an injustice to its vastness and diversity. However, I feel it is necessary to serve as an introduction to the International Relations scholar curious to know what feminism means to the

study of International Relations. In future, I might be tempted to follow Anne Sisson Runyan's and V. Spike Paterson's lead in encouraging readers to 'undertake the extensive reading program required to become familiar with feminist theory and praxis' (A. Sisson Runyan and V. Spike Peterson, 'The Radical Future of Realism: Feminist Subversions of IR Theory', *Alternatives*, vol. 16, no. 1, 1991, p. 102, note 41).

2 D. Coole, *Women in Political Theory* (Brighton: Wheatsheaf, 1988); and C. Pateman, 'Feminism and Democracy', in G. Duncan (ed.), *Democratic Theory and Practice* (Cambridge: Cambridge University Press, 1983); and C. Pateman, *The Sexual Contract* (Oxford, Basil Blackwell, 1988).

3 C. Enloe, *Bananas, Beaches and Bases: Making Feminist Sense of International Politics* (London: Pandora, 1989), p. 195.

4 Readers wanting to learn more about feminist theory would be advised to begin by consulting texts such as, H. Eisenstein, *Contemporary Feminist Thought* (London: Unwin Paperbacks, 1988); A. M. Jagger, *Feminist Politics and Human Nature* (Brighton: Harvester, 1983); and R. Tong, *Feminist Thought: A Comparative Introduction* (London: Unwin Hyman, 1989).

5 S. Harding, *The Science Question in Feminism* (Milton Keynes, Open University Press, 1986).

6 *Ibid.*, p. 25.

7 J. Flax, *Thinking Fragments: Psychoanalysis, Feminism and Postmodernism in the Contemporary West* (Berkeley and Los Angeles: University of California Press, 1990), p. 29.

8 F. Halliday, 'Hidden from International Relations: Women and the International Relations Arena', *Millennium*, vol. 17, no. 3, 1988, p. 419.

9 *Ibid.*, p. 423.

10 *Ibid.*, p. 426.

11 *Ibid.*, p. 427.

12 J. Ann Tickner, 'Hans Morgenthau's Principles of Political Realism: A Feminist Reformulation', *Millennium*, vol. 17, no. 3, 1988.

13 *Ibid.*, p. 432.

14 C. Gilligan, *In a Different Voice: Psychological Theory and Woman's Development* (Cambridge, MA.: Harvard University Press, 1982).

15 S. Ruddick, *Maternal Thinking: Towards a Politics of Peace* (New York: Ballantine Books, 1989).

16 Tickner, 'Hans Morgenthau's Principles of Political Realism', p. 438.

17 R. O. Keohane, 'International Relations Theory: Contributions of a Feminist Standpoint', *Millennium*, vol. 18, no. 2, 1989.

18 S. Brown, 'Feminism, International Theory and International Relations of Gender Inequality', *Millennium*, vol. 17, no. 3, 1988.

19 *Ibid.*, pp. 464–5.

20 *Ibid.*, p. 472.

21 S. Whitworth, 'Gender in the Inter-Paradigm Debate', *Millennium*, vol. 18, no. 2, 1989, pp. 265–72.

22 Enloe, *Bananas, Beaches and Bases*, p. 4.

23 *Ibid.*, p. 197.

24 C. Sylvester, 'The Emperors' Theories and Transformations: Looking at the Field Through Feminist Lenses', in D. Pirages and C. Sylvester (eds.),

Transformations in the Global Political Economy (London: Macmillan, 1990), p. 230.

25 *Ibid.*, p. 235.

26 Brown, 'Feminism', p. 473.

27 Sylvester, 'The Emperors' Theories', p. 241.

28 M. Daly, *Pure Lust: Elemental Feminist Philosophy* (Boston: Beacon Press, 1984).

29 Sylvester, 'The Emperors' Theories', p. 246.

30 J. Bethke Elshtain, *Women and War* (London: Pandora Press, 1987).

31 C. Sylvester, 'Feminist Postmodernism, nuclear strategy and international violence' (Unpublished paper presented at the International Studies Association Meeting, London, March 1989).

32 S. Harding, *The Science Question in Feminism* (Milton Keynes: University Press, 1986), p. 25.

33 L. Alcoff, 'Cultural Feminism versus Post-Structuralism: The Identity Crisis in Feminist Theory', *Signs: Journal of Women in Culture and Society*, vol. 13, no. 3, 1988, p. 405.

34 I am grateful to Steve Smith for suggesting the phrase 'exile on main street' (he acknowledges prior use of the phrase by the Rolling Stones, circa 1971).

35 J. Flax, 'Postmodernism and Gender Relations in Feminist Theory', *Signs: Journal of Women in Culture and Society*, vol. 12, no. 4, 1987, p. 625.

36 Some would claim that post-modernism is not necessarily nihilistic (see Sisson Runyan and Peterson, p. 102 note 35). However, this is not an uncontentious claim, see the exchange between Hawkesworth and Hekman in *Signs: Journal of Women in Culture and Society*, vol. 15, no. 2.

37 Y. Lapid, 'The Third Debate: On the Prospects of International Theory in a Post-Positivist Era', *International Studies Quarterly*, vol. 33, no. 3, 1989, pp. 235–54.

38 Here I would include, for example, the changes in Eastern Europe, the Gulf War and the breakup of the Soviet bloc.

39 Halliday, 'Hidden from International Relations', p. 423.

40 As Sisson Runyan and Peterson do in their article, 'The Radical Future of Realism' p. 71.

41 Whitworth, 'Gender in the Inter-Paradigm Debate'; and Mark Hoffman, 'Critical Theory and the Inter-Paradigm Debate', *Millennium*, vol. 16, no. 2, 1987, pp. 231–49; and Mark Hoffman, 'Conversations on Critical International Relations Theory', *Millennium*, vol. 17, no. 1, 1988, pp. 91–5.

7 NO LONGER 'A TOURNAMENT OF DISTINCTIVE KNIGHTS'? SYSTEMIC TRANSITION AND THE PRIORITY OF INTERNATIONAL ORDER

N. J. RENGGER

That we should be born in interesting times is, of course, a well-known curse. By this standard we have been well cursed indeed in the late 1980s. In this chapter I shall attempt to pick out some trends from the 1980s and suggest which might be most important in the consideration of what I would claim is one of the most crucial areas of contemporary international politics – the problem of international and world order.

There are, unquestionably, an enormous range of events that would be relevant to any consideration of this question and I do not pretend that this chapter touches upon them all. My intention is rather more modest. It is to sketch an approach to the question of international order in the 1990s rooted in what I take to be the relevant trends of world politics manifested in the 1980s. In the course of this I shall look also at some other approaches to this question with which I differ. Most especially, I shall glance briefly at three general positions on the question of international and world order that I characterise, with all due recognition of the likely simplifications and distortions such characterisation involves, as Realist, Institutionalist and Critical.

Order and world politics in the 1980s

Order is traditionally one of the most fundamental concerns of international relations. There has been a longstanding view that international politics does not really display order at all, but more usually the existence, establishment and maintenance of international order has been recognised as a vital concern of theorists and practitioners of international relations from at least the sixteenth century onwards.[1] Where there is no overall authority, no Leviathan to institute and sanction the rules that create order, then clearly how order emerges, if at all, is a vital question in the explanation and consideration of international politics.

In modern times a distinction has grown up between international order and world order. Hedley Bull, one of the writers who has most fruitfully explored the concept of order in world politics, has defined them in the following manner: 'By world order I mean those patterns or dispositions of human activity that sustain the elementary or primary goals of social life among mankind as a whole'.[2] 'By international order', he writes, 'I mean a pattern of activity that sustains the elementary or primary goals of a society of states, or international society'.[3] He also believes that the former is crucially prior to the latter: 'World Order ... is not only wider than international order, or order among states but also more fundamental and primordial than it, and morally prior to it'.[4]

As John Vincent has pointed out, Bull's view has a long pedigree but it also has several critics. E. H. Carr, for example, characteristically defines order as 'the doctrine of satisfied powers'.[5] While order may involve satisfying powers (and may certainly be maintained by satisfied powers) I think that Bull is correct to attribute something more to it. We need only look to the sense in which the term has been deployed recently to understand that, at least putatively, it is intended to carry a wider normative meaning than Carr would allow it.[6] To this extent I think that Bull has provided the best general description of the difference between two crucial senses of order in world politics, though we shall have to modify his claims a little later on.

Bull believes that international order is maintained primarily by the balance of power and international law, the actions of each being largely determined by the great powers of the day in six distinct ways. These are:

(1) preserving the general balance of power;
(2) seeking to avoid or control crises in their relations;
(3) seeking to limit or contain wars;
(3) unilaterally exploiting any local preponderance they might have;
(5) agreeing to respect each others spheres of influence;
(6) occasional joint action as in a great power concert.[7]

Let us look for a moment at the experience of the 1980s with these categories in mind. The collapse of the Soviet hegemony in Eastern Europe in 1989 and the growing internal crisis of the Soviet state itself has made manifest what is certainly the serious weakening, if not the complete collapse, of one of the two 'poles' that allegedly dominated the world after 1945. The remaining 'superpower' (a term that might have outlived its usefulness) while still hugely powerful, seems uncertain of what this development implies. The United States also, of course, faces huge domestic problems, for example, drugs, crime, debt and a decaying social infrastructure. It therefore faces an uncertain future both domestically and internationally.

The events of the 1980s have had tremendous knock-on effects. In Europe, for example, these events, including the unification of Germany, have resulted in changes that will affect the future of European security and international politics for many years.[8] In the Middle East, the ending of the Cold War and the thaw in relations between the United States and the Soviet Union has permitted the largest overseas deployment of US troops since the end of World War Two and a war that, had it been fought five years ago, might have brought the world to the brink of nuclear catastrophe, if it had happened at all.[9] Moreover, the last decade has seen the re-emergence of Islam as a potent political force in the Middle East and elsewhere.[10] In East Asia and the Pacific the rise of 'trading states' like Singapore, Taiwan, Hong Kong, South Korea and, most importantly, Japan has helped to bring about the gradual erosion of US economic dominance in the region, while Soviet military redeployments and changing foreign policy agenda coupled with the rise of China as both a military and an economic power have all helped to produce a changing balance of power in this region.[11]

In all these cases it has seemed as if traditional patterns of international politics might be breaking through after the forty-year freeze caused by the Cold War and the consequent bipolar structure of international relations. We have seen a weakening (at the very least) in the need for the US to 'balance' its great power rival, due to the internal and external weakness of that rival. The avoidance of overt conflict is partly due to the USSR's 'new thinking' and at least partial change of attitude (despite the strains that, for example, the Gulf War put on it). Equally the USSR has given up its 'local preponderance' in Eastern Europe, spheres of influence (NATO, the Warsaw Pact) have either unravelled or begun to do so and the US and the USSR have worked more cooperatively together than at any time since the end of the Second World War, notwithstanding the very real differences that still exist between them. Examples are the negotiations over the ending of the Iran–Iraq war, the independence of Namibia and on issues such as arms control.[12]

The result of these shifts has been, some say, a return to 'business as usual': the politics of multipolarity. We are told that this will mean that the future will be like the past; in the words of one advocate of this position, John Mearsheimer, we are heading 'Back to the Future' as far as the international system is concerned. Frozen into an artificial bipolarity for the last forty years, the system will return to its more common multipolar shape and, as a result, its former problems will become familiar once again, to add to the new ones.[13]

Conversely, however, events have also encouraged the hope that the international institutions that the victorious allies set up after the Second World War, most particularly the United Nations, may now be in a position to actually work as their creators intended them to and that a new era of international cooperation may be at hand.[14] If so, then it has come none too soon, for the 1980s has seen the emergence of issues of a global provenance. The environment and ecological concerns while present for some time became major issues on the international agenda. These concerns, diseases like AIDS, instances of starvation in parts of Africa (currently nearly 20 million in Sudan, Ethiopia, Liberia, Angola and Mozambique) and a massive and rapidly expanding refugee problem in many parts of the world seemed to reinforce a growing sense that we were all part of (as one BBC series put it) 'One World' and that, therefore, traditional ways of managing international relations are no longer appropriate.

On either of these readings, the international system and, as a consequence, the nature of international order as we have experienced it over the last four and half decades is said to be changing. The first view, largely (though by no means exclusively) adopted by 'Realist' analysts of the international system, suggests that while it is clear that the pattern of international events suggest a qualitative change, it is a change that is taking place within relatively familiar parameters. As Robert Gilpin has suggested:

> The distribution of power among states constitutes the principal form of control in every international system. The dominant states and empires in every international system organize and maintain the network of political, economic, and other relationships within the system and especially in their respective spheres of influence. Both individually and in interaction with one another those states that historically have been called the great powers and are known today as the superpowers establish and enforce the basic rules and rights that influence their own behaviour and that of the lesser states in the system.[15]

Note that Gilpin does two things of especial interest here. First, he suggests that not just processes and behaviour but 'rights' are set by the great powers and, secondly, he equates great powers with superpowers. On this latter point he agrees with (non-Realist) writers like Hedley Bull but distances himself from Realists like Morgenthau, who have argued that, whereas a great power 'is a state which is able to have its will against a small state which in turn is not able to have its will against a great power', a superpower is 'a great power which has no rival capable of preventing it from imposing its will upon small powers'.[16] The logic of this position, of course, is that there can be only one superpower which suggests that Morgenthau saw the notion of a superpower as being akin to hegemony. This is not, however, the sense in which it has been traditionally used in the postwar period.

This view concludes that, *pace* Bull, it is international order which is prior to world order, indeed, that international order is all there truly is, at least as long as the system continues in its present form. Realists of this sort stress that international order must be prior to any other systemic considerations. As one such analyst, Henry Kissinger, has put it 'if history teaches anything, it is that there can be no peace without equilibrium and no justice without restraint'.[17] This view emphasises the fragility of order and thereby provides a justification of attempts to preserve it, if necessary by force. Order in world politics is thus dependent on a precariously maintained balance between states. International order is a desired end in world politics because it provides the opportunities for social life within states to go on relatively untouched by the anarchy that blows, chill and unchecked, in international relations. It is a moral end for the same reason. Without it neither domestic social existence nor international exchange could take place at all and those places that are least stable and least ordered, in this sense, are precisely the places where environments conducive to other human goods do not exist (a case in point might be the contemporary Middle East).[18]

Such order can only be maintained by great powers, though certainly they are a necessary but not a sufficient condition of international order. Thus the major powers of the contemporary international system rightly seek to cooperate more fully with one another but such cooperation can only be properly understood as an element in a complex structure in which the primary tools are still the traditional ones: influence, coercion and eventually, if necessary, war. World politics is still a 'tournament of distinctive knights', where the knights compete on the 'strategic-diplomatic chessboard' for power, prestige, influence and security.[19] Thus the law of chivalry for this tournament is the language of great power politics.

The second view suggests that the major characteristics of the contemporary system are in important respects new and original and that, as a consequence, our notion of order in world politics must change from the aforementioned concentration on international order

149

to a concern with world order. This view has a very wide set of assumptions which can vary, according to taste, from the ethical to the political to the economic. Most commonly, this view is that associated with liberals or institutionalists though the terminology is somewhat hazy.[20]

On this view, the 1980s were the decade when the originality of the situation we now find ourselves in was made unambiguously clear. This originality is manifested in a number of different ways and it is worth emphasising them.[21] The contemporary system is the first world-wide system; it is the first system in which the possibility for complete global societal extinction exists through nuclear, biospherical or environmental effects; it is a system characterised by the highest ever degree of social, cultural, economic and technological inter-dependence. Indeed, the levels of the system are now so differentiated that at least one writer (Rosenau) talks of the emergence of a 'post-international' politics, profound changes in the nature of world politics driven by the turbulence aroused by the clash of centralising and decentralising forces which has now produced two worlds of world politics, a state-centric world and a multi-centric world.[22]

Many liberal or institutionalist writers would not go this far. All would claim, however, that there are sufficient new factors to make existing structures of both international and world order deeply problematic and that, therefore, we must modify talk of transitions from 'bipolarity' to 'multipolarity' if this transition is seen merely as a change in degree rather than a change in kind. We must try to erect both a world order that provides proper support for 'the goals of social life among mankind as a whole' and an international order that reflects this. The agenda here, therefore, is that in the 1990s we must, for example, look at the opportunities open for multilateralism, the growth and development of international regimes and institutions and prospects for conflict resolution and amelioration where the elements of the traditional agenda of international order are still powerfully present (as they often will be).[23] To do this we can and will use many of the traditional concepts and tools of international rela-tions but we must also realise that we are using them in a new situation and that therefore, to use just one example, the transition of Europe from a bipolar world (the Cold War) does not automatically mean the return of 'multipolarity', if by that is meant traditional balance of power politics, after the practice of the European great powers of the nineteenth century. Too much else has changed for this to be the likely result.[24] A good example of this sort of reasoning, from the neo-Realist end of the institutionalist spectrum, is Lawrence Freedman's recent argument that a new situation has arisen with regard to the expectations of the use of military force; and a second, this time quite close in certain respects to critical theory, is Ken Booth's recent articulation of a 'Utopian realism'.[25]

This brings me to the third view that has come more sharply into focus in the 1980s. I shall call this view 'critical' and subsume within it, for the purposes of this discussion of international order, various alternative, radical and interpretive approaches to international relations. It would include writers as otherwise diverse as Robert Cox, Richard Ashley, Richard Falk, R. B. J. Walker, James Der Derian, Andrew Linklater, Mark Hoffman and, in certain respects and on certain issues, some of my own work.[26] Essentially it agrees with the second view that the position we now find ourselves in is in important respects new and original, but adopts a rather different set of strategies for relating this realisation to questions of international and world order. It tends to emphasise a complete change in the system (or at least of perceptions of it and actions within it) rather than the ameliatory prescriptions of the second view. As will be seen, however, on the question that concerns me here, I take a somewhat different tack.

I think that each of these three views have something to recommend them but each also contains significant weaknesses. In what way this is so will become clearer after I have outlined my own view of the changes within the international system in the 1980s.

Order and stability in the international system in the 1980s

In what I want to say here, I start with the assumption that, at the very least, changes in technology, the spread of information, the expansion of the states system to what Martin Wight called a 'closed' states system (i.e. there is no state or body that is, in principle outside it) and the globalisation of the world economy have produced a situation so different from the world of the nineteenth century that whatever change occurs, a simple repetition of 'multipolarity' in the sense implied by Mearsheimer, for example, is highly improbable.[27]

There are also, I think, clear senses in which the situation as we have seen it develop in the 1980s possesses features that do not fit state-centric models of world politics at all. The main stress of the second view lies rightly on the change in social and political structures that interdependence is alleged to be encouraging. For example, Keohane and Nye, in the second edition of their rightly acclaimed *Power and Interdependence*, point out that their intention was to integrate aspects

151

of the Realist and the liberal traditions and that, therefore, they do not disregard the power of states or the role of individuals or organisations. They merely say that these two must be understood in a framework of institutions which shape preferences and policies.[28] Regimes, at least when they work well, perform four valuable functions. They facilitate burden sharing, provide information to governments, help great powers to keep multiple and varied interests from getting in each other's diplomatic way and they introduce greater discipline into foreign policy.[29]

This type of argument, as is also the case with other similar analyses, such as Stanley Hoffmann's, depends crucially on the assumption, not always explicitly stated, that the structure of the system *as a whole* is changing under the impetus of the developments they outline.[30] Hence Keohane and Nye's subtitle *'World Politics* in transition' (emphasis added). James Rosenau, on the other hand, believes that the multi-centric world has evolved 'independently of the one in which states function' and he seeks 'to avoid the "interdependence accounts for disarray" tendency by pointing to new organising principles, structures, and processes in this multi-centric world that are no less patterned and effective than those of the state-centric world'.[31]

However, I would suggest that the evidence of the 1980s raises very serious questions about both versions. For example, there are many different types of states in contemporary world politics. While technically (i.e. legally) all states may be the same, in fact their functions and purposes as well as their capabilities and structures seem to be divergent. One does not have to go so far as Elie Kedourie and call the new states 'imitation states', to recognise that many states in the contemporary world possess structures that have very different functions in practice, if not always in theory (though sometimes here too), than the European nation-state in whose image they were created.[32] One writer, Robert Jackson, has recently suggested that certain states in the international system be termed 'quasi-states' as they bear only juridical sovereignty, rather than actual sovereignty.[33] This raises questions about how far it is any longer even appropriate to assume an unambiguous state-centric world at all. Jackson's argument goes on to suggest that, in certain respects, we have seen two competing worlds of sovereignty develop since the Second World War. These are positive sovereignty, the traditional understanding of international relations, and negative sovereignty, that which obtains, very largely, in the developing world.

Somewhat analogously, Peter Calvocoressi has argued that of the two most crucial changes in world politics since the end of the First

World War the process of decolonisation (the other is the invention of nuclear weapons) has changed 'both the ambit and the nature' of the international system. 'The erstwhile colonies have become areas of opportunity: opportunity spells competition: competition has an aggressive edge.'[34] Calvocoressi argues that due to these features 'the flux of international politics is back', a quite clear 'return to multipolarity argument' but he also emphasises that the 'states' that have been created will often have a completely different agenda than those he terms the 'big boys' who have a 'League (of Nations)' mentality concerned with war and how to prevent it. 'Like the world it mirrors', he writes, 'the UN contains big boys and lesser fry ... by and large the big boys have what may be called a league mentality, while the lesser fry have an UNCTAD mentality. The former see the UN as an instrument for peace, the latter as an instrument for justice or equity.'[35]

This analysis assumes a degree of what we might call linear change in the international system which fits the first view I sketched above rather better than the second. One could argue also that the events of the 1980s have, in fact, made both the two key determinants that Calvocoressi mentions somewhat out of date. The emergence of new states has surely given way as a problem to their maintenance, character and mutual relations. It is not *that* the system has changed that is now at issue but *how*.

Two conclusions can be drawn, however. Firstly, 'international order' in such a system is going to be increasingly difficult to maintain over the longer term since it requires 'a pattern of activity that sustains the elementary or primary goals of a society of states'. While it is probably true to say that the institutional arrangements of the international system provide a good deal of the requisite underpinning for this, the 'pattern of activity' is likely to be increasingly difficult to maintain given that (differentiated) states have different and often incompatible primary goals.

Secondly, the different patterns of activity that are likely to emerge have a good deal to do with the fragmentation of the notion of international society, the conceptual and ideological fragmentation of world politics since 1945, made obvious in the 1980s.[36] One of the key assumptions of Keohane and Nye's model of complex interdependence, for example, is that the multiplicity of goals and difficulty of arranging them hierarchically are the results of the long-term development of the welfare state and the consequent relevance of the many dimensions and definitions of economic welfare.[37] As a description of the advanced industrial states this has some force but if it is meant to stand as an argument for the transformation of world politics ('world

153

politics in transition' as the subtitle says) then its suppressed premise is the claim that the rest of the world is increasingly going to resemble the West, at least in developing a bureaucratised welfare state and the type of political economy that that brings with it.

This claim is highly disputable as, for example, increasing resentment at Western models of economic development, not just their structure or rationale but their entire rationality, show.[38] In its most extreme form such resentment can be seen in some of the attitudes of the groups in Iran that overthrew the Shah and continue to play an important part in Middle Eastern politics in Iran, Lebanon and elsewhere.[39] James Piscatori, in one of the most thoughtful recent studies of the relationship of Islam to nationalism and the international system, has pointed out that there has evolved a consensus over the last few centuries in Islamic thought that accepts at least the principle of territorial pluralism, but he has also emphasised the degree of challenge that has arisen to that consensus from (at the moment) largely Shi'a sources. His warning is a salutary one: 'Feeling that Islam's decline is due chiefly to the adoption of Western ideas and culture, all express pessimism and suggest a radical restructuring of the world order.'[40] Different versions of this dissent are observable in other key areas of the international system, for example East Asia, where, at least in the view of some scholars, a rather different path is being mapped out which, while not currently as inimical to Western norms, might easily develop that way.[41]

This gives rise to a further and uncomfortable observation. It suggests that whatever the status of the pattern of activity that marks out the terrain of the society of states there must be a very large question mark over the 'pattern of activity' that is supposed to be prior to it. *Pace* Theodore Von Laue it does not seem to be that *The World Revolution of Westernization* has 'completed its work' and there is precious little evidence that it can be relied upon to do so.[42] As Adda Bozeman has rightly commented: 'In the absense of a common language, a common pool of memories, and shared ways of thinking, reasoning and communicating, it is hard to fathom a "world culture" ... the evidence points instead to a plurality of frames of reference.'[43] Thus, while it is certainly true that many Western norms, ideas and practices have (contingently) become universal, many have not, and even those that have a near universal character have hugely different manifestations. Human rights, for example, a Western idea now enshrined in a universal charter, are manifested and understood in many different ways.[44] The idea of the state may now be universal but, as I have already said, the character, purpose and type of states are

154

hugely diverse. This rise of ideological and cultural fragmentation and plurality in world politics makes it clear that there is fundamental disagreement over what counts as a 'basic pattern of activity' that would sustain the goals of social life as such because there is equally fundamental disagreement about what these goals are. At the same time, interdependence and technological change potentially make the incidence of conflict and competition greater and potentially more deadly. Thus, the growing instability of world politics in the late 1980s, however much we might welcome aspects of it (the renaissance of Eastern Europe for instance, or the reduction in the threat of gen- eralised nuclear war) is, in this sense, a foretaste of things to come.

This brings me to an important distinction that I should like to emphasise, that between stability and order. Stability is not the same as order in international relations, for all the fact that they are very often conflated. I have already offered a definition of order in world politics, let me now offer one for stability. Stability here should be understood to imply an international system that is not prone to violent disputes at least among the great powers (the powers that should maintain inter- national order as well as international stability). Thus, the events discussed above do indicate, I think, that world politics is becoming less stable at a global level (i.e. more volatile and given to peaks and troughs) but this, in and of itself, is not a threat to international order. Lack of stability and/or an increase in conflict is not *ceteris paribus* particularly problematic for international order, as I have been using the term here. It is usually, of course, unpleasant and often deplorable but it is a threat to international order if, and only if, particular conflicts threaten, either directly or indirectly, the underpinnings of the inter- national system itself, i.e. 'the pattern of activity' that sustains the society of states. Thus, clear hegemonic ambitions or a drive to imperium would clearly constitute such a threat as would a potential collapse of the society itself.

The analysis I have offered here suggests that these sorts of conflicts might arise in the medium to long term because of the difficulty of all the disparate actors in the system agreeing to 'a pattern of activity' that would, in fact, support the 'primary goals' of the society of states because there is decreasing agreement over what those goals might be. This is also true at the level of world order. Thus the problem for the foreseeable future seems to me how to strengthen and maintain inter- national order while trying to arrive at an understanding of world order that would permit changes in international order to reflect the emergence of a pattern of activity that supports global social life. Bull suggests that the prospects for both international and world order are

155

bound up with the existence of and the strengthening of international society, involving 'among other things ... the preservation and extension of a cosmopolitan culture, embracing both common ideas and common values and rooted in societies in general as well as in their elites'.[45] However, as we have seen, such a society is largely conspicuous by its absence at present. I infer from this that, while it is not impossible to build such a society and that all attempts should be made to do so, we cannot rely on it in our current position to provide the societal glue of which Bull speaks. The logic of this, however, is that while the circumstances of which Nye, Keohane, Hoffmann and others speak are real enough, the wherewithall to create 'world order' is at present illusory, if by that we mean an understanding of, and pattern of activity conducive to, general social life as such. Obviously, therefore, this places a greater weight on the practice of international order. Here there is at least some residual 'society' (albeit a problematic one) but the international order must be understood in terms of the changing nature of the system not as though that system has remained unaltered by the social, economic, cultural and technological changes of the twentieth century.

Bull's belief that world order is morally (and, we might say) lexically prior to international order is, therefore, mistaken. A pattern of activity designed to support the goals of social life as such needs to be anchored in a coherent vision of what such goals might be. In the absence of this at a global level in the current context the 'goals of social life', as such, must, I think, be perceived largely as things to avoid. It must needs take account of issues like AIDS, threats to the environment, the spread and possible use of nuclear weapons and so on. These concerns, however, are inevitably activities of international order also. The focus of international order will remain different – its referents being fictive persons rather than real ones – but the effect of a failure of international order would be disastrous for any hope of achieving world order as well as for elements within the society of states.

Decline and 'The New World Order': the priority of international order

The above analysis, then, suggests that a two-fold strategy should be pursued in the 1990s. We should try, in so far as it is possible, to reach agreement on those areas which pose the most obvious threats to the 'basic patterns of social life as such' and seek to implement measures that avoid at least the worst excesses of these threats. It should be clear, however, that this is not really a conception of world order in Bull's terms, not a pattern of activity conducive to (in a positive sense) social life, rather it is a set of incremental measures designed, usually *ad hoc*, in order to avoid a complete breakdown of social life. These measures will be partial, incomplete and not always successful but they remain a priority. They might include, for example, the establishment of an environmental control regime which could act as a general body to oversee and guide efforts in this area and coordinate measures to enhance and build on the existing thirty-five general international agreements in the environmental field and the countless running conferences. Most probably this could best be performed under the auspices of the United Nations Environmental Programme (UNEP), already the biggest organisation in the field and responsible for a wide range of activities.[46] It should not be supposed that such a regime could be created without costs, especially for the major industrialised states, but the costs of not establishing such a regime are likely to be far higher over the longer term given the likely effect of the failure to do so on global social life as a whole. On the logic of this chapter, therefore (and leaving aside any other ethical imperatives) the costs should be borne. Similar observations could be made apropos other similar problems such as the AIDS pandemic.

To this extent the logic of institutionalist and critical theorists is relatively sound. Indeed, the critical perspective seems to me to offer more here since it has, as its fundamental *raison d'être* the rethinking of the categories of our international political experience. However, attempts to go beyond this and to find something else that is 'common' that could define or delineate the 'pattern of activity' for global social life seems to me, at the present at least, to be highly unpromising. Although I understand and am sympathetic to its motivation I am rather sceptical about the so-called 'cosmopolitan' view within theories of international relations, represented, for example, by pluralist liberals like Charles Beitz and by critical theorists like Andrew Linklater or Mark Hoffman.[47] This is not the place to fully adumbrate such scepticism, of course, but it rests on a rather more pessimistic assessment of the possibilities for a 'cosmopolitan' view of the world that might serve as a basis of global social life which in its turn rests on a view of the relative intractability and deep-rootedness of cultural, regional, ideological and national traditions and ways of acting and a belief that these will sometimes be in conflict. To transpose Martin Wight's famous comment that 'war is inevitable though particular wars can be avoided', while I think that particular instances of cultural or evaluative conflict can be mitigated, mediated or avoided I suspect

157

that, at least for the foreseeable future, such conflict itself cannot be (though this does not mean that war or violence will necessarily result from such conflict, however).[48]

This assumption leads me to suggest two things. First, that in addition to the above measures we should try and come to terms with this inevitable plurality of voices in our international system and what it implies for us. Secondly, it does, I think, place a greater emphasis on the problems of international order, in Bull's terms, than most critical theorists or liberal/institutionalists have suggested.[49]

In this respect, then, the fundamental question for international order in the 1990s is how we assess the character of the changes that are taking place as potential threats to it and how we might manage, shape and constrain them. Perhaps the first question to ask in this context is whether, for example, the ebbing of the Cold War and the rise of new centres of power in the international system (Japan, China, the EC) prefaces a threat to international order in the short to medium term?

Shifts in the power and capabilities of great powers is a usual cause of systemic instability, as Paul Kennedy, Robert Gilpin and George Modelski have all, in their different ways, recently chronicled.[50] Thus, the rise of other centres of power and influence will change the equations that might effect international stability in the 1990s. As Martin Wight might have put it, changes in the patterns of power observable in world politics will affect the balance of power but not in any determinate way.[51] It is the way it will do so that we must attempt to assess as far as threats to international order are concerned.

That there is such a rise is not, I think, disputable. The five states, or in one case confederation of states, that Kennedy mentions as the likely poles of the new 'multipolar world', the US, USSR, Japan, China and the European community are, without question the major centres of decision in world politics even if we have doubts about the efficacy or will on some of their parts.[52] These doubts have certainly been increased, for example, by the political crisis that exploded in Japan over its possible contribution to Operations Desert Shield and Desert Storm and by the differences of opinion the crisis revealed in the European Community, but the growing influence and power of these regions at least politically and economically is not in doubt.[53]

There are questions, however, as to the significance of this rise. With the possible exception of China, none of the new centres of power seems likely to want to challenge the basic 'pattern of activity' that supports the society of states in its present form. Europe, the US and Japan have serious differences over trade policy and will, no doubt, have differences of opinion as serious as those over the Gulf on other foreign policy issues in the 1990s. This might lead to increased volatility in (for example) the international financial system. Of course, such increasing conflict between established centres of power and newer ones is likely to make the international system less stable and more prone to fluctuation and conflict. The crisis in the GATT talks in December 1990, for example, has been taken as evidence of a growing degree of economic conflict between states that were previously much more willing to subsume economic difficulties or disagreements for reasons of political or military security.[54] Such conflict among major power centres (even if we do not want to use the term great powers) will, I suspect, increase in the 1990s and this will lead to greater instability. However, none of the above states have an interest in challenging the 'pattern of activity' that sustains the system itself. Were there to be a major collapse of the international system, perhaps the long-feared (and over-hyped) 'return to the 1930s', then that might well lead to powers becoming disenchanted with the nature of the system itself and, as a consequence, attempting to change it.[55] This is not imminent, however, and it seems unlikely that short of a catastrophic breakdown in relations between these three actors, it is a realistic possibility.[56]

The case of China is slightly different. As Gerald Segal has pointed out 'there are disturbing signs that in the medium term China is likely to pose a challenge to international stability'.[57] It is an increasingly influential actor in events in Africa and the Middle East, a powerful and well equipped arms trader and a growing military presence in its own region. It also has a whole series of regional territorial disputes, the most important of which involves Taiwan, some of which have resulted in considerable military action over the last decade (over, for example, the Spratly Islands, Vietnam and Cambodia) as well as a potential arms race with Japan. Coupled with the fear engendered in the ruling elite by the events of 1989 these events make it quite possible that China may be a power whose commitment to both international stability and international order are at best questionable.[58] However, for the moment at least, and in the short term, it seems that its threat to stability in the East Asian region is likely to be considerably greater than its threat to international order more generally.

In any case, the linchpin, it seems to me, of the debates about what this systemic change will result in as far as international order is concerned has been the parallel debate over the alleged decline in US power and, to a lesser degree, that over the much more precipitate decline in Soviet power.[59] In these discussions the assumption has

159

been that it is not only the rise of new centres of power that is potentially most threatening as far as international order is concerned but this coupled with the weakening or collapse of the established ones and the relative shifts in power that might occur as a result.

The case that the US is in decline has been associated most recently, of course, with Paul Kennedy.[60] His view, that in the long term the US is bound to decline, does not lead him to make facile judgements about the pace or rate of that decline. He bases his view on a detailed analysis of the relationship between military and economic factors, as he puts it, the interaction between economics and strategy, over a 500 year timespan. He concludes that the United States is in relative decline, though that decline is not inevitable and not irreversible. The US has the same array of obligations as it did twenty-five years ago but its share of world GNP, manufacturing production, military spending and population have declined markedly, giving rise to what Kennedy terms 'imperial overstretch' and what has otherwise been referred to as 'The Lippman Gap', an imbalance of resources and capabilities with obligations and commitments.[61]

Many writers have, of course, taken a contrary view. Joseph Nye, for example, has persuasively argued that the view that the US is declining fails to address the changing nature of the international system and, therefore, of the character of international and national power. As a result, the sort of analysis offered by Kennedy and others, while interesting and important in its own right, cannot be sustained as a predictor of likely US decline in the short to medium term.[62] For Nye, US leadership in the international system is still possible and desirable.

It is obvious, of course, that the thesis of decline is compatible with a Realist view. Writers such as Gilpin have emphasised that 'power transition', as he calls it, has often prefigured major instability and eventually conflict and war.[63] Historically speaking this cannot be denied but its relevance to the question of international order is rather more obscure than might at first be supposed. As I suggested above, the fact of one state's possible decline and other states' potential rise *might* pose a threat to the required pattern of activity if one or more were seeking a preponderance of power within the system. If, in other words, they were seeking to upset the system in toto. This was arguably the case with Napoleon and more clearly the case with Hitler. It was often alleged to be the case with the Soviet Union. It is certainly not the case now. Whatever the desires of the alleged 'challengers' to the United States, a desire for territorial or even economic imperium does not seem to be present, at least not yet, even in the case of China.

This point makes clear, I think, the extent to which some commentators on this question have mistaken order for stability or defence of the status quo. Such a position is unfortunately widespread. It is observable, for instance, in a good deal of journalistic comment on the post-1989 international system and, perhaps rather more seriously, in political comment as well.[64] The claims that the 'New World Order' will be a 'unipolar' world (with the United States as the one pole) mistakes the existence of power and the maintenance of 'stability' (where this is perceived as a condition favourable to the US and its allies) with the existence and maintenance of international order. In fact, while it is fair to argue that the persistence of US power is necessary for international order (because without it there is likely to be a greater imbalance in relative power between power centres, hence more of a strain on stability and thence, over the longer term, on order as well) such a situation is not sufficient for international order.

Equally, however, claims that the important characteristic of the 'New World Order' will be predicated on the 'common principles of liberal democracy and market economics' and that the economic and environmental issues that have recently been so prominent will become the new currency of great power politics in place of military force need careful qualification.[65] It is, of course, true that these features of world politics are more important now than previously, as I have already stressed, but there are many other factors that need to be borne in mind. William McNeil, for example, has emphasised the importance of demographic change and has pointed out both the precedents and the logic of this being the engine behind renewed military aggression.[66] As Walt Rostow has recently pointed out, an appropriate metaphor for the next few years in international relations might be 'the coming age of regionalism'.[67] This will mean that, taken together with an exponentially growing and developing interdependence (Rosenau, accurately I think, calls it 'cascading' interdependence), other actors than merely the so-called great powers must have crucial roles in the maintenance and strengthening of international stability and, equally, in the potential for threatening it.[68] Regions that might not appear to be crucial for 'the great powers' (for example, South Asia or parts of Africa) will therefore be more important than previously they have been perceived to be, in their turn adding to the increasing globalisation of international order. If this is the case it also gives additional reasons for doubting the wisdom of constant appeals to what Charles Krauthammer has called 'the Unipolar moment'.[69] The United States may have to come to terms with the fact that if it wishes to act in a way supportive of international

161

order it must recognize the limitations on its power due simply to the increasing power of regional actors within their own regions and the multifaceted nature of the threats to contemporary international order. This will also mean, however, that the problem of international order cannot be ignored by those states or regions which have particular forms of government, i.e. liberal democracy and market economics. Fukuyama, for example, is right to stress the fact that future 'Gulf wars' are unlikely because it was a very unusual combination of circumstances that produced that of 1991, but he is wrong to say that, therefore, 'few regions will have an impact – for good or ill – on the growing part of the world that is democratic and capitalist'.[70] Interdependence means just that – the world is becoming much less able to treat overseas problems as events 'in a far away country of which we know nothing'.

This makes it relevant for a moment to turn back to Nye's critique of the decline thesis. One of his chief assumptions is that the transformation of power has transformed the problematic for the United States (and by implication for other powers also). He puts it this way: 'the critical question for the future United States ... [is] ... to what extent it will be able to control the political environment and to get other nations to do what it wants ... the problem for the United States will be less the rising challenge of another major power than a general diffusion of power'.[71]

This power diffusion is, of course, brought about by the growth of interdependence and, if Kennedy's case can be seen as compatible at least with Realism then Nye's is broadly, and unsurprisingly, compatible with an institutionalist case. Nye suggests that the change in the nature of world politics means that 'power is becoming less fungible, less coercive and less tangible' and he introduces the notion of 'soft power' to express this change. As he says, this idea – incorporating cultural attraction, ideology and international institutions – is not new, it is simply much more important than ever before due to the originality of the contemporary international system. The conclusion of Nye's analysis is that if the United States is to retain its influence in world politics it must recognise the change that has taken place and that, as a result, this will force a growing concern with what Bull called 'world order', i.e. patterns of activity that sustain the primary goals of social life as a whole as well as international order. The significance of this is that the logic of Nye's case is that in order for this to occur there must be changes in our understanding and practice of international order.[72]

Order against Babel: a strategy for international order in the 1990s

As I indicated above, I would certainly agree with the stress on the aspects of originality in the current position. However, the inter-relationship between the changing circumstances within world politics and changing perceptions and understandings of world politics will require not simply a gentle tinkering with the practices that might maintain world order but a radical adjustment of some of the most well established institutions in the international system. This is where Realism is least able to adapt to the changing circumstances of the international system. It is also the case that many institutionalists have similar difficulties here, partly due to their tendency to concentrate on the chimera of 'world order' (whether of a new or an old kind).

Let me look at some of the most obvious institutions of the international system in the light of this statement. War, perhaps the oldest and certainly the most problematic institution of the classical states system, must be seen in a very different light than it has been as an instrument of international order. This is not to subscribe to John Mueller's view that major war is obsolete, though Mueller is right to trace a decline in the sense in which war is an acceptable policy option under *ceteris paribus* conditions.[73] Nor is it to subscribe to the view that democracies are necessarily more peace-loving than other forms of government and that, as a consequence, the increasing democrati-sation of world politics implies a decline in conflict.[74] It is merely to point out that given the fragility of the international society that underlies international order and given also the changing conditions of the international system, violent efforts to resolve conflicts are much less likely than under different conditions to secure order rather than merely to bolster, probably temporarily, stability (and will very often not do this either).[75] Here again, the protagonists of the 'new world order' seem either to overestimate the ability of war to achieve its aims in the contemporary context (Krauthammer, Kennedy) or underesti-mate the sense in which war is still a very real problem even for supposedly 'safe' liberal democracies (Fukuyama, Doyle, Keohane and Nye). In part this is also due to the fact that the language we use to talk about war is badly in need of reform. The scholars who have begun this process are largely those inclined towards a post-modern reading of the subject, but as yet the area is little explored.[76]

As with war, so with other well-known aspects of the traditional pattern of state behaviour (particularly great power behaviour). Alli-ances, for example, are clearly still a crucial instrument in international

163

politics but their purpose has traditionally been concerned with stability (either to maintain it or overturn it), I suggest, and only secondarily with order. As Stephen Walt has shown, the tendency is for states to ally in response to perceived threats and they generally balance rather than bandwagon.[77] However, such behaviour might, under certain conditions, threaten rather than maintain the pattern of activity conducive to the survival of the society of states. It might thus undermine international order rather than contribute to it. A concern for international order cannot therefore rely upon such 'traditional' instruments of interstate action as 'the balance of power' (even if it is actually, as Walt thinks, a 'balance of threat') to help maintain order; another reason for questioning readings of the contemporary system which suggest that we are seeing a 'return to multipolarity' (and all that is said to go with it).

These considerations and the emergence of the new issues mentioned above (drugs, AIDS, the environment etc.) will therefore require a change in the hierarchy of threats to international order. After all, a society of states can be destroyed as easily by plague, famine and death as by war. This will mean that to maintain international order, states will have to cooperate more than might have been the case in the past and that the stakes of failure will be correspondingly higher.

A further area where care will be needed is in the area of domestic regime change. As Andrew Hurrell, for example, has pointed out, there is more than a whiff of Western triumphalism in the air at the way that events moved in the late 1980s and an increasing segment of opinion has been won over to the view that the way that international stability and order is best maintained is by giving support, economic, institutional and, if necessary military (either overt or covert), to establish or support democratic government.[78] Moreover, there seems to be something of a convergence between Realists and institutionalists on this point. Even some critical theorists seem to incline towards this position.[79]

There are a number of problems with this. To begin with, of course, such a strategy has probably the maximum chance of providing states with a reason for changing the system or for being dissatisfied with its effects on them. While it is a perfectly fair position to suggest that states should trade with who they want to and on conditions that are mutually acceptable (and if democratic state A wishes to trade only with other democratic states, so be it) or in principle to welcome the emergence of representative, constitutional regimes (as in Eastern Europe), it is rather a different argument to suggest that large, powerful democratic state A should insist that poor, underdeveloped state B change its undemocratic system of government in return, for example, for aid. Leaving aside the thorny question of exactly how you define 'democratic' in this (or any other) context, such a practice strikes me as flying directly in the face of two of the most important conclusions of this chapter: that we learn to accept plurality and difference in the international system, and that we should try to strengthen international society and thence international order, and not develop practices that gratuitously undermine it.[80]

A second reason for caution is that it is by no means unambiguously clear that democracies, simply by virtue of their domestic political structure, will necessarily be in any better position that any other type of regime to pursue effective policies supportive of international order. It is not inconceivable, indeed, that the regimes most responsible to public opinion (as democracies tend to be) are also most likely to be those regimes which have the greatest difficulty pursuing policies that create short-term costs but have long-term gains. If, as I have suggested, policies designed to support international order (conducive to the maintenance of the society of states, let us remember) will sometimes require states sacrificing short-term interest (as with the West subsidising other states on environmental pollution, for example) then getting public support, or even acquiescence, for such policies may be very difficult.

Of course this problem does not mean that democracy is not to be desired and that those of us fortunate enough to live under political systems called democratic should not be aware of our good fortune. It simply implies that we should exercise some restraint in making assumptions about the inevitability or desirability of rapid social change towards democracy in all places or at all times or that, if this occurs, it will necessarily be a good thing from the point of view of international order. This does not imply, of course, that anything goes nor that we have to approve of many of the regimes that share the earth with us. We can, indeed must, be consistent in opposing actions, policies or governments that add to the greater sum of human misery both because we may find such action ethically repugnant but also, and just as importantly, because such action is itself a likely barrier to international order and not an aid to it. It might, of course, be objected that as I have questioned our ability to define 'democratic' surely questions of human misery or ethical repugnance are at least equally problematic. To this I reply that in many respects they are but that it is not important in this context since 'democracy' is a form of social organisation whereas our actions within all forms of social organisation will be in part determined by our sense of ethically acceptable (or unacceptable) action. Since I think that international order is a necessary ethical aim under current conditions, to support it is ethically required action. To go too far into this area here would take me a long way from my main purpose in this chapter but to give the sense of what I mean let me consider two examples.

Of the various problems that have arisen directly as a result of the decline of the Cold War since 1989, I shall look at two that provide particularly interesting questions for students of international order. The first concerns the possibility of the secession of individual republics from the Soviet Union. In 1989 and 1990 this was most acute in the three Baltic republics that had been ruled by Moscow since the Second World War. When it was clear that there was considerable desire in all three republics to secede, the question arose, how should countries in the West, especially Europe and the United States, respond to these desires? The fear was that by welcoming and encouraging such developments President Gorbachev, still viewed as essential to the continuing East–West *rapprochement*, might be placed in an increasingly difficult position *vis-à-vis* his own conservative opposition. Moreover, it was widely reported that officials in, for example, the British Foreign Office and the US State Department were concerned less instability in the Baltic region and possible secession set off a chain reaction elsewhere that would threaten the fragile stability in the newly liberated Eastern Europe and perhaps the East–West relationship more widely.[81] Surely, one prominent trend of Western opinion suggested, it was as well to acquiesce in the Soviet desire to retain its Baltic possessions in order to maintain stability. However much the West might prefer a democratic and free Baltic region in principle, too much was at stake to risk rocking the boat for it in 1989 or 1990. An alternative position, also widely supported, was to suggest that as the West supported Gorbachev only so long as he was trying to democratise the Soviet Union, if he ceased to do that (i.e. did not let those republics that wanted to secede do so) then support for him was pointless anyway.

These two positions represent variants of the Realist and institutionalist positions already discussed. The former position is essentially a traditional Realist view, the latter could be defended on either realist or institutionalist grounds. The problem is that neither really considers the question from the standpoint of international order as I have used the term here. To do this we have to look at what we might identify as the basic pattern of activity that sustains the society of states. To begin with this must mean a principle of legitimacy. With James Mayall I think that it is a mistake to completely divorce the question of legitimacy in international politics from its provenance in domestic politics and in contemporary terms; this means that the essential principle of legitimacy is still sovereignty as defined through national self-determination.[82] A pattern of activity that supports this must accord due weight to national self-determination.[83] In the Baltic case, the first view suggested we sacrifice the Baltic states on the altar of potential future stability. This is clearly an activity that negates this principle of legitimacy and is consequently threatening to international order. Therefore, it should be opposed. The second view, while supportive of the notion of democracy (and therefore, presumably, of 'national self-determination') is ambiguous about the principle of sovereignty to which the self-determination principle must be wedded. Thus, while not necessarily opposed to international order its manifestations would need to be very carefully worked through in order to ensure that support for democracy does not turn into opposition to sovereignty and thence become such a threat. As Elie Kedourie has noted 'A government's title to rule cannot simply depend on a plebiscite ... plebiscites are shifting sands and the stability and good order of a society cannot be erected upon them.'[84] Quite: no more can that of international society.

If we turn to my second case, the Gulf war and its aftermath, we can see similar problems arising. The initial opposition of the international community to Iraq's invasion of Kuwait is perfectly easy to justify on grounds of international order (on traditional grounds, let it be noted; we do not need to posit a 'new world order' at all).[85] It is clearly threatening to the society of states to allow a recognised member of that society to be violently absorbed by a neighbour. That does not, of course necessitate particular forms of response. The type of response is at the discretion of the international community. The response that is followed should, however, itself be congruent with international order. There is always ground for legitimate disagreement, of course, but given what I said above about resort to war it does seem to me that war should only have been used after all other possible (and plausible) options had been exhausted. This does not appear to me to have been the case in this instance. That having been said, it is the situation that existed after the war that was perhaps most interesting for my present concern.

The appalling tragedy that afflicted the Kurdish people after the war posed a very stark choice for the coalition powers that had initiated the military response to Iraq's invasion of Kuwait. It became clear after only a relatively short time that the Iraqi forces were more than a match for the Kurdish and other rebels that opposed them. The question therefore arose: should the coalition powers, specifically the United States, be prepared to use military power to redress the balance and help prevent the collapse of the rebellion and the probable brutal repression of the Kurdish and Shi'a districts that had been in the forefront of it? The Bush administration's initial policy, supported by all its allies, was to emphasise that it had no UN mandate beyond the liberation of Kuwait and that it could not intervene in the internal affairs of Iraq as this violated international law.[86]

On the surface this might look like a policy in tune with international order. In fact, it is the most flagrant abandonment of such a policy. One can understand that President Bush and his allies had many conflicting pressures on them. Turkey and Syria (and Iran, though Iran was not part of the coalition) had powerful and vocal Kurdish minorities and would not want an independent Kurdistan; President Bush would not want to risk further US battle deaths and his own domestic popularity; the Soviet Union, having lurched back towards a more conservative stance, might not have accepted further military intervention with equanimity. All of these were important considerations. However, it is a longstanding aspect of international society that, as Christian Wolff put it, intervention is most justified when it is done on behalf of the *civitas maxima*, that is to say on behalf of the international community.[87] Moreover, there are a number of articles of the UN charter which could, in principle, legitimate action that involves intervention in the internal affairs of a member state.[88] Intervention is not, therefore, against international law. On the contrary, there are occasions when it would be a necessity. Would it, however, have been supportive of international order in the case of the Kurds? I think the answer is yes. Remembering what I said earlier about the principle of legitimacy in international and domestic politics being related, it cannot be supportive of the society of states to allow such gratuitous acts of brutality to go unpunished or, if it is possible (as in this case it was) unprevented. Such a view also draws on my earlier claim that in an interdependent world such behaviour is inevitably exceedingly dangerous as it *ipso facto* sucks in outside forces (as the Kurdish exodus inevitably did). In an interdependent world, and with apologies to Donne, no state is an island entire unto itself. All are a part of the main and, as such, are concerned with the internal, as well as the external practices of each other. Thus, taking a strong line against Iraq over the question of the Kurds would have been supportive of, not disruptive of, international order.

A strategy for international order for the 1990s must, therefore, concentrate on building a shared understanding of what 'patterns of activity' might constitute support for social life as such (however remote or difficult such a project might sound) but, primarily, on ensuring that in the meantime the structure of international order itself does not crumble but is maintained and, if possible, strengthened. To this extent the agenda of building and strengthening international regimes and institutions is indeed an important one. However, it must be seen for what it is: part – and only part – of a policy designed to keep an international system in transition afloat, with no guarantee that the passage will be easy or short. Moreover, the more important and by far the more difficult task, is to use the breathing space thus achieved to try to provide a grounding for human social life that can form a basis for 'world order' in a much more developed sense. However, this is likely to be successful only if the plurality of contemporary world politics is acknowledged and faced up to. We should remember, however, that the recognition of plurality does not accord *carte blanche* for any or all actions in a system. This plurality therefore need not resemble Babel. It will do so, however, if we think that we can build a conceptual tower in which to escape from it or overcome it. If it is true that the arrival of the millennium has the effect of concentrating peoples minds on both what should be preserved from the past and what should be hoped for in the future, then the arrival of this millennium, at least for students of international relations, might well have come none too soon.

Notes

I am very grateful for the comments of Robin Brown, Fred Halliday, Eric Herring, Steve Smith and Gerry Segal on earlier versions of this paper and for discussions with Andy Hurrell. None of them are, of course, responsible for the result.

 1 This tradition is part of the Realist tradition to which I shall turn in more detail in a moment. It is usually perceived as a 'Vulgar Realism', however, to be opposed by a more sophisticated version of realism with which I shall chiefly be concerned here. For a discussion of this see Robert Gilpin's article, 'The Global Political System' in R. J. Vincent and J. D. B. Miller (eds.), *Order and Violence: Hedley Bull and International Relations* (Oxford: Clarendon, 1990), especially p. 120. See for general discussions of order and international relations, Arnold Wolfers, *Discord and Collaboration* (Baltimore, MD: Johns Hopkins, 1962); Raymond Aron, *Peace and War* (New York: Praeger, 1967); Marcel Merle, *Sociologie Des Relations Internationales*, 4th edn (Paris: Dalloz, 1988).
 2 Hedley Bull, *The Anarchical Society: A Study of Order in World Politics* (London: Macmillan, 1977), p. 20.

3 *Ibid.*, p. 8.

4 *Ibid.*, p. 319.

5 See R. J. Vincent, 'Order in International Politics', in Vincent and Miller (eds.), *Order and Violence*, p. 44. Vincent expressly mentions Hume and the Stoics as being ancestors of this view of Bull. I would agree with Hume, up to a point, but would seek a much more recent starting point for the tradition in the thought of the early sixteenth century. E. H. Carr, *The Twenty Years Crisis* (London: Macmillan, 1939).

6 See for example the discussion in 'A New World Order', *Newsweek*, 11 March 1991.

7 Bull, *The Anarchical Society*, p. 207.

8 For a representative sample of the debate that these events have ignited see 'The Future of Europe: A Debate', *International Affairs*, vol. 66, no. 2, April 1990; see also Barry Buzan, et al., *The European Security Order Recast* (London: Pinter, 1990); William Wallace (ed.), *The Dynamics of European Integration* (London: Pinter, 1990). See also John Mearsheimer's article in *International Security* referred to in note 13 below and the ensuing debate.

9 On this see virtually every world newspaper between August 1990 and March 1991.

10 On perhaps the most celebrated issue that has highlighted this see James Piscatori, 'The Rushdie Affair and the Politics of Ambiguity', *International Affairs*, vol. 66, no. 4, October 1990.

11 For a full discussion of this phenomenon, see Richard Rosecrance, *The Rise of the Trading State: Commerce and Conquest in the Modern World* (New York: Basic, 1986); see also Gerald Segal, *Rethinking the Pacific* (Oxford: Clarendon, 1989).

12 On Iran–Iraq and Namibia see, for example, Geoff Berridge, *Return to the UN* (London: Macmillan, 1991); also N. J. Rengger, *Treaties and Alliances of the World* (London: Longmans, 1990), see especially ch. 2.

13 See John Mearsheimer, 'Back to the Future: Instability in Europe after the Cold War', *International Security*, vol. 15, no. 1, Summer 1990. A similar type of argument is outlined by Samuel Huntington in 'America's Changing Strategic Interests', *Survival*, vol. 33, no. 1, January–February 1991. The Mearsheimer article has sparked a long debate in the pages of *International Security* involving Robert Keohane and Stanley Hoffmann.

14 For a discussion of international cooperation that is broadly optimistic from a largely realist position, see Joshua Goldstein and David Freeman, *Three Way Street: Strategic Reciprocity in World Politics* (Chicago: University of Chicago Press, 1990). On the contemporary position of the United Nations, see Adam Roberts and Ben Kingsbury (eds.), *United Nations, Divided World* (Oxford: Clarendon, 1989).

15 Gilpin, 'Global', pp. 29–30. See also Gilpin, *The Political Economy of International Relations* (Princeton, NJ: Princeton University Press, 1987).

16 Bull equates the two, *The Anarchical Society*; Hans J. Morgenthau, 'From Great Powers to Superpowers', in B. Porter (ed.), *The Aberystwyth Papers* (London: Oxford University Press, 1972), pp. 129–30.

17 Henry A. Kissinger, *The White House Years* (London: Michael Joseph/ Weidenfeld and Nicolson, 1979), p. 55.

18 For a first rate account of the politics of the contemporary Middle East, see Thomas Friedman, *From Beirut to Jerusalem* (London: Fontana, 1989).

19 This felicitous phrase is Stanley Hoffmann's, *Primacy or World Order: American Foreign Policy since the Cold War* (New York: McGraw Hill, 1978), p. 110, he takes the latter expression from Aron.

20 See Robert Keohane, *International Institutions and State Power* (Boulder, CO: Westview, 1989). Writers who would be included within this position include Keohane, Ernst Haas, Stanley Hoffmann, Joseph Nye, John Groom, Paul Taylor, Mark Imber, Hylke Tromp. There is also a link to earlier writings on international relations that stress international law and collective security for example. Such a realization is strengthened by the growing awareness that 'idealism' was far more 'realistic' than many of its critics allowed, see Cornelia Navari, 'The Great Illusion Revisited', *Review of International Studies*, vol. 15, no. 4, October 1989 and David Long and Peter Wilson (eds.), *Thinkers of the Twenty Years Crisis* (London: Macmillan, 1991).

21 This list draws on the work of Hoffmann, Keohane and Rosenau.

22 James N. Rosenau, *Turbulence in World Politics* (Hemel Hempstead: Harvester, 1990), chs. 1, 10.

23 Robert Keohane, 'Multi-Lateralism: An Agenda for Research', *International Journal*, vol. 45, no. 4, Autumn 1990.

24 See the debate sparked by Mearsheimer cited above.

25 Lawrence Freedman, 'Escalators and Quagmires: Expectations and the Use of Force', *International Affairs*, vol. 67, no. 1, January 1991; Ken Booth (ed.), *New Thinking About Strategy and International Security* (London: Harper Collins, 1991).

26 These characterizations are partially derived from the work of Richard Falk, see 'Normative International Relations' in *The End of World Order* (New York: Holmes and Maier, 1983) examples of 'critical' writing include, Robert Cox, *Production, Power and World Order* (New York: Columbia, 1987), Richard Ashley, 'Living On Borderlines: Man, Poststructuralism and War', in James Der Derian and Michael Shapiro (eds.), *International/ Intertextual Relations: Postmodern Readings of World Politics* (Lexington, MA: Lexington, 1989), Andrew Linklater, *Beyond Realism and Marxism: Critical Theory and International Relations* (London: Macmillan, 1990). N. J. Rengger and Mark Hoffman (eds.), *Critical Theory and International Relations* (London: Harvester, 1991), R. B. J. Walker, *One World, Many Worlds* (London: Zed, 1988).

27 Martin Wight, *Systems of States* (Leicester: Leicester University Press, 1977); Mearsheimer, 'Back'.

28 Robert O. Keohane and Joseph S. Nye, *Power and Interdependence*, 2nd edn (Glenview: Scott Foresman, 1989), p. xi.

29 Keohane and Nye, *Power and Interdependence*, pp. 271–2.

30 In addition to *Primacy or World Order*, see Hoffman, *Janus and Minerva* (Boulder, CO: Westview, 1987).

31 Rosenau, *Turbulence*, p. 97.

32 In Hedley Bull and Adam Watson (eds.), *The Expansion of International Society* (Oxford: Clarendon, 1984). He is explicitly echoing Michael Oakeshott. See also Mostafa Rejai and Cynthia H. Enloe, 'Nation States and

State Nations', *International Studies Quarterly*, vol. 13, no. 2, 1969; Vernon Hewitt, *The International Politics of South Asia* (Manchester: Manchester University Press, forthcoming); a contrary view is Charles Tilly, *Coercion, Capital and European States* (Oxford: Blackwell, 1990).

33 Robert H. Jackson, *Quasi-States* (Cambridge: Cambridge University Press, 1990).

34 See Peter Calvocoressi, 'World Power, 1920–1990', *International Affairs*, vol. 66, no. 4, October 1990, pp. 663, 666.

35 Calvocoressi, 'World Power', p. 667.

36 See N. J. Rengger, 'Incommensurability, International Theory and the Fragmentation of Western Political Culture', in J. Gibbins (ed.), *Contemporary Political Culture* (London: Sage, 1989); and Bull and Watson, *Expansion*.

37 Keohane and Nye, *Power and Interdependence*, p. 227.

38 See Elie Kedourie, 'Development and Politics' in Kedourie, *The Crossman Confessions* (London: Mansell, 1984).

39 See James Piscatori, *Islam in a World of Nation-States* (Cambridge: Cambridge University Press, 1986), Jackson, *Quasi-States*.

40 Piscatori, *Islam*, pp. 144, 145.

41 Segal, *Rethinking*.

42 T. H. von Laue, *The World Revolution of Westernization* (New York: Oxford, 1987).

43 Adda Bozeman, 'The International Order in a Multi-Cultural World', in Bull and Watson, *Expansion*, p. 391.

44 See R. J. Vincent, *Human Rights and International Relations* (Cambridge: Cambridge University Press, 1986).

45 Bull, *The Anarchical Society*, p. 317.

46 For a summary of current environmental treaties see Rengger, *Treaties*, pp. 53, 115–16.

47 Beitz, *Political Theory and International Relations* (Princeton: Princeton University Press, 1979); Hoffman, 'States, Cosmopolitanism and Normative International Theory', *Paradigms*, vol. 2, no. 1, 1988, Linklater, *Men and Citizens in the Theory of International Relations* (London: Macmillan, 1990), a sceptical view is Chris Brown, 'Cosmopolitan Confusions', *Paradigms*, vol. 2, no. 2, Winter 1988–9.

48 Martin Wright, *Power Politics* (Harmondsworth: Penguin, 1979), p. 143.

49 These problems are recognised by Stanley Hoffmann among the institutionalists and by R. B. J. Walker and Mark Hoffman among the critical theorists.

50 Paul Kennedy, *The Rise and Fall of Great Powers: Economic Change and Military Conflict from 1500 to 2000* (London: Unwin Hyman, 1988); Robert Gilpin, *War and Change in World Politics* (Cambridge: Cambridge University Press, 1981); George Modelski, *Long Cycles in World Politics* (London: Macmillan, 1986).

51 Wight, *Power Politics*, chs. 15–16.

52 Kennedy, *Rise*, ch. 8.

53 For assessments of the influence of these states or regions see *The Economist*, 30 June 1991; Wallace, *Dynamics*; Karl Kaiser, 'German Unification', *Foreign Affairs*, vol. 70, no. 1, 1991; Segal, *Rethinking*; Rudolf Kirshlager, 'Auf dem Weg zu einem grosseren Europa', *Europäische Rundschau*, 1, 1988.

54 *The Economist*, 1 December 1990, pp. 16, 101.

55 Gilpin, *Political Economy*, ch. 10.

56 For evidence of this see, for example, the efforts to rescue the GATT talks after the near collapse of December 1990, the increasing talk of European and Allied cooperative security action after the Gulf War and continued pressure as successive G–7 summits towards at least some economic policy coordination. I am not suggesting that these measures will necessarily succeed, merely that they display a willingness, indeed a desire, to keep the system going in roughly its present form.

57 Gerald Segal, 'As China Grows Strong', *International Affairs*, vol. 64, no. 2, Spring 1988, p. 217.

58 Segal, *Rethinking*, chs. 13, 14.

59 Gilpin, *War and Change*, pp. 42–3.

60 Kennedy, *Rise*.

61 Kennedy, *Rise*, ch. 8; Samuel Huntington, 'Coping With the Lippman Gap', *Foreign Affairs*, Winter 1987–8.

62 Joseph S. Nye, *Bound to Lead* (New York: Basic, 1990).

63 Robert Gilpin, 'Where Does Japan Fit In' *Millennium*, vol. 18, no. 3, Winter 1989.

64 For example Neal Ascherson in *The Independent on Sunday*, 17 February 1991; also *The Economist*, 28 February 1991, and *The Guardian*, 3, 8 April 1991.

65 *The Guardian*, 8 April 1991.

66 William H. McNeill, *Population and Politics Since 1750* (Charlottesville: University Press of Virginia, 1990).

67 W. W. Rostow, 'The Coming Age of Regionalism', *Encounter*, June 1990.

68 Rosenau, *Turbulence*, p. 24.

69 In *Foreign Affairs*, vol. 70, no. 1, 1991.

70 *The Guardian*, 8 April 1991.

71 Nye, *Bound to Lead*, p. 175.

72 *Ibid.*, p. 188.

73 John Mueller, *Retreat From Doomsday* (New York: Basic, 1989).

74 On this view see Michael Doyle, 'Liberalism and World Politics', *American Political Science Review*, vol. 80, no. 4, December 1986, 'Kant, Liberal Legacies and Foreign Affairs', Parts 1 and 2, *Philosophy and Public Affairs*, vol. 12, nos. 3, 4, Summer, Fall, 1983. It also forms part of Francis Fukuyama's argument in 'The End of History', *The National Interest*, 16, Summer 1989; for a critique see Mearsheimer, 'Back'.

75 See Mueller, *Retreat*.

76 See Der Derian and Shapiro *International/Intertextual*.

77 On the background to alliances see Rengger, *Treaties*, ch. 1, see also Stephen Walt, *The Origins of Alliances* (Ithaca, NY: Cornell, 1986). The terms balancing and bandwagoning are used by Kenneth Waltz in *Theory of International Politics* (Reading, MA: Addison-Wesley, 1979), similar terms are used by others, see Walt, *Origins*, p. 17.

78 Andrew Hurrell, 'International Support for Democracy and International Order', Paper to the LSE Seminar in International Political Theory.

79 See Charles R. Beitz et al. (eds.) *International Ethics* (Princeton: Princeton University Press, 1985).

80 Democracy fits W. B. Gallie's notion of an 'essentially contested concept', *Philosophy and Historical Understanding* (London: Chatto, 1964).

81 *The Economist*, 27 January 1990.

82 James Mayall, *Nationalism and International Society* (Cambridge: Cambridge University Press, 1989), pp. 26–32.

83 I am deeply suspicious about this principle, however it is broadly accepted.

84 Kedourie, *Crossman*, p. 82.

85 I do not suggest that the action of the coalition powers was actually motivated by these considerations; only that it could, without contradiction, have been so motivated.

86 It is of course clear that a large number of US officials from General Schwartzkopf down were very uneasy with this policy. President Bush stuck to it in its essentials although it was, of course, modified in the light of the huge Kurdish exodus and the subsequent international outcry.

87 For Wolfe see his *Ius Gentium* (Halle, 1750); see also the discussion in Hedley Bull (ed.), *Intervention in World Politics* (Oxford: Oxford University Press, 1984), pp. 181–95, and *passim*.

88 See for example, article 39, article 42, the Genocide Convention, Rengger, *Treaties*, pp. 40–4.

FURTHER READING

Books

Armstrong, David and Erik Goldstein (eds.), *The End of the Cold War* (London: Frank Cass, 1990).

Balzer, Harley D. (ed.), *Five Years that Shook the World: Gorbachev's Unfinished Revolution* (Boulder: Westview Press, 1991).

Booth, Ken (ed.), *New Thinking about Strategy and International Security* (London: Harper Collins, 1991).

Bowker, Mike and Phil Williams, *Superpower Detente: A Reappraisal* (London: Sage, 1988).

Brzezinski, Zbigniew, *The Grand Failure: The Birth and Death of Communism in the Twentieth Century* (London: McDonald, 1990).

Bull, Hedley, *The Anarchical Society: A Study of Order in World Politics* (London: Macmillan, 1977).

Buzan, Barry, Marten Kelstrup, Pierre Lemaitre, Elizbieta Tromer and Ole Weaver, *The European Security Order Recast* (London: Pinter, 1990).

Cox, Robert, *Production, Power and World Order* (New York, Columbia, 1987).

Der Derian, James and Michael Shapiro (eds.), *International/Intertextual Relations: Postmodern Readings of World Politics* (Lexington, MA: Lexington Press, 1989).

Enloe, Cynthia, *Bananas, beaches and bases: Making Sense of International Politics* (London: Pandora, 1989).

Gaddis, John Lewis, *The Long Peace: Inquiries into the History of the Cold War* (New York and Oxford: Oxford University Press, 1987).

Gati, Charles, *The Bloc That Failed: Soviet–East European Relations in Transition* (Bloomington and Indianapolis: Indian University Press, 1990).

Gill, Stephen and David Law, *The Global Political Economy: Perspectives, Problems and Policies* (Hemel Hempstead: Harvester Wheatsheaf, 1988).

Gilpin, Robert, *The Political Economy of International Relations* (Princeton, NJ: Princeton University Press, 1987).

Halliday, Fred, *The Making of the Second Cold War* (London: Verso, 1983).

Holsti, K. J. *The Divided Discipline: Hegemony and Diversity in International Relations* (Boston, MA: Allen and Unwin, 1985).

Kegley, Charles W. (ed.), *The Long Postwar Peace* (New York: HarperCollins, 1991).

Kennedy, Paul, *The Rise and Fall of the Great Powers: Economic Change and Military Conflict from 1500 to 2000* (London: Unwin Hyman, 1988).

Keohane, Robert, *After Hegemony: Cooperation and Discord in the World Political Economy* (Princeton, NJ: Princeton University Press, 1984).

Keohane, Robert (ed.), *Neorealism and its Critics* (New York: Columbia University Press, 1986).

Keohane, Robert and Joseph S. Nye Jr, *Power and Interdependence* (Glenview: Scott Foresman, 2nd edn, 1989).

LaFeber, Walter, *America, Russia and the Cold War, 1945–1990* (New York: McGraw-Hill, 6th edn, 1991).

Linklater, Andrew, *Beyond Realism and Marxism: Critical Theory and International Relations* (Boston, MA: Allen and Unwin, 1985).

Morgenthau, Hans J. *Politics Among Nations: The Struggle for Power and Peace* (New York: Knopf, 5th edn, 1973.

Nye, Joseph S. Jr *Bounds to Lead: The Changing Nature of American Power* (New York: Basic Books, 1990).

Olsen, William C. and A. J. R. Groom, *International Relations Then and Now: Origins and Trends in Interpretation* (London: Harper Collins, 1991).

Rosenau, James N. (ed.), *Contending Approaches to International Politics* (Princeton, NJ: Princeton University Press, 1969).

Shaw, Martin (ed.), *War, State and Society* (London: Macmillan, 1984).

Thompson, E. P. et al., *Exterminism and Cold War* (London: Verso, 1982).

Wallerstein, Immanuel, *Historical Capitalism* (London: Verso, 1983).

Waltz, Kenneth, *Theory of International Politics* (Reading, MA: Addison-Wesley, 1979).

Articles

Cox, Michael, 'Whatever Happened to the "Second Cold War"? Soviet–American Relations, 1980–1988', *Review of International Studies*, vol. 16, no. 2, 1990, pp. 155–72.

Doyle, Michael, 'Liberalism and World Politics', *American Political Science Review*, vol. 80, no. 4, December 1986, pp. 1151–69.

Fukuyama, Francis, 'The End of History?', *The National Interest*, vol. 16, Summer 1989, pp. 3–18.

Halliday, Fred, 'The Ends of Cold War', *New Left Review*, no. 180, March–April 1990, pp. 5–23.

Kubalkova, Vendulka and Albert A. Cruickshank, 'The "New Cold War" in "Critical International Relations Studies"', *Review of International Studies*, vol. 12, no. 3, July 1986, pp. 163–86.

Little, Richard, 'International Relations and the Methodological Turn', *Political Studies*, vol. 39, no. 3, September 1991, pp. 463–478

Mearsheimer, John J. 'Back to the Future: Instability in Europe after the Cold War', *International Security*, vol. 15, no. 1, Summer 1990, pp. 5–56.

Rengger, N. J., 'Serpents and Doves in Classical International Theory', *Millennium*, vol. 17, no. 2, Summer 1988, pp. 215–25.

Schopflin, George, 'The End of Communism in Eastern Europe', *International Affairs*, vol. 66, no. 1, 1990, pp. 3–16.

Singer, J. D. 'The Level of analysis problem in International Relations', in K. Knorr and S. Verba (eds.), *The International System* (Princeton, NJ: Princeton University Press, 1961), pp. 77–92.

INDEX

abortion, 139, 141
Acquired Immune Deficiency syndrome,
148, 156, 157, 164
Afghanistan; soviet casualties in, 104;
soviet invasion of, 1, 43, 106; Soviet
withdrawal from, 91, 95, 104, 107
Africa, 104, 148
Aganbegyan, Abel, 102
AIDS, *see* Acquired Immune Deficiency
Syndrome
Akhromeev, Sergei, 92
Alcoff, Linda, 136
Alksnis, Viktor, 91
alliances, 26, 164
anarchy, 2, 4, 8, 13, 149; contrasted with
domestic politics, 13
Andreeva, Nina, 93
androcentrism, 120–1, 133, 135
Andropov, Yuri, 101, 103
Angola, 148
anti-Americanism, 38
anti-systemic movements, 31, 32
apartheid, 139
Arbatov, Georgi, 91, 101
arms control, 42, 147
arms race, 1, 21, 41; fuelled by US, 41–2
Arrighi, Giovanni, 31
Ashley, Richard, 12–13, 136, 151
Axelrod, Robert, 8

balance of power, 3, 4, 7, 27, 32, 73, 146,
158, 164
Baltic Republics, 94, 166, 167
behaviouralism, 2, 25
Beitz, Charles, 157
bipolarity, 4, 5, 26, 62, 147, 150;
preferability of, 64; Waltz on, 62
Bogomolov, Oleg, 101
Booth, Ken, 151
Bozeman, Adda, 154
Brandt, Willy, 100; *Ostpolitik* of, 64
Brezhnev, Leonid, 93, 96, 101; and
economic problems, 99; and 'stability of
cadres', 100

Brezhnev Doctrine, 106, 107
British Boradcasting Corporation, 148
Brookings Insitution, 86
Brown, Sarah, 127–8, 133
Brzezinski, Zbigniew, 40, 82, 83, 84, 85
Bull, Hedley, 24, 149, 155, 157; on gret
powers, 146; on international order,
146; on world order, 146, 156, 162
Burlatsky, Fedor, 93, 101
Burton, John; cobweb approach of, 129
Bush, George, 35, 50, 109; administration
of, 168

Calvocoressi, Peter, 152–3
Cambodia, 37, 159
capitalism, 4, 9, 12, 24, 25, 26, 30, 32, 83;
development of, 15; dynamic of, 28, 31;
elimination of, 44, 118
Carr, E. H., 146
Carter, Jimmy, 37; human rights policy
of, 40
Catherine the Great, 85
Caucasus, 92, 94
change, 14; in Cold War System, 15, 73;
historical, 14; in international system,
148, 151
Chase-Dunn, Christopher, 9
Chernenko, Konstantin; funeral of, 50
China, 22, 26, 37, 100, 105, 139, 147, 158,
159, 160
Chinese Empire, 14, 32
Chomsky, Noam, 22, 36, 39, 44, 45, 50
Chowdry, Geeta, 140
class, 9, 10, 118; abolition of, 117
Clausewitz, Carl von, 28
Cold War: consequences of end of, 52, 59;
as contest between social systems, 73;
costs of, 77; debates over, 21, 35; end of,
25, 53, 69; First, 21; in Europe, 59;
inter-systemic view of, 23–33;
internalist view of, 22, 25; orthodox
view of, 36; post-revisionist view of, 37;
Realist view of, 22; responsibility for,
21, 36; revisionist, views of, 36, 44;

177